VIETNAM WARRIORS

by
Charles Melson
and
Gordon Rottman

Vietnam Warriors

* A combined volume specially bound for the Veterans of Foreign Wars of the United States through TN Marketing L.L.C.

* Made up of:

Warrior 23 US Marine Rifleman in Vietnam 1965-73, by Charles Melson

Warrior 28 Green Beret in Vietnam, by Gordon Rottman

Warrior 98 US Army Infantryman in Vietnam, by Gordon Rottman

This edition created in 2006 for TN Marketing L.L.C. by Osprey Publishing Ltd.

Contains material first published in Great Britain by Osprey Publishing Ltd, Midland House, West Way, Botley, Oxford, OX2 0PH as Warrior 23 US Marine Rifleman in Vietnam 1965-73, by Charles Melson, © 1998 Osprey Publishing Ltd; Warrior 28 Green Beret in Vietnam, by Gordon Rottman, © 2002 Osprey Publishing Ltd; and Warrior 98 US Army Infantryman in Vietnam, by Gordon Rottman, © 2005 Osprey Publishing Ltd.

Printed in the United States of America.

406 West 34th Street
Kansas City, MO 64111

CONTENTS

PART 1

US INFANTRYMAN IN VIETNAM 1965-73

US ARMY INFANTRYMAN IN VIETNAM 1965–73

INTRODUCTION

The image of the infantryman busting through the brush, startlingly young, gaunt, sunburned and often looking oddly clean as grime was sweated off, is what most often comes to mind when Vietnam is mentioned. Of the hundreds of thousands of troops deployed in Vietnam, it was the light infantryman, the 11B[1], who bore the heaviest burdens of a distant, controversial war. Commonly called an "11 Bravo," "11 Bush," "11 Bang," "11 Bullet-stopper," "ground-pounder", or "crunchy" (for crunching through the brush), the infantryman was more often simply called a "grunt" – from the the sound a soldier makes when hoisting a rucksack on to his back or rising to his feet, helped by a buddy.

Vietnam was truly an infantryman's war, in which he fought an elusive, dedicated, and crafty enemy in a wide range of environments, from forested mountains, open plains, rolling triple-canopy jungles, to vast delta swamps. Eighty-one infantry battalions of all types fought in a harsh environment with frequently changing weather conditions. While it was mostly hot and humid, infantrymen could also be inundated with endless rains or even chilly nights.

Not all infantrymen "busted brush" through the jungle, at least not all the time. Many rode in, or, more accurately, on, armored personnel carriers, and all rode in helicopters – some more than others. Others were transported by heavily armed river assault craft; still others were paratroopers. But these were merely the delivery means – all infantrymen spent time with "boots on the ground." Their experiences differed depending on the type of unit they were assigned to, where they served, and when. It was a long, evolving war, and the life of the infantryman in Vietnam was extremely harsh, brutal, and mind numbing. Endless days in the "boondocks" (rough or isolated country)

Reception Station, US Army Training Center, Infantry, Ft Polk, LA. Recruits would see signs bearing the shoulder-sleeve insignia of units in Vietnam all over the training center as a means of instilling esprit de corps.

---

1   11B is the military occupation specialty code for light infantryman. The first "1" means combat arms, the second "1" infantry, and the "B" light infantryman, a rifleman. Prior to 1965 the MOS code was 11100.

in what they called the "lost year," a year out of their lives away from home and family, was a year lost to a cause few understood and many questioned.

The Vietnam infantryman was a product of his society, as are all soldiers, but the political atmosphere, the sudden and sweeping changes in American culture, and the complex and confusing nature of the war made the American infantryman a very different kind of soldier than found in other American wars.

Although the US was militarily involved in Vietnam to an increasing degree from the early 1950s, infantry units were not deployed until 1965 and then rapidly increased. Units began to withdraw in 1969, and most combat units were gone by late 1971, with the last to leave a year later.

It has recently become popular in some political circles, even those that in the past shunned or even despised them, to be supportive of veterans of the Vietnam War. This is one reason why this book is so important at this point in time – to provide a means of understanding what the grunt endured and what his life was like, which transcends one's view of the war or political affiliation.

Inspections were conducted on Saturday mornings. While most were in the barracks, an occasional "full field layout inspection" was conducted. The "pup tent" was assembled by buttoning two shelter halves together, one carried by each soldier, along with a three-section tent pole and five tent stakes. These were seldom used in Vietnam, as soldiers had to make do with ponchos.

CHRONOLOGY 1954–75

July 21, 1954	Vietnam divided at the 17th Parallel as the French withdraw.
March 1955	First US military advisors arrive in Vietnam.
January 1959	North Vietnam issues resolution that changes its "political struggle" in South Vietnam to an "armed struggle."
May 1959	North Vietnam begins major improvements on the Ho Chi Minh Trail to supply its struggle in the south.
December 1960	National Liberation Front (Viet Cong) formed.
February 6, 1962	Military Assistance Command, Vietnam (MACV) formed to control all US armed forces in RVN (Republic of South Vietnam).
November 22, 1963	President John F. Kennedy is assassinated. Lyndon B. Johnson becomes president.
June 20, 1964	Gen William Westmoreland assumes command of MACV.
August 2–4, 1964	Destroyers USS *Maddox* and *C. Turner Joy* allegedly attacked by North Vietnamese torpedo boats in the Gulf of Tonkin.
August 7, 1964	US Congress passes Gulf of Tonkin Resolution to counter North Vietnamese aggression.
November 3, 1964	Johnson elected president.
February 7, 1965	VC attacks US installations in Pleiku. Johnson authorizes air attacks on North Vietnam, which commence on February 24.
March 8, 1965	First US Marine ground combat troops arrive in RVN.
April 6, 1965	US ground troops authorized to conduct offensive operations.
May 7, 1965	First US Army conventional ground combat troops arrive in RVN: 173d Airborne Brigade.
July 30, 1965	US Army, Vietnam (USARV) is formed to control Army forces.
September 11, 1965	1st Cavalry Division (Airmobile) arrives in RVN.
October 2, 1965	1st Infantry Division arrives in RVN.
March 28, 1966	25th Infantry Division arrives in RVN.
September 25, 1966	4th Infantry Division arrives in RVN.
December 16, 1966	9th Infantry Division arrives in RVN.
September 25, 1967	AMERICAL[2] Division activated in RVN.

---

2   The AMERICAL Division was formed in World War II; its name was derived from 'Americans in New Caledonia'

November 19, 1967	101st Airborne Division arrives in RVN.
December 1967	Anti-war protests increase in the US.
January 30, 1968	VC and NVA initiate Tet Offensive, which ends on February 26.
March 16, 1968	My Lai massacre.
March 31, 1968	US government announces de-escalation of its war effort and halts bombing of North Vietnam.
May 12, 1968	Peace talks begin in Paris.
July 1, 1968	Gen Creighton Abrams assumes command of MACV and Gen Westmoreland becomes Chairman of the Joint Chiefs of Staff.
November 6, 1968	Richard M. Nixon is elected president.
June 8, 1969	US initiates Vietnamization Program to completely turn the war effort over to RVN forces.
November 16, 1969	My Lai massacre is publicly revealed.
April 29, 1970	Offensive operations into Cambodia to neutralize NVA/VC sanctuaries.
November 7, 1970	Nixon is re-elected.
January 15, 1973	US announces halt of all offensive ground actions.
January 27, 1973	Ceasefire agreement is signed in Paris and US conscription ceases.
March 29, 1973	Final US troops are withdrawn from RVN, and MACV is disbanded.
August 9, 1974	Nixon resigns and is replaced by Gerald Ford.
April 29, 1975	US Embassy in Saigon is evacuated.
April 30, 1975	Saigon falls to NVA forces.

CONSCRIPTION AND ENLISTMENT

The draft, or, officially, Universal Military Service, had been a fact of American life since before World War II. How the possibility of involuntary military service sat with young men varied greatly. Some strongly opposed it; others viewed it as something necessary, if unpleasant; most thought little about it until being surprised when called to the colors.

It was a period that saw perhaps the most sweeping changes ever to American society and culture, a disjointed revolution of sorts: civil rights for minorities, women's rights and the feminist movement, the drug subculture, the so-called sexual revolution, the Hippie subculture (not as widespread as imagined), and the growing anti-war movement. Motion pictures, television, and popular music "spread the word" of new ideas as never before. It was a period of youthful defiance. It became popular to disdain patriotism, distrust the government, and question authority. Race and anti-war protests, as well as protests against just about everything else in society, were widespread, ranging from peaceful demonstrations to boycotts to sit-ins to vicious riots requiring National Guard and even active Army suppression. These actually involved only a small percentage of Americans.

The Selective Service Act required all males to register for conscription on reaching 18, making them eligible for the draft until 27. At the beginning of US ground combat in 1965 less than one-third of the Army was composed of conscripts. Of the 9,087,000 men and women of all armed services serving during the Vietnam War (1964–73), 2,594,000 were actually deployed in Vietnam. Only 1,766,910 of those serving throughout the world were drafted, with most going into the Army and fewer than 42,700 into the Marine Corps; the Navy and Air Force did not accept draftees. The numbers of draftees serving in

A C-ration lunch was standard fare when training in the field. In Vietnam infantrymen would live on Cs for weeks on end. Here cartons of milk were issued with the Cs, or "meal, combat, individual." These trainees wear the old black-on-OD US Army and black-on-white nametapes. By 1967 black-on-OD versions of both were being worn in Vietnam and Stateside.

combat units varied over time. In 1965, after the first ground combat units were introduced, it was about 20 percent. At the time the withdrawal began it was almost 70 percent.

Upon turning 18, individuals reported to their local draft board, filled out a classification questionnaire, and underwent a pre-induction physical to determine their status and eligibility for deferments or exemption. The over 4,000 draft boards were assigned monthly quotas. There was a complex system of deferments and exemptions based on physical qualifications, education, essential employment situations, family hardships, and religious beliefs. Some played the system, but most made little or no effort to do so, not knowing what to do or simply leaving things to fate. Essential employment included law enforcement officers, firemen, medical professionals, teachers, ministers and divinity students, and certain categories of scientists and engineers. Married men with or without children, post-graduate students, men caring for elderly parents, and other hardship situations, were usually given a lower priority I-A status, but by 1966 when the draft was increased to 30,000 a month such individuals began to be called. The peak year for induction was 1966 when new divisions, brigades, and support units were raised and existing units brought up to strength for Vietnam deployment: 382,000 were drafted. After that it was well over 200,000 per year until dropping off in 1970.

A Class I-A classification meant eligibility for induction. I-C, D, O, S, W, and Y were deferments for police, ROTC, conscientious objectors, high-school students, conscientious objectors performing civil work, and those qualified only in time of declared war, respectively. II-A, B, and S were deferments for critical occupations, agricultural workers, and students. III-A was a deferment for extreme hardships or children. IV-A, B, C, D, and F were individuals with prior military service or a sole surviving son, government officials, resident aliens not liable for service, ministers or divinity students, and physically or mentally unqualified. Registrants received a Registration Certificate: the infamous "Draft Card."

If grades seriously dropped, a student could lose his deferment, and once a deferment was rescinded it could not be reapplied for. Upon graduation, college students lost their education deferment and were just as eligible for the draft as an 18-year-old unemployed Black from Georgia. In fact, prior to 1967 they were even more likely to be drafted because draft boards selected the oldest first from their list of eligible 18–25-year-olds. This practice was reversed in June 1967 and 18-year-olds headed the list. This, it was felt, was less disruptive to the lives of younger men recently out of high school, who had not yet begun college, or had become established in jobs and careers, or had started families.

In 1970, in an effort to improve fairness, a World War II-type lottery system was established. The first lottery was drawn on December 1, 1969 for 1970, when 366 capsules were drawn in random order and the dates announced in newspapers. Each date was assigned a number from 1 to 366 in the order drawn. I-As born between 1944 and 1950 were called in the order their birth date was drawn. This was repeated each year, with the age bracket moved up until the draft was cancelled in 1973.

The issues of minorities and the poor are often broached when discussing combat service in Vietnam. It is true that the poor or lower middle class would more likely be assigned to the infantry, and a large percentage of minorities fell into that category. However, studies have shown that the numbers of minorities serving in combat units and killed in action were almost identical to the national population percentage. In fact it was the service support units that typically possessed a higher percentage of Blacks. It was true, however, that the better educated one was, the less chance there was of going to Vietnam or being assigned to a combat unit. Only about 40 percent of college graduates went. Over 60 percent of high-school graduates went and fewer than 70 percent of the dropouts.

Some volunteered for the draft. They had little better chance of receiving a non-combat assignment than other inductees, but they could time their induction, get their inevitable service out of the way, and get on with their lives. This was beneficial to those planning for college, pursuing a career, or starting a family.

Conscription was for two years, followed by four years in the Standby Reserve after "separation" from active duty. Technically Standby Reservists were liable for call-up in the event of war or national emergency, but they were simply a manpower pool, were not assigned to Reserve units, and never mobilized. Once their six-year-military obligation had been fulfilled, they were "discharged" from the Army.

Throughout the war, large numbers volunteered for the Regular Army and three years' active duty. Numbers dwindled as the war dragged on. Obviously it was the route chosen by those seeking a military career. Volunteering for the Regular Army also had benefits over waiting to be

The confidence course was yet another form of physical fitness, but also built self-confidence and agility. Both it and obstacle courses were run without combat equipment to allow the necessary freedom of movement.

drafted. Volunteers could pick their MOS in a specialty skill, many of which were closed to two-year draftees, and were almost guaranteed exemption from combat if that was their desire. Almost 90 percent of the Army was assigned to non-combat positions. Volunteers not remaining in the Army after their three years' active duty were assigned to the Standby Reserve, the same as draftees. A man could enlist at 17 with both parents' permission, but the normal age was 18. Seventeen-year-olds could not be deployed to Vietnam.

Over 1 million served in the National Guard and Organized Reserves during the war. As draft quotas sank after 1970, the numbers enlisting in the Guard and Reserves fell. This was another way to beat the draft, with waiting lists to join units. Joining the Army National Guard or Army Reserve meant six years assigned to a drilling unit. They undertook up to six months' active duty training alongside Active Army trainees and returned home to carry on jobs or schooling. A Guard infantryman undertook roughly four months' active training. He then attended one weekend drill a month and a two-week summer camp as well as occasional specialty or NCO schools. A Guardsman or Reservist missing three weekend drills could technically be assigned to active duty, though this was rare. Only a very small number of Guard and Reserve units were mobilized for active duty and fewer were deployed to Vietnam. Guardsmen and Reservists are often criticized for avoiding Vietnam or active duty, but such criticism is unjustified. Units in Europe, Korea, and elsewhere were often under-strength, and the US needed backup forces to discourage threats in other regions.

Men volunteering for three years in the Regular Army enlisted through local Army Recruiting Stations. They could pick their MOS (military occupation specialty) based on their Armed Forces Classification Test (AFCT) scores. Test scores evaluated one's aptitude in such areas as Clerical, Electronics, General Maintenance, Mechanical Maintenance, and Skilled Technical. The most important was the General Technical (GT) score, similar to an IQ score. An infantryman was required to achieve at least a 70 GT score, Special Forces 100, and Officer Candidate School 110.

The tear gas chamber served to familiarize trainees with the effects of tear gas, or CS, but also taught them the value of the M17 protective mask's proper use and demonstrated that it actually worked. The first step had the trainees enter the chamber wearing a mask, removing it, and reciting their name, rank, service number, and date of birth before being allowed to flee the building. CS was used extensively in Vietnam and it was essential that soldiers be familiar with its effects.

Many Blacks and Hispanics volunteered for the airborne, either because it was an opportunity to prove themselves or simply because it enabled them to send extra money home to their families. The GI Bill, paying for a college education once active service was completed, was a major motivator for many, regardless of ethnic group or social status. In the long run the GI Bill[3] provided the country with a large number of more mature and educated citizens, many of whom would not have been able to obtain a degree without it.

Volunteers could enlist via the Delayed Entrance Program, even while a high-school senior, and delay their entry up to six months. Delay time did not count toward their service obligation, but did count toward time in grade for promotion. They would take a physical prior to enlisting and then another when they reported for duty to ensure that they still met requirements. There was also a Buddy Program where two or more friends could enlist and be guaranteed to attend at least BCT (Basic Combat Training) together and perhaps AIT (advanced individual training) if they drew the same MOS.

Draftees received an Order to Report for Armed Forces Physical Examination to assess their fitness as well as take the AFCT and other tests. The in-depth physical examination tested agility, sight, hearing, teeth, blood, chest, urine, etc. For a recruit to be assigned to a combat arms branch (infantry, armor, combat engineers – artillerymen were allowed a 2 for hearing) he was required to possess a physical profile 111111 meaning no physical limitations: a "picket fence profile." The PULHES profile consisted of: P – Physical capacity or stamina, U – Upper extremities, L – Lower extremities, H – Hearing and ears, E – Eyes, and S – Psychiatric.

When selected, inductees received an Order to Report for Induction, usually about a month before their reporting date. It began with, "GREETING: You are hereby ordered for induction into the Armed Forces of the United States, and to report at ..." followed by the address of an Armed Forces Induction Station usually located in the Federal Building or main Post Office of a nearby large city. They would receive another physical, more tests, complete more forms, and wait. They were sworn in en masse – draftees, volunteers, Guardsmen, Reservists from all armed services – by an officer not necessarily from their assigned service. With right hand raised they pledged to defend America from all enemies, foreign and domestic, and to obey all lawful orders of those appointed over them. "Congratulations, you are a member of the Armed Forces of the United States." For anyone thinking this would not happen to him, he had now entered reality.

They had been told to bring three days' clothes, toilet articles, $20, and their Social Security card (or to apply for one if they did not have it). Either that same day or the next they were on a chartered bus for one of seven infantry training centers – Ft Benning, GA; Ft Dix, NJ; Ft Gordon, GA; Ft Jackson, SC; Ft Ord, CA; Ft Polk, LA; Ft Riley, KS. Most had said their farewells to family and friends at home prior to reporting. They left the bus station without fanfare, a small suitcase or gym bag – what they learned to call an "AWOL bag"– in hand, full of apprehension.

---

3   The Servicemen's Readjustment Act of 1944, better known as the "GI Bill of Rights," was instituted by President Franklin Roosevelt to assist veterans' education and job training assistance; home, farm or business loans; unemployment pay, job-finding assistance, and other post-discharge assistance.

Training was of course the focus during Basic and AIT, but work details were a necessary part of Army life. A company mess hall required six or so KPs a day to clean the dining room and kitchen, wash dishes and cooking utensils, clean garbage cans, and help man the serving line. Only cooks could serve meat to prevent serving-line KPs from slipping extra to their buddies.

And what of those who actively avoided the draft – the draft dodgers? Some simply failed to register, chancing the risk of being caught and prosecuted. Others took extensive measures to change their identity or openly defied authorities and burned their Draft Cards. Others left the country, with an estimated 50,000–125,000 running to Canada, which included deserters as well. Estimates of the numbers of Canadians drafted or volunteering for the US armed forces vary just as much, but at least 2,500–5,000 served in Vietnam, including a Medal of Honor winner. An unknown Marine wrote, "The worst of ours are going north, and the best of theirs are coming south."

TRAINING

Charles Legg had volunteered for the Army out of high school, signing up for the Delayed Entrance and Buddy Programs with a friend, William Peters. They delayed their entry until school began in the fall and enjoyed their summer. They had gone through high school together, becoming fast friends in the Junior Reserve Officer Training Corps (JROTC). That had been a bit of a challenge, as ROTC was far from popular in the late 1960s. They were generally excluded from the usual cliques of want-to-be "hippies," "goat-ropers" or "cowboys," "surfers," "rockers," "jocks," and the "popular." ROTC, however, taught them much of what they would learn in Basic Combat Training and had prepared them well. While the strange new world the recruits were about to enter would confuse and perplex them, Legg and Peters would take it in their stride.

They were middle-class 18-year-olds from blue-collar families, hard working, patriotic, and religious, with solid values. Their fellow recruits on the bus reflected a cross-section of American society from all economic levels, ethnic groups, religions, and employment, from major urban, suburban, or rural areas, and small towns. For many it would be the first time they had mixed with such a diversified group of young men of their own age. Schools had only recently desegregated, and many had had little close exposure to Blacks, and vice versa.

The bus was quiet and the recruits wide-eyed, staring at everything as the Greyhound rolled into the United States Army Training Center, Infantry, Ft Polk, Louisiana, late at night. They passed rows of darkened barracks on empty, well-lit streets. The bus pulled into an asphalt parking lot before a group of two-story barracks. A sign proclaimed, "US Army Reception Station: Welcome Soldier to the United States Army – Stand Proud!"

The bus door hissed open and a shadowy figure stepped aboard: "Get off my bus!" There was a mad scramble. They lined up on a yellow stripe and were informed by a sergeant wearing a black helmet liner that they would be here for several days for administrative processing, to receive a hair cut, more testing, inoculations, and uniforms. This was "Zero Week" and did not count toward Basic. They lined up and marched past an amnesty barrel in which they were to drop prohibited items without fear of repercussion: drugs, firearms, ammunition, alcoholic beverages, knives with a blade exceeding 2.5 inches, and straight razors. Their adaptation to military life began immediately as they learned how to fall into formation, wait in lines, pay attention to instructions, make it quick, make their bunk beds, roll their socks and underwear for locker display, and how to behave in the mess hall. There was no real harassment and they were not expected to march or even appear soldierly. They were rushed and chewed out for being late, too slow, or not paying attention. They learned to hurry up and wait, that they had to do everything "ASAP" (as soon as possible – "a-sap"), and discovered Army chow was not too bad. A $25 advance, the "flying 25," was made to their first month's pay to buy toothpaste, razor blades, cigarettes, boot polish, etc.

Wearing new uniforms and toting heavy duffel bags, the recruits, about to become trainees, assembled on the parking lot. Their drill sergeants were en route to pick them up. Names were called off and they formed into groups of 120. Soon a column of olive-drab school buses rolled into the parking lot. Wearing starched fatigues and "Smokey Bear hats," Drill Sergeants stepped off the buses and appeared inexplicably angry – actually a display to cower the recruits and not a genuine annoyance. They marched to the different groups with clipboards in hand and again called off names. Rushed on to the buses, they were driven to their new home for the next two months. There were rows and rows of World War II wooden barracks surrounded by mowed lawns. In the company area were three cream-colored barracks, perched low to the ground on piers, with high green-shingled pecked roofs and a 3-foot-wide wooden awning over the first-floor windows. In one side near the end was a door with another in the far end. Beside that door a fixed ladder led to a tiny porch before a second-floor door. The company admin building was one-story. In the front end was the orderly room, domain of the first sergeant and the company clerk, and small offices for the CO, XO, training officer, etc. The larger portion of the rear was the supply room with the arms cage. The mess hall was next door. A large dining room with a stainless-steel serving line dominated the building, with a kitchen outfitted with all the appliances and facilities found in a moderate-sized restaurant. Scattered about the small company area were various physical training apparatus.

The drill sergeants had been curt but civil on the short ride from the reception station to the company area. "Get off my bus!" They scrambled off to find more drill sergeants and black-helmeted soldiers waiting for them. Screaming at the stumbling trainees,

Much time was spent on the disassembly, assembly, and maintenance of the M14 rifle. It was stressed that the rifle was the most important piece of equipment in the hands of an infantryman.

they herded them into a low-crawl pit filled with sawdust and sand and told to crawl back and forth "until I'm tired of watchin' ya!" With their new uniforms now filled with the pit's contents, the trainees were broken down into three platoons by alphabetical order. Platoons lined up in four equal ranks by height. "If you're taller than the man in front of you, move up." They then faced to the right and repeated the procedure. The men who had been in ROTC were moved to the head of each rank to be squad leaders. Legg found himself at the head of a squad and was later given an armband with two chevrons. Willie Peters, simply because he was the tallest of the ROTCers, was made platoon guide, an acting platoon sergeant with three chevrons. The rest of the day was spent being told what life would be like and what they could and could not do. Bunks were then assigned. They were restricted to the company area. Squad leaders received a mimeographed sheet with diagrams of how wall and footlockers were to be arranged. Men were picked for kitchen police (KP) and they were told about fireguard. The cooks ("spoons") were sometimes tougher on KPs than the drill sergeants. Each night a squad was assigned fireguard, with the squad leader assigning men to walk the floor for an hour and then waking their reliefs. The almost 30-year-old wooden barracks would burn down in minutes if a fire started.

Two squads were housed on each floor with one squad to a side. Bunk beds were double-stacked. On the first floor were two small cadre rooms at one end and the latrine at the other with a larger cadre room above the latrine. One or two drill corporals or other company cadre might use these. The latrine was simply a large room with toilets on one wall without stalls, and sinks on the other plus a few urinals. A large shower room with three walls sprouting showerheads occupied one end of the latrine. Squads

Eight hours of hand-to-hand combat, consisting mostly of defensive moves, was taught in Basic. It was yet another means of achieving physical fitness, agility, aggressiveness, and self-confidence – just enough to give one the confidence to start a bar fight and get his butt kicked, as the drill sergeants cautioned against.

cleaned their own areas and alternated cleaning the central aisle daily. A water fountain sat at the latrine end of the aisle and fire extinguishers and butt cans hung on support posts. Butt cans were red-painted 1-gallon cans with an inch of water in the bottom for cigarettes. Latrine clean-up was rotated between all squads.

The drill sergeants, usually sergeants and staff sergeants, were not called Drill Instructors (DI); that was a Marine Corps term. They were specially selected NCOs who attended a six-week Drill Sergeant School. With shortages of drill sergeants, "drill corporals" and even PFCs were employed. Tactical NCOs ("TACs") were newly graduated sergeants of the NCO Candidate Course assisting drills to gain troop experience. Others were Vietnam veterans with a few months remaining in their enlistment, for whom it was not worth assigning to a troop unit for such a short time. None had attended Drill Sergeant School, and they wore black helmet liners rather than the distinctive "Smokey Bear hats," being known as "hardhats." It was a tough job, requiring longer hours than that put in by the trainees.

The first days were a nightmarish blur of unceasing harassment and adaptation to the new life. Much of the harassment was sophomoric, and, so long as one

Basic Combat Training G-3 Testing Score-card.

understood that it was seldom personally directed and just part of the game, it was not unendurable. Of course individuals who were screw-ups or had an attitude were singled out for special treatment. If errant trainees failed to change their ways they might receive a late-night "blanket party" from their squad, in which the victim was pinned down by a blanket and subjected to a barrage of punches. One also did not want to be tagged as a "ghost," i.e. one who disappeared when work was to be done. Harassment was directed mostly at the platoon or the company as a whole. There was a great deal of shouting, push-ups, and runs. Drill sergeants were prohibited from striking a trainee and were supposed to keep their language clean, which most of them found impossible. It was difficult for most trainees in the first couple of weeks, but they adapted, and the harassment gradually declined, except when deserved, rather than mindlessly directed at the platoon. The reason for harassment and group punishment was to help trainees understand that they had to respond immediately to orders, pay attention to detail, anticipate what needed to be done, and work as a team. It was not about individuals, as the trainees learned: it was for the good of the group.

Young American men are mostly competitive, sports-minded, and individualistic. Platoons competed against each other in everything from having the cleanest barracks to running a mile in the fastest time. In the first confused days individuals were always asking where they were going, what they would be doing, as they loaded in buses, or trucks, or marched down a road. Such questions dwindled after the first couple of weeks. They learned that wherever they were going might not always be fun, but it would be interesting and that everything was organized.

Basic Combat Training

The Basic Combat Training program of instruction called for 352 hours, 44 hours a week, but it was actually many more hours, with additional reinforcement training provided by the ever-present drill sergeants into the evenings and on the weekend "off" days. What little "free time" was allotted was mostly spent cleaning the barracks, washing clothes, polishing boots, and working in the yard. After the third week trainees were allowed to leave the company area after duty hours, and after the fifth they were given off-post 24-hour passes. Days began at 0500 hours with a rushed visit to the latrine, dressing, readying equipment as relayed from the drill sergeants through the squad leaders, a hasty breakfast, and formation at 0700 hours to depart for training. Besides marching to the tune of Joddie calls (often raunchy in these pre-PC days), 18-wheeler tractor-trailers were employed. Flatbed trailers fitted with sidewalls and bench seats could haul a platoon. Known as "cattle trucks," they were also called "watermelon trucks," as only the tops of the seated passengers' green helmets could be seen above the sides.

Basic Combat Training[4] was just that. Virtually everyone entering the Army undertook Basic to learn the bare skills necessary to become a

---

4 "Basic" was sometimes called "Boot Camp," but this is a Marine Corps and Navy term.

soldier. "Combat" was included in the syllabus title, as all soldiers, regardless of their duties and their type of unit, were expected to be able to defend themselves. It served as an orientation to Army and military life in general, got them into physical shape, conditioned them to accept orders and authority, and taught them how to work as a group and how to shoot. Commander's time was devoted to orientation, safety briefings, make-up and reinforcement training, and pay call. They learned about the Uniform Code of Military Justice, the legal system they were now under; the Code of Conduct, guiding their conduct in combat and as a prisoner; and the General Orders, dictating the requirements of guard duty. Drill and ceremonies taught them how to march in formation. First-aid training was sufficient to help keep a wounded man alive until evacuated. Only 30 hours were allotted to physical training (PT), but this was actually a continuous process, with all the intense activity, marching to training areas, and so forth. Push-ups were frequently dealt out by the drill sergeants, unit runs were common occurrences as were the "Army Daily Dozen" – a series of exercises – and pull-ups on the horizontal ladder were practiced as the men stood in line outside the mess hall. The 26 hours of physical contact confidence training included obstacle and confidence courses, pugil-stick exercises in which head and groin protection was donned before battering one another with padded poles using bayonet techniques, plus several hours of bayonet instruction. Considered impractical in modern warfare, bayonet training provided an additional means of PT, thereby learning agility, and instilling aggressiveness. Also included was eight hours of hand-to-hand combat instruction. The focus of the chemical, biological and radiological warfare training was the entering of a tear gas-filled room, removing the protective mask, and experiencing the effects personally. Another exercise saw trainees entering a chlorine-gas-filled room (non-lethal levels), removing their masks, and then re-donning and clearing them to provide confidence. Individual tactical training included day and night movement techniques, camouflage, and concealment.

Besides push-ups, no more than 10 at a time although this was often exceeded, other punishments might be dealt out by the drill sergeants. The front-leaning rest, the up position of push-ups with a straight back, was held for lengthy periods as was holding up a barracks. This was a position in which one's legs were outspread four feet from the wall, leaning forward at a steep angle, and arms widespread. Hugging a tree required one to wrap one's arms and legs around a coarse-barked pine tree and hang on tightly. Failure to shave could result in a "dry-shave," literally shaving without shaving cream or water. In order to pass the Army Physical Fitness Test (APFT) at the end of Basic, trainees were tested almost weekly. Those failing in different areas were assigned to the dreaded

Pugil-stick training encouraged achieving physical fitness, agility, aggressiveness, and self-confidence. It was also supposed to reinforce bayonet-fighting techniques, but it usually turned into a battering match, allowing trainees to vent some pent-up stress.

Basic Combat Training Subjects

Subject	Hours
Administrative processing	24
Commander's time	23
Proficiency test	4
Achievements & traditions of the Army	2
Military courtesy & customs	3
Character guidance	4
Code of conduct	1
Geneva Convention	1
Basic map reading	6
Military justice	3
Command information	1
Dismounted drill & ceremonies	34
Personal hygiene	1
First aid	8
Chemical, biological & radiological warfare	4
Guard duty	4
Inspections	28
Physical training	30
Orientation in counter-insurgency operations	1
Physical contact-confidence training	26
Hand grenades	4
Basic M14 rifle marksmanship course	83
Close-combat course	4
Infiltration course	3
Individual tactical training	14
Marches & bivouacs	30
Combat firing	4
Driver education	2

Motivation or Duffel Bag Platoon. They would receive additional PT in their problem areas after duty hours.

Lunch was at noon. If in the field or on a range it was "Mermited" out in insulated food containers and served on mess-hall trays, which were returned and then cleaned in the mess hall. Mess kits were not used, as these were difficult to clean in the field. Training was completed by 1700 and dinner was in the mess hall. If night training was undertaken, the troops either returned to the field or again the chow was Mermited out. Much of the 30 training hours allotted to marches and bivouacs was consumed marching to ranges and training areas. Only a night or two were spent on overnight bivouacs, where the men learned field sanitation and how to pitch pup tents. Lights out (no talking) was usually at 2130 or 2200 hours, providing about seven hours of sleep.

Two full weeks were dedicated to M14 rifle training, assembly/disassembly, care and cleaning, zeroing, known-distance range firing, and combat firing. The latter was known as Trainfire I and consisted of the firer engaging targets from standing, kneeling, squatting, prone, and foxhole positions. The targets were green waist-up, man-sized silhouettes. The downrange firing lane was rough ground covered by brush and trees, as would be encountered in combat. Targets would pop-up in irregular sequences from 50- to 300-meter ranges, requiring the shooter to first detect the target and engage it before it dropped to "safety" after a few seconds' exposure. This would also be the method used for rifle-qualification firing. Another eight hours was dedicated to conducting combat firing as a squad, and a close-combat assault course run by two trainees covering each other with live ammunition. They were taught how to identify hand grenades, and every trainee threw at least one live grenade. Trainees were taught the "Quick-Kill" technique from 1967, with one man tossing half-dollar-size aluminum discs into the air and his partner shooting at them with a BB (pellet) gun without sights. Many could actually hit a coin in flight with an M14.

The infiltration course offered a high degree of realism, stress, and confidence building. At night, the trainees entered a trench running perpendicular to several machine guns' lines of fire. Crawling out of the trench they advanced toward the machine guns, which fired bursts of live tracers over their heads as they low-crawled through barbed-wire obstacles and detonated demolition pits. Periodically pole-mounted floodlights would flash on, simulating flares, and the crawling trainees would freeze and wait for them to be extinguished before continuing.

Military rank and pay

Aside from all the physical training, one of the most difficult things to adjust to was the perplexity of military ranks. Officer ranks were quickly understood, though it was at first confusing that the silver bar and oak leaf of 1st lieutenants and lieutenants colonel were senior to the gold bar and oak leaf of the more junior 2nd lieutenants and majors. Trainees soon learned that 2nd and 1st

The infiltration course, with live machine-gun fire zipping overhead, required trainees to low-crawl through obstacles and exploding demolition pits, and was a tremendous confidence builder. Trainees were told to hug the ground or risk being hit. While the tracers streaking overhead appear inches away, the machine guns were firing 8 feet above the ground.

lieutenants were both addressed as "lieutenant," and that lieutenant colonels and "full" or "bird" colonels were collectively called "colonels." Not that it made much difference; they were all called "Sir" and seldom seen. To simplify things, they learned to informally refer to officers by their pay grade rather than rank titles: O-1 for 2nd lieutenants and O-6 for colonels, pronounced "Oh-Six." The "O" meant officer.

Enlisted ranks were more complex. Enlisted pay grades ran from E-1 to E-9. There were two private grades, E-1 and E-2, or PV1 and PV2. Prior to 1968 both grades lacked insignia, and were thus known as "slick sleeves." Private first class (PFC) E-3 wore a single point-up chevron until mid-1968 when this insignia was given to PV2s and PFCs added a rocker to their chevron. The next rank was specialist 4 (SP4) E-4 or "spec 4." His insignia was an odd-shaped backing with an indented downward point and an arched top. A spread-winged eagle, as on the cap badge, was centered. Specialists were just that and filled technical positions, though spec 4s in the infantry were generally grenadiers, machine gunners, mortar gunners, etc. Specialists did not have supervisory responsibilities and they fell below the NCO rank of the same pay grade in authority. Corporals ((CPL) E-4), two chevrons, were rare. The only corporal positions in a division were senior pathfinders and artillery assistant gunners. Sergeants reduced in grade to E-4 were usually made corporals, resulting in more legitimate corporals being asked why they had been busted.

Next up was specialist 5 ((SP5) E-5), identified by a spec 4's insignia with an arched bar across the top. In an infantry battalion spec 5s were first cooks, senior radar operators, senior vehicle mechanics, and senior medical aidmen. Sergeants ((SGT) E-5, three chevrons), were commonly called "buck sergeants" to differentiate them from other sergeant ranks. They were fire team and mortar squad leaders. Specialist 6s ((SP6) E-6) had two arches over the eagle. The only spec 6s in an infantry battalion were medical assistants. Three chevrons with a rocker across the bottom identified staff sergeants ((SSG) E-6) leading rifle and weapons squads. Specialist 7s ((SP7) E-7) were only found in higher echelon support units and had three arches over their eagle. The two NCO E-7 ranks, sergeant first class (SFC) and platoon sergeant (PSG), were identified by three chevrons and two rockers. SFCs were in battalion and higher staffs and support units.

There were two E-8 ranks: master sergeant (MSG) with three chevrons and three rockers, and 1st sergeant (1SG) with the same chevrons but with a diamond in the center. Master sergeants were on battalion and brigade staffs, while the "first shirt" was the senior company NCO.

Likewise there were two E-9 ranks: sergeant major (SGM) and command sergeant major (CSM), identified by the master sergeant's chevron with a star in the center; the CSM, however, had a smaller wreathed star. Sergeant majors were on division and higher staffs while the CSM was the senior NCO and advisor on enlisted affairs to the commander of battalion and larger units. Within enlisted ranks their word was "God's."

Collectively, sergeants were called "sergeants" – "hard-stripers" as opposed to specialists, regardless of

Enlisted Rank		
Rank	**Abbreviation**	**Pay Grade**
Private 1	PV1	E-1
Private 2	PV2	E-2
Private first class	PFC	E-3
Specialist 4	SP4	E-4
Corporal	CPL	E-4
Specialist 5	SP5	E-5
Sergeant	SGT	E-5
Specialist 6	SP6	E-6
Staff sergeant	SSG	E-6
Specialist 7	SP7	E-7
Sergeant first class	SFC	E-7
Platoon sergeant	PSG	E-7
Master sergeant	MSG	E-8
1st sergeant	1SG	E-8
Sergeant major	SGM	E-9
Command sergeant major	CSM	E-9

Trainfire I rifle qualification firing was conducted in the sixth week. During the many hours of practice, range-firing pairs of trainees would fire while the other coached. During qualification firing they scored for each other. Here the coach wears a yellow steel helmet so that the safety NCOs can maintain better control. Safety measures on range were extreme.

rank, with the exception of 1st sergeants and sergeant majors, who were addressed as such. NCOs more often though were simply referred to by their pay grade, E-5 through E-9, while specialists were spec 4 through spec 7. Hard-stripers were promoted to the next NCO rank and specialists to a higher specialist rank, but they could be "promoted" to the parallel NCO rank within the same pay grade or promoted to the next pay grade's NCO rank if they assumed supervisory responsibilities.

As Legg and his buddies low-crawled and marched their way through Basic they gradually changed. Their stomachs flattened out and those needing some weight gained it while others with less need lost it. It was no longer all so strange. The drill sergeants began complimenting them on their accomplishments; they were not hopeless losers after all. All still looked forward to the end of Basic, but it had not actually been the ordeal many feared. It was demanding to be sure, but they were gaining confidence, taking things in their stride, and developing teamwork. There were three tests they had to complete to graduate. The APFT required a one-mile run, push-ups, pull-ups, sit-ups, horizontal ladder, dummy hand grenade throw, low-crawl, and the completion of a run, dodge and jump course, all timed or requiring a minimum number of repetitions. This was taken in the last week, as was G-3 Testing – proficiency tests where trainees demonstrated skills and knowledge before a committee. The other was rifle qualification requiring a Marksman rating of at least 26 hits out of 40 on the Trainfire I range. Sharpshooter required a score of 33 and Expert 38. If one failed to qualify, he "boloed," and would be re-cycled to another training company to re-qualify.

Graduation day was held on the post parade ground with the companies uniformed in khakis or greens depending on the season. They marched past

G-3 proficiency testing was conducted in the final week of Basic. Trainees demonstrated their skills and ability to perform tasks under pressure. Here a trainee applies a field dressing to a dummy to show his knowledge of treating a gunshot wound and to halt bleeding. A group number is chalked on his helmet liner.

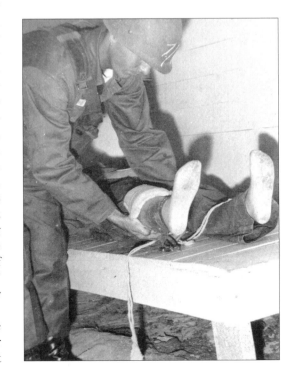

the post commander, with a band playing, listened to a short speech about duty and what they had accomplished, and found out that their drill sergeants thought they had done well after all. They had found out their future assignments during the previous week; Legg and others destined for infantry training at Tigerland felt sobered. Occasionally those realizing that infantry might mean Vietnam went AWOL. For the majority, there were heart-felt goodbyes and sincere handshakes with the drill sergeants. Legg was stunned to realize that he had actually come to like some of them. It was sad too when it was realized that he would never again see most of his fellow trainees. Up until 1967, Basic graduates received two weeks' leave, but in the rush to produce troops, leave was not granted until after AIT. The one exception was that trainees in Basic and AIT received a two-week Christmas leave if their cycle fell at the year's end. Soldiers were authorized 30 days' paid leave per year.

Military Pay

Pay call was on the last Friday of the month. The company commander, with a loaded .45-caliber pistol, paid Legg and his fellows in cash. Before income tax, Social Security, and optional Savings Bond deductions, the Base Pay for soldiers with less than two years' service (1968 scale) was:

$102.30	E-1 less than 4 months
$109.50	E-1 over 4 months
$113.40	E-2
$137.70	E-3
$190.20	E-4

Married soldiers without children received $55.20 Basic Allowance for Quarters, and another $30 Family Separation Allowance when deployed overseas. When overseas, including Vietnam, they additionally received $16 Overseas Allowance and in Vietnam $65 Hostile Fire Pay ("Combat Pay"). Paratroopers received $55 Hazardous Duty Pay ("Jump Pay"). Paratroopers were required to jump once every three months to receive Jump Pay, but they continued to receive it in Vietnam, as aircraft and parachutes were unavailable for parachute proficiency jumping. In Vietnam there were no income tax deductions, but Social Security deductions were still withheld.

After graduation

The graduates went in all directions. Some stayed at Ft Polk to be trained by the 4th Combat Support Training Brigade as truck drivers, wiremen, cooks, and clerks. Others were dispersed throughout the Army school system to be trained in one of the over 350 MOSs. Of the seven infantry training centers, six were Vietnam-oriented, with Ft Dix, NJ, being the sole exception. There infantrymen bound for Germany, Korea, Alaska, and Panama, as well as many destined for OCS and Special Forces, would later receive Vietnam-oriented training. Not enough infantrymen could be pushed through the training system to feed units in Vietnam. Peters and a small number of graduates who had demonstrated leadership ability attended the two-week Leadership Preparation Course prior to AIT, and Legg and his friend parted company. They would serve as platoon guides and squad leaders in AIT and often go on to the NCO Candidate Course.

Two of Ft Polk's BCT brigades and the CST (Combat Support Training) brigade were located on South Fort, but the 3d Infantry AIT and 5th BCT Brigade were at North Fort. BCT graduates were assembled from different companies and bused a few miles to Tigerland, as North Fort was known. While Tigerland had the reputation of being one of the toughest AIT brigades, it was not all that much different from the others, and certainly nothing like that depicted in the motion picture bearing the same name.

There was the usual harassment to let the infantry trainees know they were still trainees and who was in charge. More of the drill sergeants were Vietnam veterans than in Basic. Overall though it was milder, but the training was intense, fast-paced, and more technical. Training companies had four platoons, one of which was filled with either indirect fire crewmen (mortarmen – MOS 11C) or direct fire crewmen (recoilless rifle gunners – MOS 11H). They conducted common-skill training with the three rifle platoons (light weapons infantrymen – MOS 11B), but much of their training was conducted separately.

The main focus was on weapons. Three weeks of rifle marksmanship in Basic prepared them well, along with the many hours of combat firing. They fired the 40mm M79 grenade launcher, the 3.5-inch M20A1B1 bazooka, the M72 LAW, and the .50-caliber M2 machine gun for familiarization. A great deal of instruction was spent on the 7.62mm M14A1 automatic rifle, which Legg found was difficult to qualify on even as Marksman; Expert was seldom achieved because the weapon was so inaccurate. The 7.62mm M60 machine gun was a different matter and an entire week was spent on this weapon. They also fired the .45-caliber M1911A1 pistol for qualification.

The Viet Cong village at Peason Ridge, north of Ft Polk, LA, provided a fairly realistic setting for exposing infantry trainees to Vietnam. It did not replicate a typical Vietnamese village, but rather a fortified VC village.

Tactical training consisted of 56 hours of squad techniques of fire and tactics, 32 hours of patrolling, 15 hours of individual combat skills, and 15 hours of map and compass work. It was realistic, and Vietnam veterans from specialized training committees conducted most of the training. Survival, evasion, and escape training included a night escape and evasion (E&E) course, as squads attempted to exfiltrate through "enemy" patrols. They learned how to operate squad and platoon radios, became familiar with radio procedures, and learned the phonetic alphabet (words substituted for letters to prevent misunderstandings through static). In land-mine warfare they learned how to emplace, arm, disarm, and recover anti-personnel and anti-tank mines as well as make and deal with booby traps.

Infantry AIT was 352 hours, but Vietnam-oriented AIT entailed an extra week of patrolling, land navigation, countering booby traps, field sanitation, enemy tactics, and the cordon and search of a simulated village.

AIT did not make the same impression on Legg as Basic. Basic was that first memorable taste of military life, what seemed like impossible challenges overcome, and an episode often remembered with a certain degree of fondness. In the final week of AIT they learned their destination. Most were headed for Vietnam, but small numbers found they were assigned to other overseas units and some even in the States, though they might be levied for Vietnam themselves within six months, leaving draftees with sufficient time to serve their year in Vietnam. Three-year volunteers not bound immediately for Vietnam had a year and a half to sweat out a levee. Those bound for Vietnam received a 30-day leave, most others two weeks. Many graduating AIT were promoted to PV2.

During AIT, trainees had the opportunity to volunteer for the Basic Airborne Course ("Jump School") at Ft Benning, GA. They had to first pass the Airborne Physical Fitness Test. This was a three-week course more physically demanding and intense than the eight weeks of Basic, requiring five parachute jumps. These men would go on to the many airborne units in Vietnam, the States, Germany, Panama, and Alaska.

E-1s through E-4s attending the NCO Candidate Course (NCOCC) had to have proven leadership skills, at least a 100 GT score, and at least 13 months' service remaining after graduation. Willie Peters took this route. There were such serious shortages of NCOs that a means of providing additional junior leaders was necessary. The shortage was due to NCO casualties, retirements, and the requirement that unless a soldier volunteered he could not be redeployed to Vietnam for 25 months. The NCOCC was conducted in two phases, the first being 13 weeks of leadership instruction, combat skills, weapons employment, and squad and platoon tactics. NCO candidates were made corporals, but could not wear the rank. Graduates were promoted to sergeant and a few honors graduates to staff sergeant. They were assigned to a troop or training unit for 9–10 weeks as leader "understudies" or as TAC NCOs to gain practical experience. The program was begun in late 1967 and ran through early 1972, producing 20,000 infantry NCOs (other combat arms also ran NCOCC). (To give an idea of the chance of an infantryman being killed in Vietnam, 1,002 of the graduates were KIA.) Graduates were eligible for OCS, but most declined.

There was resentment of the "Instant NCO Course" in some circles. Dubbed as "Shake n' Bakes," "Instant NCOs," and "Whip n' Chills," senior NCOs resented the fact that soldiers could receive the stripes in a year that it took them 4–6 years to earn. E-4s and below with several months in Vietnam were resentful of a newly assigned sergeant who had been in the Army for less time than they taking over their squad. The program did not prevent other enlisted men from progressing in rank though. It was true that the new NCOs lacked the years of practical experience gained by traditional NCOs, but most did well, especially if first broken in when assigned to a squad rather than taking over directly.

APPEARANCE

In an era when the Beatles-style haircut was in vogue, the idea of having one's head nearly shaved bare was almost unbearable. Marched to the barber shop and begrudgingly plopping down into the chair, PV1 Legg was asked, "Ya wanta keep those sideburns, trainee?" There

grunt v. 1. To utter a deep guttural sound, as does a hog. 2. To utter a similar sound, as in disgust, annoyance, indifference, strain, or effort. 3. An infantryman.

Light Infantry Advanced Individual Training Subjects	
Subject	Hours
Administrative processing	10
Commander's time	27
Character guidance	2
Command information	4
Physical training	24
Drill and ceremonies	12
Inspections	14
Land navigation	18
First aid	4
Graduation	1
Bayonet	2
Field fortifications	3
M1911A1 pistol	8
M79 grenade launcher	4
3.5-inch rocket launcher	6
.50-caliber machine gun	8
Land mine warfare	8
Survival, evasion & escape	9
Individual combat actions	15
Introduction to armored personnel carrier	1
Technique of fire & tactics, rifle squad	56
Proficiency test	4
Weapons demonstration	2
Communications	10
M14A1 automatic rifle	28
M60 machine gun	40
Patrolling	32

Vietnam's terrain varied widely, with the variations often extreme. This photograph demonstrates this with an open rice paddy, edged by dense jungle, beyond which are steep forested hills, all within a few hundred meters.

appeared to be hope after all. "Yes, sir!" "Then hold out ya hand." To add insult to injury, the recruits had to pay 50 cents for the haircut. Less than a quarter of an inch remained on top, and around the ears and nape of the neck it was "white sidewalls." Regardless of the reasons given – sanitation in a hot, dusty environment with no time to spend on grooming – the real reason was simply uniformity. Everyone was different, but nobody was special, and no one needed to stand out. Shaving was mandatory every day whether one had a beard or not.

The first thing that struck PV1 Legg when the day came to be issued uniforms was a sign over the entrance to the warehouse-like quartermaster building: "Through these doors pass the world's best-dressed soldiers." Aside from snide remarks by some, Legg reasoned that this was possibly true – the uniforms looked sharp. They stripped down to underwear and placed their "civvies" in sacks to be mailed home. They did not realize that it would be months before they donned civvies again. Civilians quickly and efficiently measured, fitted, and issued the men's uniforms in a whirlwind, assembly-line process.

The second surprise was the quantity of uniforms that filled Legg's arms: four sets of fatigues, two of short-sleeve khakis, a set each of summer- and winter-weight Army green "Class A" uniforms, three tan shirts to wear with the greens, two field caps, two envelope-like Army green garrison caps, and a visored Army green service cap, referred to respectively as "baseball," "overseas" or "c**t," and "bus driver" or "flying-saucer" caps; five pairs of white boxer shorts, undershirts, and handkerchiefs; five pairs of black cushion-sole socks, three pairs of black dress socks, black leather glove shells with two pairs of olive-drab wool inserts, two black web belts, an M1951 or M1965 field jacket, an Army green overcoat, and a leaky taupe raincoat – a grayish brown that turned lilac when wet. Two pairs of black leather combat boots were issued with much discussion on how best to break them in. A can of white paint was provided and a little square painted at the top edge of the back reinforcing strap on one pair. The drill sergeants directed that boots would be alternated each day. Another white rectangle was painted inside and marked with name and serial number. Plain black low-top dress shoes were to be worn with khakis and greens, known simply as "low-quarters."

It was a massive armload of clothing and accessories, and when stacked beside Legg's duffel bag it appeared impossible for it all to fit. The NCOs said it had better. He packed a layer in and slammed the bag on to the floor a few times to compact it before shoving in more. It did all fit, barely. Gold-on-black US ARMY tapes were already sewn on the fatigue shirts, but black-on-OD nametapes had to be sewn on by a battery of speedy women behind sewing machines. Recruits wore no other insignia. A passing sergeant asked a group waiting in line what the US Army meant. Reluctant to take the bait, no one admitted knowing. Pointing to each letter on his own chest he said, "Uncle Sam Ain't Released Me Yet." It was their first hint that sergeants were human too.

After arrival at their training company, recruits were issued two additional items for which they had filled out forms at the reception center. One was a black plastic nameplate with their last name etched in white. This was worn on the flap of the right breast pocket on khakis and greens. The other was the personal identity tag, or "dog tag." One of the stainless steel rectangles with rounded ends was attached to a beaded neck chain and the other to a shorter chain attached to the longer. A religious medal could be attached to the chain, but no other form of jewelry. The drill sergeants taught that if a man was killed, the tag on the long chain remained with the body and the other was detached and turned in with the casualty report. They dispelled the lingering myth that one of the tags was jammed between a dead man's teeth. Dog tags were part of the uniform and were to be worn at all times. Stamped on the tag was: LEGG, CHARLES (NMI). "NMI" meant No Middle Initial. Beneath this were his serial number, blood type and group, and religious preference. At the PX he bought a pair of "dog tag silencers," stretch-plastic frames that fitted around the tags' edges to keep them from clinking. The silencer set included a length of clear plastic tubing through which the long chain was threaded. Some soldiers simply taped the tags together. Most soldiers can still recite their seven-digit serial number preceded by two letters: RA – Regular Army (three-year volunteers), US – United States (conscripts), ER – Enlisted

A patrol parallels a stream (described as a "blue line" in radio conversation), moving in the open rather than attempting to move through the dense elephant grass and brush on the far side. Elephant grass can grow up to 9 feet high (3m), but most is from three to six feet (1–2m).

Reserve, or NG – National Guard. If an enlisted man was commissioned through OCS he received a new serial number preceded by an "O." From January 1968 Social Security numbers replaced serial numbers and the letter prefixes were dropped.

The olive green utility uniform, more commonly known as "fatigues," was the daily duty wear. The loose-fitting uniform was worn with the shirt (officially a jacket) tucked into the trousers, sleeves down, and the trouser cuffs bloused (tucked) into the boots. Many used blousing garters or "blousing rubbers" rather than tucking them into the boot tops. The garters, purchased at the PX or Quartermaster Clothing Sales, consisted of a twisted elastic cord with a small hook at both ends. They were fastened around the ankles over the top of the socks and the trousers cuff rolled up under it. Large rubber bands were sometimes used, but were not as durable. The term "blousing rubbers" came from World War II when a couple of condoms were tied together end-to-end and used for the same purpose. Some drill sergeants would not allow their trainees to blouse their trousers in this manner, requiring them to be tucked into the boots instead.

Trainees simply washed their fatigues at a self-service Laundromat equipped with washers and dryers and wore them un-pressed and un-starched. Drill sergeants and permanent party (cooks, clerks, etc) had their fatigues starched and pressed and would daily "break starch," that is, force their legs and arms into the trousers and shirtsleeves to peel the heavily starched fabric apart. Later, as soldiers purchased additional sets of fatigues, they learned that wearing an older faded shirt with new darker trousers or vice versa was called a "golf suit" because of the mismatched shades, and was frowned upon.

The helmet – "steel pot," "piss pot," or "brain dome" – was worn with its helmet liner. Basic trainees did not wear camouflage covers, just the bare olive-drab helmet. Trainees in AIT wore the reversible cover. A complete helmet assembly weighed almost 3.5 pounds, but the men found that within a week they became used to it. The unpopular hot-weather field cap, or "baseball cap," was worn in the company area and off-duty. Headgear was removed indoors, and the cap's visor was folded into the crown and the cap stuck into the back of the trousers.

Khaki uniforms were 100 percent cotton and required heavy starch and military creases: three creases down the back, centerline and parallel on either side aligned with the shoulder blades, chest creases aligned down the center of the chest pockets, sharply creased trousers. It was a sharp-looking uniform until worn for a few hours and then it looked like one had slept in it. Later some purchased tan tropical worsted wool uniforms ("TWs"), authorized in lieu of cotton khaki, and these were distinctively presentable uniforms. The well-tailored Army Green uniform, especially the 100 percent wool winter weight, was also a presentable uniform.

Once training was completed, hair could be grown out somewhat, but it was still "high-and-tight." Mustaches were out in most cases. Few first sergeants

Streams were common in many areas and crossing them a frequent occurrence. Here infantrymen ford a stream for a short local security patrol on the far side. They have stripped down to the bare minimum, as it is of only short duration. They carry only a bandolier with seven M16A1 rifle magazines.

allowed them, often saying, "You can have a mustache if you're wearing one in your ID card photo," which of course was an impossibility, a "Catch 22." Sideburns were not to extend below the level of the ear opening, a restriction frequently tested.

The PX sold such items as higher-quality-than-issue branch-of-service collar insignia, rank insignia, award and decoration ribbons, unit patches and crests. Brass-like branch-of-service insignia and belt buckles could be purchased that did not require polishing. The Quartermaster Clothing Sales Store sold "Army-issue" versions of the same items at a lower cost as well as all uniform and individual equipment items, which could be purchased as replacements for lost or worn-out items.

Grubby in the bush

Legg's appearance was to alter drastically in Vietnam. It was an altogether different army and environment. The uniforms and equipment infantrymen donned there would thus be different from those worn elsewhere.

He reported to the overseas replacement station wearing travel-crumpled khakis and a couple of sets of fatigues; everything else was left at home. One of the first activities was the issue of tropical uniforms. He received three sets of tropical combat uniforms, two pairs of tropical combat boots, five sets of olive-green undershirts and shorts, and two olive-green towels. He was told that he had to have a baseball cap and to buy one at Quartermaster Sales if he had reported in without.

The loose-fitting, many-pocketed "jungle fatigues" or "fatikees" were probably one of the most popular uniforms worn by the US Army. Comfortable, lightweight, and fast-drying, they proved a practical design. The lightweight canvas-topped "jungle boots" with punji stake protection in the soles, drainage eyelets protecting from leeches, and cleated soles also proved popular. The men rushed to on-post dry cleaners to have their name and US Army tapes, and any special skill badges, sewn on. Unit patches would wait until they found out their assignment in Vietnam. They might have sewn on sleeve rank insignia, but from 1968 small black pin-on collar rank insignia were authorized. In 1968 subdued unit shoulder patches and special skill badges were also authorized. During the transition period through 1970, both full-color and black or OD subdued insignia could be worn mixed on the uniform depending on what was available.

In Vietnam, dress and appearance standards were somewhat relaxed owing to the limited laundry facilities, the climate, and the overall primitive conditions. Undershirts and shorts were usually dispensed with as they trapped moisture and caused rashes, immodestly called "crotch rot" or referred to as a disease: "rot-ya-crotch-off." Jungle fatigue shirtsleeves were usually rolled up above the elbows, but Legg learned that when busting dense brush, bamboo, thorn thickets, and elephant grass it was best to keep them rolled down. This helped keep out ants and leeches as did tie-tapes on trousers cuffs. An olive-green towel or triangular bandage was often worn around the neck to sop up sweat: a "drive-on rag." While Legg and his buddies generally went shirtless in firebases or wore undershirts, at nightfall they were required to don shirts with sleeves rolled down to deter malaria-bearing mosquitoes.

Once assigned to a unit the shoulder patch would be sewn on in a local Vietnamese tailor shop, one of the many "mamasan" shops outside larger bases. Often it was a wasted effort to sew on nametapes, badges, and so forth. In the field, filthy uniforms were direct exchanged (DXed) for new uniforms devoid of insignia or for laundered uniforms with someone else's nametape.

Little was carried in pockets because any item with bulk and weight would bounce when the soldier ran. Seldom were the shirt's skirt pockets used because they were inaccessible when wearing web gear. Leaders carried plastic-wrapped maps in a trousers cargo pocket and a compass in a chest pocket, dummy-corded to a shirt buttonhole. Wallets were placed in a small plastic bag secured by a rubber band. Typical contents were:

- Armed Force Identification Card ("Military ID Card")
- Geneva Conventions Identification Card
- MACV Ration Card
- US Government Motor Vehicle Operator's Identification Card ("Military Driver's License;" few infantrymen possessed this)
- Home-state driver's license (did not have to be renewed while in the service)
- Personal photos (family, wife, children, girlfriend)
- Military Payment Certificates

The steel pot was habitual wear in the field and became an equipment carrier and billboard. The camouflage cover was worn green-side-out in most areas and it was seldom reversed if the vegetation changed – too much trouble. Personal names and nicknames, home towns and states, slogans, and unit mottoes were commonly written on the cover with grease pencils or felt markers. Various symbols too were crudely marked, ranging from rank, unit patches or crests, state outlines or flags, peace symbols, or short-timer calendars. The elastic camouflage band was seldom used to attach foliage, but instead to stow small personal items making them easily accessible and out of reach of water when wading streams: cigarette pack, matchbook, C-ration spoon, insect repellent bottle, P38 can opener, and field dressings are examples.

The full-brimmed tropical hat was issued, and locally made versions were often bought from mamasan shops. It was seldom worn in the field, even on reconnaissance patrols. However, soldiers were often sentimentally attached to their "boonie hat," to the point where the replacement depots allowed them to retain Army-issue ones rather than try to collect them up when departing.

OD 550-pound parachute suspension line ("550 cord") often replaced bootlaces. Rather than wearing the dog tags around the neck, men often threaded them through the bottom end of their boot laces, one on each boot. The theory was that both tags would not be separated from the body, as would be the case

Stream crossing often required the aid of a buddy because of the irregular bottom, deep mud, and sometimes swift current. The infantryman in the foreground wears the nylon rucksack with aluminum frame. The frame precluded wearing any equipment on the belt other than on the front. Large water leeches and smaller land leeches were more a nuisance than a hazard.

Besides jungles, swamps, and hills, the infantryman also sometimes fought in built-up or urbanized areas. Most of the urban construction was reinforced concrete to endure the harsh tropical climate.

with decapitation – a rare occurrence. It was more frequently done to be different rather than for practical reasons. Those wearing dog tags in the normal manner invariably had a P38 can opener attached.

With time there were efforts by some to assert their individuality, protest their plight (real or perceived), or make some statement. Such efforts increased as the war wore on, small-unit leadership deteriorated, and as the war became increasing unpopular at home. More anti-war and peace symbols[5] and slogans appeared, some sported headbands, beads or necklaces with peace symbols, and braided or bead bracelets made their appearance. Some sported longer hair, especially long sideburns, and mustaches sprouted. The extent of such practices varied from unit to unit, and the degree to which it was tolerated depended on the unit leader.

WEAPONS AND EQUIPMENT

The day after their assignment to the training company the recruits were fallen in in front of the supply room. Each man picked up a footlocker filled with an assortment of bags, pouches, straps, and belts. Each item was called off as trainees held it up for confirmation. Drill sergeants walked through the formation coaching them on what unfamiliar items were. They signed an individual clothing and equipment record. Back in their barracks a drill sergeant explained that the bewildering tangled pile of OD canvas and webbing was called "TA-50," after Table of Allowance 50, specifying how many of what items were issued. They were talked through assembling and adjusting the M1956 load-bearing equipment (LBE) or load-carrying equipment (LCE) or "web gear."

The heavy-duty pistol belt had a pair of universal ammunition pouches ("ammo pouches") on the front, a first-aid pouch with a field dressing, a plastic canteen in a carrier on one hip, and a small combat pack ("butt or ass pack") attached to the back of the belt. A pair of heavy-duty suspenders took the weight of the gear off the hips. Its front straps were attached to the belt and the back strap to tabs on the butt pack. If the butt pack was not worn, the back straps were extended and fastened to the belt. Two 20-round M14 rifle magazines were carried in each pouch and there were small straps on the sides for hand grenades. Another strap on the pouch clipped to a ring on the front of the suspenders to support the weight. Magazines were only issued on the rifle range. Trainees soon learned that the drill sergeants would check

---

5 The peace symbol began life as an icon for the British Campaign for Nuclear Disarmament (CND) in 1958. It represents the semaphore flag signs for "N" (inverted "V") and "D" (vertical line). Its original meaning subverted, it soon appeared in US civil rights marches and later in anti-war demonstrations. It also happened to be the 1940 insignia of the German 3d Panzer Division.

The enemy, here an NVA sapper, reconnaissance-commando, armed with the 7.62mm AK-47 assault rifle. He is a defector, a Chieu Hoi (pronounced "choo hoy"), who demonstrates sapper techniques to American troops. The Local Force VC appeared to be local peasants wearing black "pajamas." Main Force VC and NVA regulars mostly wore green uniforms and were well equipped for the most part.

pouches to ensure that cigarettes and "poggy bait" (candy and snacks) were not carried. A canteen cup with a folding handle nested on to the bottom of the one-quart canteen. Legg would find this to be a valuable item for heating coffee and cocoa, cooking C-rations, for washing and shaving, and even for bathing. A folding entrenching tool was carried on the left hip when necessary. A man in Legg's squad made the mistake of calling it a "little shovel," immediately setting off an outraged drill corporal, who told him it was an "e-tool," not a shovel, and that if he heard such a blatant unauthorized nomenclature being used for an e-tool he might be going to the stockade for murdering a trainee. A bayonet could be fastened to the e-tool's carrier, but these were issued only during bayonet training. On a daily basis nothing was carried in the butt pack other than a rolled up poncho and a pair of socks.

Legg soon learned to rattle off the description of what was officially designated the US rifle, caliber 7.62mm, M14: a "lightweight, air-cooled, gas-operated, magazine-fed, shoulder-fired weapon." Having handled only .22 rifles and bolt-action deer rifles he was surprised by its 11.25 pounds loaded with a full magazine. Regardless of the fact that large numbers of Americans owned firearms, only a comparatively small number had more than just minimal experience with them, many none at all. None had experienced semi-automatic assault-type weapons, as they were not yet widely available on the commercial market. They quickly learned that it was called a "rifle" or "weapon," never a "gun," which is an artillery piece. Rifles were issued after breakfast from the arms room cage and turned in at day's end. Legg was given yet another number to remember: his rifle's serial number.

Gear in 'Nam

When PV2 Legg arrived at the 1st Cavalry Division's FIRST TEAM Academy, he was issued with a full set of LBE. His platoon sergeant or squad members told him what was essential and what was unnecessary; the bare minimum was carried. Tramping over the rugged terrain and the enervating climate made this necessary. The ability to conduct frequent resupply by helicopter helped keep loads light with only a few days' rations carried and no need for spare clothing. Occasionally a new platoon leader or company commander would have some idealistic desire to make soldiers carry everything specified "by the book," much of which was unnecessary, such as shelter-halves and mess kits. Most leaders were more practical and allowed troops to carry what they felt was needed and dispense with the "nice to have" items. Experience and observation of how other platoon members carried their gear led to Legg making refinements during his tour.

M1956 gear provided the basis for LBE in Vietnam. Even when more durable rot-proof nylon gear began to be fielded in 1967, it was similar in design to the earlier cotton web gear. There were three areas in which the earlier gear, designed for temperate environments and supported by traditional supply lines stretching from a secure rear area, differed from Vietnam:

1. Soldiers had to carry rations for several days rather then receive the next meal when consuming the last.

2. According to manuals the basic load of ammunition for an M14 rifle was five 20-round magazines, and nine 20-round magazines for an M16A1 (30-round magazines used today were not available). This was completely insufficient for close-range firefights that might turn into prolonged battles. Helicopter resupply of ammunition was erratic and not always timely because of weather and enemy fire. Two or three times as much ammunition might be carried.

3. Water was another concern. In a conventional environment soldiers carried a single one-quart canteen. Four to six quarts was typical in Vietnam.

The official temperate climate fighting load was 65 pounds and only a single C-ration meal was carried. Much of the extraneous items were eliminated in Vietnam (13-pound sleeping bag, gas mask, mess kit, bayonet, and other items), but made up for by additional rations, water, ammo, and other munitions. Efforts were made to reduce individual loads by sharing a single item between two men. Soldiers would buddy-up, with one carrying an air mattress ("rubber bitch") and the other a poncho liner and mosquito net. One carried an e-tool and both a poncho.

The small butt pack was totally inadequate for carrying necessary loads. Either the lightweight rucksack with an aluminum frame or the later tropical rucksack was used. "Rucks" accommodated the minimum three days' rations, a gallon or more of water in one- and two-quart canteens, and the additional munitions distributed through squads. Four M16 ammunition pouches might be carried, and extra magazines were sometimes carried in one-quart canteen carriers or Claymore bags. Many soldiers carried up to two-dozen magazines. Besides the short ammo pouches made for M16 magazines, sometimes only deeper M14 pouches were available. Both carried four M16 magazines. To raise the shorter M16 magazines up to the M14 pouch's top opening, a field dressing was placed in the bottom. M16 ammunition was issued in seven-pocket cloth bandoliers with two 10-round stripper clips per pocket. A loaded 20-round magazine was often carried in each pocket. Two magazine-filled bandoliers were often the only means used by some to carry ammo, and allowed the elimination of the pistol belt and other belt-carried gear, with canteens being attached to the ruck.

Toilet articles (razor, razorblades – disposable razors had not yet appeared – bar of soap in a plastic box, toothbrush, toothpaste), a few pairs of socks in a plastic bag (dry socks were heaven), letter-writing materials in a plastic bag or a grenade packing tube, and not much else, were carried. At least two field dressings were carried, as a gunshot typically resulted in entry and exit wounds, and mortars, grenades, RPGs, and booby traps often caused multiple fragmentation wounds.

Besides two to four frag grenades, soldiers carried a significant amount of munitions for the platoon. This was divvied up and included machine-gun belts, 40mm rounds, Claymore mines, LAWs (light anti-tank weapons), colored smoke grenades, trip flares, "pop-up" signal flares, 1.25-pound C4 demolition blocks (different individuals carried detonators and safety fuse), radio batteries, and special-purpose grenades such as WP, concussion, and thermite.

Scout-dog teams search a "hooch" of typical construction. When ordered to burn a village that had been supporting the VC, most soldiers felt that it was no great loss to the Vietnamese as the houses could be quickly and easily replaced. A cheap, simply built hut it might be, but to the Vietnamese it was home, and such acts often did more harm than good.

Weapons in 'Nam

Up until late 1969 Legg and other trainees used the M14 rifle. It was not until then that M16A1s were provided to training units. Most Army units in Vietnam received the 5.56mm M16A1 in 1966 and it officially replaced the M14 in February 1967, but it remained in use by most of the Army outside of Vietnam for sometime. Airborne and airmobile units had received the still experimental XM16E1s prior to deploying to Vietnam in 1964 as a lightweight more compact weapon.

Vilified by some, praised by others, the M16 was arguably the most controversial weapon to enter US service. Its advantages over the M14 were its lighter weight (7.6 pounds compared to 9.3 pounds unloaded), compactness, and more room for ammo to be carried. There were problems with early M16s: the bolt would sometimes not fully close after excessive firing, it had poor extraction, and the open prong flash suppressor often caught on vegetation, thus fouling the weapon. Many of these problems were rectified in the M16A1, providing an improved bolt and recoil spring, a forward assist plunger on the receiver's side to ensure that the bolt fully locked, a chrome-plated chamber to improve extraction, and a closed-type "birdcage" suppressor. It still required meticulous cleaning, but this was somewhat offset by a less fouling propellant.

Other problems were experienced with M16s because of their extremely high-velocity lightweight bullet. It achieved very poor penetration through brush, bamboo, sandbags, foxhole parapets, etc. It was easily deflected by vegetation and there were frequent reports of it inflicting light wounds that should really have been kills. There were equally numerous reports of horrendous wounds and fatal 5.56mm hits that would have been less severe if a 7.62mm M60 machine gun had been used. Such disparity in effects was caused by the light bullet's erratic behavior. One might make a

The VC and NVA often left propaganda signs and scattered leaflets in abandoned camps, urging surrender when they heard free-world units approaching. American soldiers treated these rather simplistic efforts with disdain.

clean passage through a target and the next would tumble after impact. However, the bullet did not tumble in flight, as so often reported, unless it had been deflected by vegetation.

Because of the M16's poor penetration, the platoon's 7.62mm M60 machine guns played an important role. The M60 was heavy, 23 pounds, but able to put out a high rate of fire that could chop through dense vegetation. Up to 1,200 rounds would be carried for each M60, with the 100-round assault bags distributed through the platoon. While the M60 had a quick-change barrel for overheating, spare barrels were seldom carried by the two-man crew.

The M14 saw initial use in Vietnam along with the M14(M) and M14A1 (M14E2 1963–66) automatic rifles. While heavy, the M14 offered good penetration and man-stopping capabilities. The basic rifle, while capable of full-automatic firing, was fitted with a selector lock to allow only semi-automatic firing. The M14(M) (Modified) was fitted with an M2 bipod and the selector lock removed. It was too light, resulting in it being extremely inaccurate. An effort was made to improve its accuracy in the form of the M14A1 by providing a straight-line stock, rear and forward pistol grips, and a muzzle compensator. It was still notoriously inaccurate and quickly overheated.

The US Army employed thousands of helicopters in Vietnam. They were essential for transportation, resupply, medical evacuation, command and control, reconnaissance, and fire support. The French operated only 54 helicopters in the whole of Indochina. Here Hueys extract a company after completing a search-and-clear mission.

The 40mm M79 grenade launcher – "blooper" or "thumper" – was an extremely effective and versatile weapon. A good grenadier could easily put a high explosive fragmentation round on a small target at 150 or more meters and area targets up to 350. It could also launch various colored signal smoke and pyrotechnic ("pyro") signals and illumination flares. The M79 was light, 6.2 pounds, but grenadiers carried up to 30–40 rounds. These might be carried in an 18-pocket vest or in a combination of M14 ammunition pouches, Claymore bags, one-quart canteen carriers, or the six-round bandolier the cartridges were issued in.

Squads had two M79s, and one problem was that each M79 meant one less rifle. Grenadiers carried a .45-caliber M1911A1 Colt pistol, but that was strictly a self-defense weapon and contributed nothing to platoon firepower; a few grenadiers carried an M16 though. Development began on a 40mm grenade launcher that could be attached beneath an M16's handguard. The first attempt was the XM148, which saw limited field testing in 1966. It was plagued with mechanical problems and the project was dropped. The XM203 was field tested in 1968 and standardized the following year, although the M79 continued in use.

Certain precautions were necessary with the M79. Early HE (high explosive) rounds armed within 8–12 meters, and if the round struck vegetation or the launcher was accidentally fired with the round impacting among nearby troops, friendly casualties resulted. The causality radius was 5 meters, although casualties occurred within 15 meters. New rounds armed within 14–28 meters, making them safer to friendly troops.

A rifleman prepares to leap off the skid of a Huey. His aluminum-frame rucksack demonstrates the sometimes haphazard collection of gear infantrymen carried. In most units it was very much left up to the individual how he arranged his gear.

The M72 light anti-tank weapon (LAW) was a 5.2-pound single-shot, disposable 66mm rocket launcher with a high explosive anti-tank (HEAT) warhead. Intended as an anti-tank weapon, it was less than effective against personnel. One problem encountered was that if it struck the ground at a low angle, a given because of the flat trajectory, it often failed to detonate. Early models were prone to moisture, humidity, and dust affecting the firing system, resulting in failures to fire. Regardless, many platoons carried a small number of LAWs to engage bunkers. They were also barrage-fired into trees containing a sniper. Maximum effective range was 325 meters, but 150–200 meters was more practical, although they were typically employed at much closer ranges.

There were lots of hand grenades of all types. Legg's introduction to grenades in training had been minimal, but he became adept at identifying and employing them. The most common were the several models of fragmentation grenades or "frags." They were filled with composition B and contained an internal fragmentation liner inside the smooth bodies with 4–5-second delay fuses. The earliest models were lemon-shaped, the M26, M26A1, M26A2, M57, and M61. In 1967 the "baseball" shaped frag was issued to provide a more even all-around fragmentation pattern. These were the M33, M59, M67, and M68. The M57, M61, M67, and M68 were identical to the M26A2, M26A1, M33, and M59, respectively, with the addition of a safety clip. This wire clip was rotated to allow the arming lever to fly off once the arming pin was pulled and the grenade thrown. It helped prevent accidents if the grenade was dropped at the wrong time. Of course there were instances in the excitement of combat when rotating the clip would be forgotten. The M26A2, M57, M59, and M68 were impact-detonating frags. They too had a 4–5-second delay, but if they struck the ground before that time they detonated on impact. They proved very dangerous if accidentally dropped once armed, and worse, would detonate if striking intervening vegetation, something impossible to avoid. Many troops simply refused to use impact grenades. They were identified by a squatter fuse and marked IMPACT on the lever and body. Other grenades are depicted in Plates D and G.

M18A1 Claymore anti-personnel mines were used extensively in Vietnam, some 80,000 per month. It was a 3.5-pound directional mine in a rectangular, slightly curved fiberglass box with 1.5 pounds of C4 plastic explosive backing an epoxy matrix in which were embedded 704 7/32-inch (6mm) diameter ball bearings. It was either electrically detonated by command or rigged with a tripwire to be activated by an intruder. When detonated the ball bearings were blasted out in a 60-degree fan with an optimum range of 50 meters, but dangerous up to 250. Blast and secondary fragmentation were

Infantry Battalion Weapons, 1965–73
.45-caliber M1911A1 pistol
7.62mm M14 rifle
7.62mm M14(M) and M14A1 automatic rifles
7.62mm M21 sniper rifle
5.56mm M16 and M16A1 rifles
5.56mm XM177E1 and XM177E2 submachine guns ("CAR-15")
7.62mm M60 machine gun
.50-caliber M2 machine gun
40mm M79, XM148, and M203 grenade launchers
66mm M72 and M72A1 light anti-tank weapons (LAW)
3.5-inch M20A1B1 rocket launcher ("bazooka")
90mm M67 recoilless rifle
106mm M40A1 recoilless rifle
81mm M29 and M29A1 mortars
4.2-inch M30 mortar

A: Recruit, Ft Polk, Louisiana

35

B: Viet Cong village, Tigerland

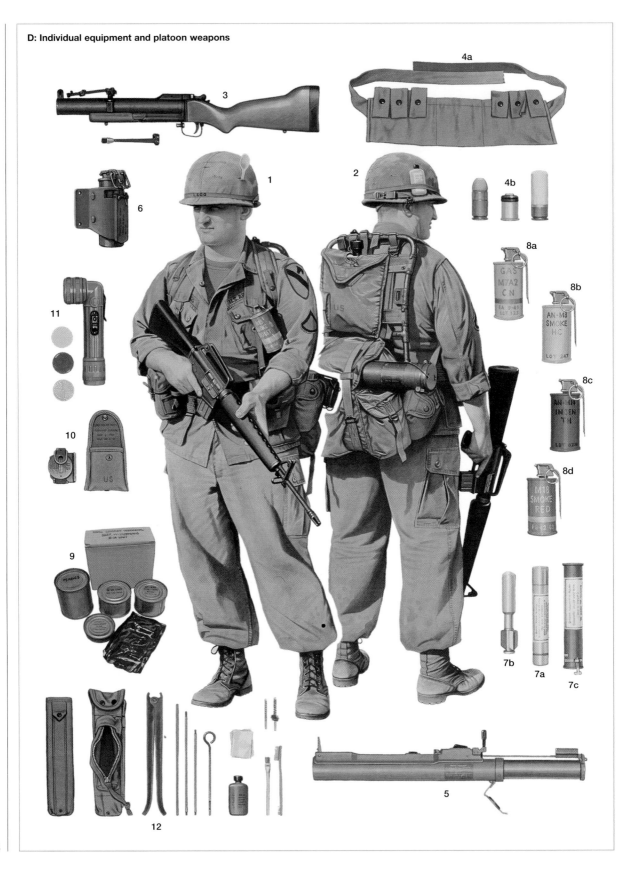

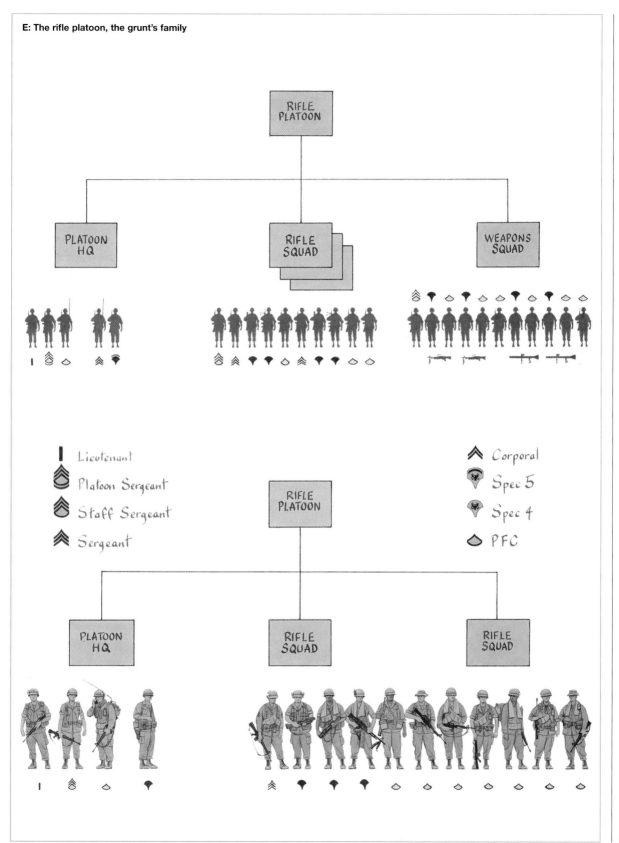

F: Firefight – the "seven-minute war"

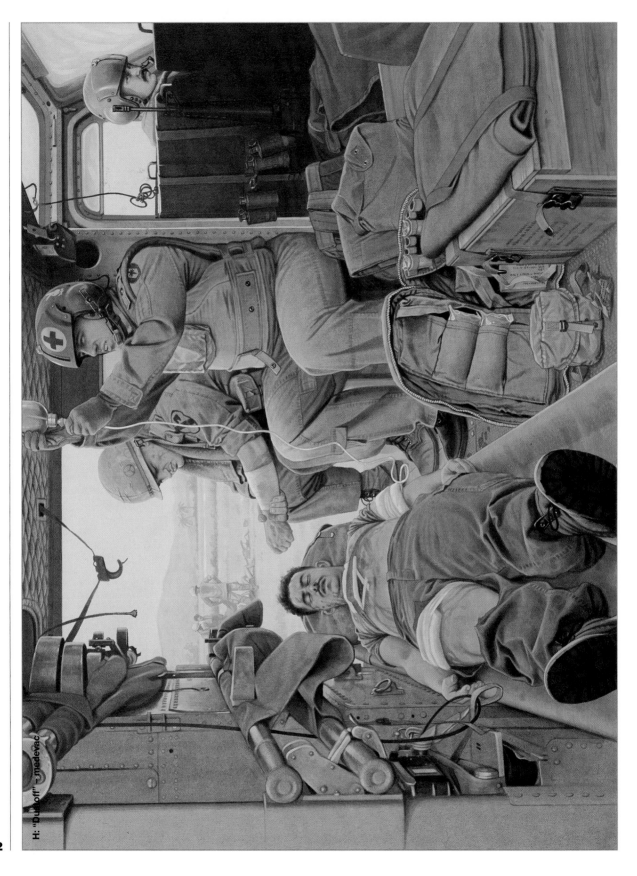

H: "Dust off" – medevac

dangerous within 100 meters in all directions, and they were devastating to assault troops and those caught in an ambush kill zone.

The M49A1 trip flare was 1.5 inches in diameter, almost 5 inches long, and weighed 15 ounces. They were attached to barbed-wire pickets, stakes, trees by a mounting bracket, or simply wired to a stake without the bracket, several inches above the ground within wire entanglements or on likely enemy approaches to a unit's night position, and rigged to be activated by an up to 40-foot tripwire. When activated the magnesium flare immediately ignited, burning for 55–70 seconds at 50,000 candlepower at 4,200°F and illuminated up to a 300-meter radius area. They could also be thrown by hand by removing the arming pin, gripping the grenade-like arming lever, and throwing it. It ignited immediately upon release of the lever, but cleared the hand by several feet. This was useful for illuminating a close-in area that the enemy was suspected of infiltrating, or to ignite fires.

WELCOME TO VIETNAM ... FNG

The Boeing 707, chartered from a commercial airline and bearing stewardesses and the usual amenities, rolled down the Cam Ranh Bay runway. After processing at Ft Lewis, WA, the recruits' airliner had departed McChord Air Force Base, refueling in Alaska and Japan. The day they took off marked the beginning of their 365-day tour in 'Nam, and the countdown to DEROS (Date Eligible for Return from Over Seas – "de-ros") had begun. Others would fly over after processing at Oakland Army Base (Oakland Army Terminal before July 1966), CA, from Travis Air Force Base to arrive at Saigon's Ton Son Nhut Airport and at the 90th Replacement Battalion at Long Binh Army Base outside of the city. Of the almost 2,600,000 who served in Vietnam, only some 7,000 failed to report for deployment.

Worn out from the whirlwind processing, 18–20 hours' flying and jetlag, the first thing that struck Legg was the absence of the half-expected rocket attack, followed by the realization of just how hot and humid it was. There were Vietnamese civilians everywhere, workers on the base, and not a single one suddenly threw a grenade. Columns of gray smoke rose over the base, indicating that they had just missed a rocket attack. The 160 troops off-loading the plane felt vulnerable being unarmed, especially when the steel mesh-covered windows on the buses were noted. They were driven to the 22d Replacement Battalion and along the way saw the three most common sights in Vietnam: barbed wire, sandbags, and motorbikes, sometimes with an entire Vietnamese family clinging on.

Housed in simple two-story barracks similar to their Stateside counterparts, the replacements were rushed through a week of processing and filling out more forms, including a next of kin (NOK) notification. They could check a box saying "not to notify

A Pathfinder ground-guides a Huey as it off-loads infantrymen. Choppers preferred not to actually land on the ground, as rocks or stumps hidden in the grass and brush could damage the underside. All infantry units became equally proficient at airmobile operations, whether they were airmobile, airborne, light, or standard "straight-leg" infantry.

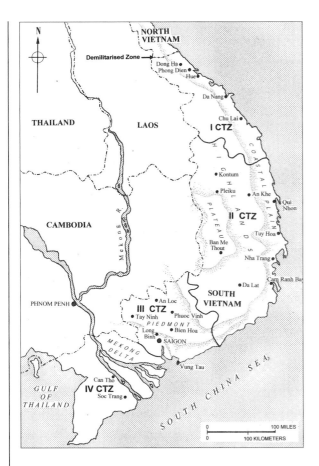

The diversity of Vietnam's terrain is demonstrated by this map of the Republic of Vietnam (South Vietnam). The ARVN divided Vietnam into four corps tactical zones (CTZ) for command and control purposes. US command arrangements were overlaid on this. When a veteran is asked where he served in Vietnam he will say Eye Corps, Two Corps, Three Corps, or Four Corps and others will know the approximate area.

NOK" if they were lightly wounded, but if seriously wounded, killed, or missing their NOK would be notified. They found that if KIA (killed in action), MIA (missing in action), WIA (wounded in action), or taken prisoner, an officer and chaplain would notify their NOK in person. Servicemembers' Group Life Insurance paid the beneficiary $10,000 plus burial expenses.

They were issued Geneva Conventions and MACV Ration Cards (limiting purchases of electrical appliances, cameras, liquor, and cigarettes, for black market control). American dollars were exchanged for Military Payment Certificates (MPC – "monopoly" or "funny money") and they were informed that the possession and use of US dollars was illegal. MPCs could not be spent on the local economy either; they were required to be converted to piasters, "pees," at military pay offices and banks (US$1.00 = 115$VN in 1969). MPCs could only be spent in PXs, military clubs, Army post offices, and Vietnamese concessionaires on bases (barbers, launders, etc.). Most men had much of their pay deposited in the First National City or Chase Manhattan Banks in check or savings accounts. Legg drew $50 a month in MPCs and banked the rest. Money could also be sent home by postal money order through Army post offices. Coming as a surprise, all E-2s were promoted to PFC upon arrival.

The men learned that letters could be sent home postage free by simply writing "FREE" on the envelope. If mailed to a friend in another unit they wrote "IN COUNTRY." It was popular to use the tops of C-ration cartons as postcards. Full postage had to be paid on packages. They had to brush their teeth with special one-time-use fluoridated toothpaste and sternly told to take their daily and weekly malaria pills. In some cases individuals were charged with an Article 15 (a small fine or reduction in rank) for failure to follow orders if they contracted malaria, as they had obviously failed to take the pills. Venereal disease was a major problem in Vietnam, and replacements were warned not to partake of local offerings. They were told about incurable "black syphilis," and that if they contracted it they would be sent to an island off Vietnam to spend the rest of their lives and their families notified that they were KIA. Few believed this myth.

They finally found out to what division or separate brigade they were assigned; Legg drew the 1st Cavalry Division (Airmobile). It was a bit unsettling to be told, "Only the ARVN (Army of the Republic of Vietnam – "Ar-vin") have been in 'Nam longer than the CAV." Loaded on a C-130 transport, 40 replacements were flown southwest to Phong Dien in the extreme north of Vietnam. The sprawling base was the CAV's home and included an airfield with some of the Division's 400 helicopters, vehicle and aircraft maintenance facilities, communications sites, artillery positions, motor pools, unpainted barracks and mess halls, and everywhere bunkers in which to take cover from the occasional rocket attack. They had electrical power, clubs, PXs, a post office, troop clinics for sick call, outdoor movies. It was not unlike a Stateside base, just more austere. Steam baths ("steam and cream") and low-cost prostitutes (500 pees for "short-time," 2,000 for "longtime" – all night) were readily available in the off-base "vil." The large division and brigade base camps were relatively secure. They might be rocketed and mortared, but seldom was a ground attack attempted.

They were surprised that Vietnamese civilians pulled most KP and served as hooch maids, cleaning barracks, polishing boots, washing uniforms (strictly hands-off, though that did not prevent some girls from earning extra piasters). Legg had soon found that columns of gray smoke were common on all bases and were not the result of "incoming" – rockets or mortars. Latrines were wooden outhouses with toilet seats over a compartment containing a cut-down 55-gallon drum. The shit-burning detail involved pulling the drums out of a door in the back, stirring in diesel fuel, and burning it. Not a pleasant detail, but the pungent odor was masked by the diesel. Urinals were pipes or plastic mortar round tubes inserted at an angle in a gravel bed sprinkled with DDT powder to keep down flies.

Since 1966, divisions and separate brigades were required to conduct a week or two orientation and acclimatization course. At the FIRST TEAM Academy, replacements were given a bit of the CAV's history, acclimatized through marches and runs, refresher first aid, "helicopter" rapelling from a tower, and land navigation. They also received instruction on booby traps, Claymore mines, ambushes, and patrolling; they familiarization-fired the M79 and M60, were issued gear, and received training on and zeroed their M16A1s. Sometimes they ran a patrol and set up a night ambush outside the base. It was disconcerting to be told, "Forget everything you learned in the States." This was an exaggeration, but their previous training was mostly oriented to a conventional environment, and 'Nam required different tactics and techniques.

There were several types of infantry battalion in Vietnam: "standard" infantry and light infantry, the latter structured for Vietnam, but the former similarly modified – "straight-leg" – infantry. Mechanized battalions were equipped with M113A1 armored personnel carriers (APCs or "tracks"), one per squad, which they rode on top of, rather than inside, for fear of mines and rocket-propelled grenades. Airborne infantry battalions were of course parachute-qualified, but there was such a shortage of parachutists that many units were designated "airborne" only on paper and sometimes converted to airmobile. Airmobile divisions (1st Cav, 101st Airborne from 1969, AMERICAN Divisions – though not so designated) possessed enough "organic" helicopters (ones permanently assigned to the unit) to lift one-third of the division at once, giving them unprecedented tactical mobility. All other infantry battalions were just as proficient in air assaults using abundant non-divisional aviation battalions. There were even

While UH-1D/H Hueys were used for combat assaults and many other missions, when troops were transported into a secured area or firebase the CH-47 Chinook, or "Shithook," was used. They could carry up to 33 troops, although in Vietnam it was fewer because of high temperatures, the infantrymen's loads and extra armament, and armor. Troops took a deep breath before loading or off-loading a Chinook, as the exhaust blasting from the engine housings above the tailgate scorched the air like a blast furnace.

Ten cent Military Payment Certificate (MPC) or "funny money." Also issued in five, 25 and 50 cent as well as one, five, ten, and 20 dollar denominations.

A CH-53 Tarhe, or "Skyhook," heavy-lift helicopter delivers a 155mm M114A1 howitzer to a ridge-top firebase. A firebase such as this was often in place only for a few days to support an operation and was then relocated to another hilltop. Defenses were hasty and sometimes not even concertina wire was strung.

A rifle-platoon leader and his radio-telephone operator (RTO). Lieutenants selected their RTO with care from the sharpest men and they performed as a team. Many platoon leaders did all the talking on the radio. Others relayed to the RTO and he did the talking. The soldiers wear body armor vests, "flak vests," which were not too commonly worn by Army troops.

riverine battalions transported in armored troop transports – armed and armored landing craft in the Mekong Delta. 11Bs were not specifically trained for the different types of battalions, other than paratroopers; they learned their duties on the job.

Meals on the large bases were mainly B-rations: canned, dehydrated, and preserved foods, mostly in #10 (1-gallon) cans. Some A-rations – fresh and frozen foods (mostly steaks, pork chops, chicken, fish) – were served, and bread was baked in base bakeries. Iced tea, fruit juice, and coffee were also served. Even milk was available. Filled milk – powdered milk reconstituted with water and fat – came from a plant at Long Binh. Eggs were mostly powdered. Some fresh vegetables and canned fruits were available. Similar fare was served on fire support bases, but no A-rations because of lack of refrigeration.

On graduation day the men were told which battalion they were assigned to. Legg and four others were loaded in a Huey, their first chopper ride, and flown to a firebase. This was their first chance to view the terrain they would be working in – horizon to horizon of vivid green jungle. From their seat it looked beautiful, but then they would see kilometers-long swathes of shattered trees and craters from B-52 Arc Light strikes and burned-out villages.

The firebase was a sad sight, a ragged muddy or dusty scar of a clearing gouged into the jungle. There were one or two coils of meandering concertina wire around an irregular-shaped bulldozed earthen berm, green sandbag bunkers – no two alike – donut-like artillery positions, dozens of radio antennas, columns of gray smoke from shit-burning and endlessly howling generators, helicopters constantly arriving and departing among blowing dust. All this promoted the response: "It hits home, we're really in it now." The troops lived in rat- and roach-infested, wet and overly hot sandbag bunkers or slept beneath culvert pipe sections covered with a couple of layers of sandbags.

Soldiers on the firebase were lean and gaunt-looking, their uniforms, boots, web gear, hair, and skin tinted pale maroon from the deep red soil. Some stared at the new guys, but most ignored them. They'd seen plenty before of what the *Army Digest* called "funny new guys."

BELIEF AND BELONGING

The men were met by an NCO and led through the base's labyrinth of bunkers and trenches to the battalion command post (CP). The sergeant major welcomed them, told them what he expected and to listen to their NCOs. They were in the CAV now and he expected them to give their best. Another NCO led them to a grubby sandbagged company CP. Here another "lifer," the first sergeant, laid down the law and welcomed them to "the best company in the battalion." They filled out

paperwork and stacked their duffel bags and rucks outside. They met the company CO, the "Old Man" or the "Six" (derived from the radio code for a CO). The "Top" showed them around the company area and then turned them over to their platoon sergeants, who may or may not have been lifer-types, most being 20-something staff sergeants. He too read the riot act and then assigned Legg to a squad.

The eight men of 1st Squad, 2d Platoon, Charlie Company, were stripped to the waist and filling sandbags, a seemingly unending task in a firebase. They were a mixed lot – Whites from across the country, one a college dropout – from a wide range of social and economic backgrounds. Two were Blacks and one a Hispanic. They had been "in-country" from three to 10 months. The buck sergeant squad leader had been in the Army over two years and in-country eight months, having served a tour in Alaska. They regarded Legg with little apparent interest, shook hands as the squad leader rattled off nicknames and last names, the names he would remember them by; for most he never knew their full names or even where they were from. Legg would get to know them closely on one level, but in many ways he would know little about most of them.

Most soldiers immediately began counting off their 365 days. Some waited until later. The six-month point was sobering to many realizing they had just as much time left as they had already spent. If not sooner, most started a "short-timer calendar" at 30 days.[6]

Few young Americans knew anything about Vietnam or the war. Few watched television news or read the papers, at least not about the war. Rare was the 18-year-old who could even show you where Vietnam was on a map, much less understand what the war was about. Some thought it was a civil war … it wasn't. The author had a couple of high-school students ask him about the war when he returned and they thought we were fighting the Japanese.

6 This was usually in the form of a woman's body or an outline of Vietnam divided into 30 or even 365 numbered
   segments to be penciled in.

The rifle platoon's two M60 machine guns, or "pigs," were a key part of the platoon's firepower. Prior to the introduction of small pin-on and sew-on collar rank insignia, subdued rank insignia were worn on the sleeves, here Spec 4.

The rifle squad's two 40mm M79 grenade launchers provided a third of the squad's firepower. On occasion all or part of a platoon's M79s were concentrated in a group for concentrated fire on enemy positions or snipers. This grenadier has hand grenade arming rings and pins inserted in his boonie hat's camouflage band. These were handy for neutralizing VC booby traps, which often utilized hand grenades. US grenade pins could be inserted in Chicom and Soviet grenades as well.

While not educated politically to any degree nor barraged with government propaganda even approaching what any communist government inflicted on its people, the average middle-American values of conservatism, God-given rights, and anti-communism were strong. Many soldiers who served in Vietnam had fathers and uncles who had fought for those same values just 20-odd years earlier in World War II.

While the war was increasingly unpopular or thought of as un-winnable or unmerited or just plain wrong, a large percentage of the population did not believe that the US should cut and run. Many did feel that it was attempting to halt the spread of communism, that the South Vietnamese people had the right to defend themselves, and that it was just that we aid them. It was at the higher military and political levels that the war was poorly conceived and managed. It was the politicians who lacked the wherewithal and not the soldiers.

Drug culture

Drugs were an increasing problem throughout the war. As opposition to the war rose at home, leadership deteriorated, and as numbers of draftees increased, drug usage grew. The use of draftees as a whole was not the cause, but it did increase the numbers of less than motivated soldiers who resented enforced military service, and felt that their lives had been disrupted, and that they would spend a "wasted" year in a war they wanted nothing of. Drugs could be purchased at low cost from Vietnamese, though a few soldiers set themselves up as dealers. Marijuana was the most common, but cocaine and heroin came into increasing use. Drugs, especially marijuana, were used on combat operations by some troops, but more often it was not tolerated by most of them, at least in the bush. It was not as widespread in infantry units as assumed, but much more prevalent in support units. Use varied from unit to unit. Up to nine soldiers supported every infantryman "beating the bush." Employed in often boring and mundane jobs, drug use, alcoholism, racism, and dissent was more common in the rear among the REMFs – "rear echelon motherf**kers," as they were known to the "grunts."

Rest and recreation

Troops need time off. A five- or six-day Rest and Recreation (R&R), non-chargeable to annual leave with free airfare, was authorized after in-country for four months, plus a three-day in-country R&R at Vung Tau or China Beach.[7] Sydney was extremely popular, and many married men met their wives in Hawaii. Though not encouraged, they could take a seven-day leave to R&R Centers or other places accessible by military hop, such as Okinawa. When a death occurred in the immediate family, individuals were flown home and granted 30 days' compassionate leave. If a soldier extended six months in Vietnam, he received a 30-day leave home and another R&R.

---

7   R&R Centers were located at Bangkok, Thailand; Honolulu, Hawaii; Manila, Philippines; Sydney, Australia; Hong Kong; Singapore; Tokyo; Taipei, Taiwan; and Kuala Lumpur, Malaysia.

Relations in the ranks

Legg met his platoon leader later in the day, a 2nd lieutenant in his mid-20s. His source of commission was college ROTC, which he had taken for four years in a state university to pay for part of his tuition and then owed six years' active duty. He attended the 12-week Infantry Officer Basic Course (OBC) at "Ft Benning School for Boys" after commissioning. Others had a college degree without having taken ROTC. Upon joining the Army they could volunteer for the 23-week Infantry Officer Candidate School (OCS) at Ft Benning, GA, with no requirement for IOBC. Most officers had served at least a year in troop or training units prior to deployment. Second lieutenants were automatically promoted to 1st after 12 months and to captain after another 12.

In most instances relations were cordial enough, but officers did have to maintain a certain distance. How well this was perceived by the troops and handled by the officers was very much personality driven and also depended on company and battalion leadership. Known simply as the "LT," in the field, the lieutenant endured the same ordeals as his platoon. In the FSB he was often quartered separately and frequently burdened with extra company administrative duties. The running of the platoon was left to the platoon sergeant, who essentially became a foreman for endless work details. Some lieutenants tried to become their men's "buddy," others remained aloof and even condescending. It was difficult under such conditions to strike an even balance – know your men, but don't become too familiar.

It was rare that relations were hostile, but it occurred. Frustration with the war and with their lot in life, constant danger, harsh conditions, drugs, and increasing racial issues contributed to the stress. Most enlisted men were destined to serve out their year in a platoon. Most lieutenants did six to seven months as a platoon leader and then went on to become a company XO or CO or drew a "softer" headquarters company assignment. This could lead to officers being viewed as a privileged class and to further resentment, but this again depended on personalities. Lax discipline was just as much a cause of problems as overly strict and unfair authority.

"Fragging," the use of grenades to murder or harass disliked leaders or other individuals, did occur, but not nearly on the scale depicted in novels and motion pictures. Fragging was usually conducted as a graduated sequence of warnings: first a smoke grenade, then a tear gas grenade, then a frag grenade without pin pulled, and finally a frag with pin pulled – the targeted individual usually got the message before the process ran its full course. There were 199 homicides from all causes within the Army in Southeast Asia (including Thailand, Cambodia, and Laos) from 1961 to 1976. One source cites 500 fragging incidents from 1968 to 1972, and another source claims 363 from 1970 to 1972. Not all resulted in death or injury. Some 62 percent were directed against officers, mostly lower ranking. Most of the remainder were aimed at staff sergeants and above.

Racial tensions increased throughout the war. It was not so much of an issue in combat units because of the shared adversity, close living conditions, and reliance on everyone within a small group. It was much more of

Troops of a rifle company's mortar platoon in the field. A mortar platoon had three 81mm mortars. Usually only one or two were carried to the field. They more often stayed in the firebase, as the mortars and ammunition were too heavy and only a limited number of rounds could be carried. Companies operated under the umbrella of artillery, gunships, and close-air support.

The 81mm M29A1 mortars normally remained in firebases for close-in defense and to support local security patrols. Besides HE and WP ammunition, they also fired parachute illumination flares, one of their most valuable uses.

The AN/PRC-25 radio, or "prick-25," was the standard platoon and company-level radio. Weighing 20 pounds, it was a substantial load coupled with rifle, web gear, smoke grenades, heavy spare batteries, and accessories, carried here in a canvas bag on the left side. RTOs were sniper targets and the radio was sometimes carried inside a rucksack or covered with a sandbag.

a problem in support units. It was occasionally seen in combat units though, and the longer a unit remained in a base the stronger the tendency for individuals to migrate toward others of their own social background, which was divided along racial lines. Whites too splintered into sub-groups, much like those found in high schools.

Maintaining the esprit de corps

Diversions in a base were few: card-playing, occasional movies, reading, the rare United Service Organization (USO) show, writing letters, and reading the much-anticipated letters from home. In 1965 the new cassette tapes were coming into use and for the first time an electronic means of sending mail was available. Cassette tapes also provided music (rock, folk, country and western, rhythm and blues). The Armed Forces Radio and Television Service (AFRTS) provided programming, mostly re-runs of popular Stateside television shows, but also local weather bulletins and public service announcements warning soldiers of the dangers of drugs and spending US dollars on the local economy. The military-run *Stars and Stripes* newspaper, *Army Digest* magazine, and divisional newspapers provided information. There were few opportunities for organized sports.

Life in a firebase consisted of endless work details: building and rebuilding bunkers and quarters, filling sandbags, stringing and repairing barbed wire, digging drainage ditches, burning out latrines, KP, unloading supplies and ammunition from helicopters, trash details, perimeter guard, radio watch, local security patrols, manning observation (day) and listening (night) posts, and more.

The Army made a major effort to provide meaningful meals during Thanksgiving and Christmas. Firebase meals were served on paper plates and cups and with plastic-wear to eliminate the health hazard of mess-kit washing. Breakfast and dinner were usually B-rations and lunch Cs. The Fourth of July was usually celebrated in the form of a more intense and colorful evening "mad minute." Religious services were available in firebases. Mail too was important to the Army, and every effort was used to get it to the troops in remote locations and while on operations.

The outlook of individuals ranged from a strong sense of patriotic duty to extreme anger at the disruption to their lives and a loathing of what they were to face. Most men called to the colors made the best of it and did their duty. Among those volunteering, and there were a great many of them, even late in the war, their reasons were varied: patriotism, sense of duty, adventure, a challenge, to gain experience, learn a technical skill, gain self-respect, or the opportunity for an education. Many wished to prove themselves to themselves or others, or had no employment prospects, who saw the opportunity for a better life than they had living in poverty or a poor relationship or a bad family situation at home, or because a judge gave them the option of the military or jail time. Many admitted they were seeking discipline and direction. Others felt the war was just, and while many could have gotten deferments, they felt strongly that if they backed the war they should prove it and not just let others fight it. Others fell for the packaged image presented by recruiters, or the picture painted by the few pro-war novels and non-fiction books. Their experiences were mixed. Some came out of the war disillusioned, feeling that they had been sold a bill of goods; others felt they had benefited and realized their expectations. For many the war would be a defining event in their lives, an experience that changed their lives and their entire view of life for good or bad. How often has one heard, "You know, he's different since he came back from Vietnam?" No kidding, what a surprise.

THE BOONIES: ON CAMPAIGN

The "Boondocks," the "boonies," the "bush," "Indian Territory"; this is where infantrymen spent most of their time. Combat operations could be of a few days' duration, or up to five or six weeks without seeing a firebase. To the grunt it was a company-size operation. It made no difference to him if his company was operating as part of a battalion, brigade, or division-level operation. He saw little of other companies. He might hear their fire, overhear radio transmissions, see dozens of helicopters flashing over, and jets "bring smoke" (bomb runs or artillery strikes), but down in the bush he had a very limited view of the world. In the forested and brush-covered northern mountains, the southern double- and triple-canopy jungles, in densely vegetated swamps, even on the elephant grass-covered plains of the central highlands, he could see little, often just a few men around him.

The climate is typically in the high 90-degree Fahrenheit range with equally high humidity. In the northern highlands it can become chilly at night, and it experiences a "wetter dry season." There are two seasons: the November to April dry season or northeast monsoon, and the June to October wet season or southwest monsoon. Soldiers claimed that there were three seasons: wet, dry, and dusty, occurring at hourly intervals. Mosquitoes, dry land and water leeches, red and black ants, scorpions, centipedes, snakes, and flies were a bother. Malaria, dengue fever, dysentery, diarrhea ("Hershey squirts," the topic of many discussions), "undiagnosed fevers," heat exhaustion, and dehydration were common ailments. Everything stung, bit, or jabbed you.

PFC Legg was assigned to Mojo, a wiry black kid from up north and a veteran of seven months. Mojo did not much care for the "buddy team" assignment, but told Legg, "Do what I say and you might make it through this crap. Play stupid, you end up wrapped up in a poncho and stuffed in a body-bag." Mojo had his "cherry" (slang for a first timer) dump out his ruck and threw out and added to its contents, and more canteens were drawn from supply.

A rifle squad cautiously advances up a trail after receiving sniper fire. Note that the rear men keep an eye on the flank. Their rucksacks have been left in the nearby patrol base.

Charlie Company was alerted that it would airmobile into an area and conduct a search-and-destroy mission[8]. As usual no duration was specified. Mojo gave Legg a 100-round M60 belt, a Claymore bag, two pop-up flares, and three colored smokes. He learned that over the radio they were not called red, yellow, green, or violet, but cherry, lemon, lime, and grape or other shades. It might fool the enemy monitoring their radios, as they would try to confuse aircraft by throwing the same color smoke. Red was only thrown when contact was made or to warn helicopters of enemy fire.

Mojo showed him how to strip down C-rats. They would receive a minor resupply every three days and a major every sixth. The minor brought Cs, water, and ammo, a quick in and out. Three days meant nine 1-pound meals, but most only ate two Cs a day. Unwanted items were discarded along with the cartons and the cans packed in spare socks to reduce rattling.

The UH-1H Huey helicopters arrived early in the morning. The company was divided into sticks of six men. In theory a Huey could carry 11 troops, but with the addition of door guns, ammunition, two gunners, and the high temperatures affecting lift capability, only six or seven could be carried. Before loading, Legg's squad leader admonished him: "Stay on your toes and pay attention to Mojo."

Piling out of the chopper the stick "chogied" (moved rapidly) through elephant grass across the landing zone (LZ) to the tree line. No enemy fire: a "hot" LZ was rare. Three lifts were required to insert the company. Once assembled they moved out in a single file, the "long green line." Movement formations and tactics were kept simple to ease control and because of inexperienced leadership. Operations entailed a lot of walking in rough terrain, slow, often boring, yet dangerous. Many assume that paths were hacked with machetes through the brush and bamboo, but this was seldom done – it was too noisy. The long green line pushed and crawled "busting brush." Short breaks were frequent. The company's position was reported hourly to "higher."

The first night in a "remain overnight" (RON) position was tough on Legg. Worn out from his first day in the bush, he took his turn maintaining the 50 percent alert: two hours on, two off, rotating with Mojo. They shared the single air mattress and poncho liner they carried. If the enemy did not appear too active, only one squad member stood guard, with each man pulling one hour. They ate a C-rat in the evening and one in the morning, maybe just C-rat "John Wayne crackers" or cookies for lunch. Water was collected from streams or from rain running off ponchos, but chlorine-tasting water was brought in by helicopter too. Water purification tablets were essential for stream water. Pre-sweeten Kool-Aid sent from home cut lukewarm turbid water. C-rats and coffee might be heated with a little burning ball of C4 or heating tablets ("heat tabs"), but more often they were eaten cold. Cs were filling, not all that bad tasting, but when cold, sometimes greasy, and

Infantrymen enter a Vietnamese village through a drainage ditch beneath a barbed-wire fence. Many villages had such barriers as a mostly ineffective deterrent to visiting VC. The VC would often make nocturnal visits to spread propaganda, collect food, extort "war tax" money, and ask villagers about American movements.

---

8   Such missions were later termed offensive sweeps or reconnaissance-in-force because of the adverse connotations implied by the media.

they became monotonous. Tabasco sauce was a favorite condiment for spicing up the flavor. "Care packages" sent from home with foods and snacks were valued and shared with one's squad. The major resupply day was often a rest day. The unit secured an LZ and might receive two lifts. If possible, hot chow was flown in in Mermit containers to be picked up by the second flight. Mail was delivered and picked up; radio batteries, fresh socks, and replacements for damaged uniforms were issued.

Units seldom moved at night: it was too slow and loud. American units were not generally known for their noise discipline and a RON was not always silent. Moving in daylight they were sometimes noisy, and radios were even fitted with speakers allowing transmissions to be heard. Americans were also notoriously lax with litter discipline. The VC scrounged up expended smoke grenades, safety levers and pins, LAW tubes, Claymore components, ammunition boxes and containers, grenade and projectile packing tubes, propellant containers, sandbags, bandoliers, loading clips, machine gun links, C-rat cans (some unopened), and expended batteries. They made munitions from them, and a "dead" battery had enough juice to detonate a mine. The VC even recycled field dressings, IV bottles, and morphine syringes. There were of course exceptions to laxness, but it was more common than the exception.

The average soldier respected the enemy, especially NVA regulars. VC Main Force were good too, but were mostly filled with North Vietnamese, even before the 1968 Tet Offensive decimated the VC. These forces were conventional light infantry. They were not guerrillas, though they employed many guerrilla techniques. From 1965 Vietnam was a low-intensity conventional conflict. The enemy may not have employed armor, artillery, or aircraft, but operations on both sides were divisional or multiple-division actions. Local VC guerrillas supported them, and guerrilla tactics were still an aspect of the war, but for the most part American solders were fighting light conventional forces. Local Force VC were more a nuisance, being typically described as "Three gooks carrying an AK, a magazine, and a grenade." The VC and NVA were commonly referred to simply as the "Cong" or "Charlie," derived from the phonetic alphabet "Victor Charlie" or "Chuck," the nickname for Charles.

The attitude of soldiers toward the Vietnamese is often discussed and was a major dynamic. Regardless of the line pitched by the US government and Army, the average grunt thought very little of the people they were fighting to protect from communism and instill democracy in. To many soldiers they were unmotivated, indifferent, lazy, unclean, selfish, uneducated, and would do anything for a piaster. There was widespread corruption within the Vietnamese government and ARVN. They thought even less of the ARVN, who often appeared unmotivated and unreliable (though there were many well-led, effective units). There was a degree of

A rifle squad advances across a clearing. This is a 1965 photograph with the troops wearing Stateside fatigues and cotton M1956 web gear. They would soon receive jungle fatigues and later nylon LBE.

Most villagers were pro-government and welcomed Americans. Most of the infantrymen here wear towels around their necks to mop up sweat, "drive-on rags." This machine gunner has taped his baggy trouser legs to help prevent them from snagging on vegetation.

racial prejudice among Americans too, and the soldiers' common names for Vietnamese were "gooks," "slopes," "dinks," and "zipperheads." Another factor was the type of Vietnamese most often encountered by soldiers. One does not develop a kindly outlook toward a people when exposed mainly to prostitutes, pimps, bargirls, and drug and pornography dealers. The population suffered from almost 30 years of war weariness and changes in corrupt governments. The attitude had evolved to make the best of it for oneself. Rural villagers did not care who ran the country; they just wanted to be left alone to continue their simple lives.

There is a tendency among critics of the war to claim incorrectly that it was common for American soldiers to carry out atrocities such as these: "personally raped, cut off ears, cut off heads, taped wires from portable telephones to human genitals and turned up the power, cut off limbs, blew up bodies, randomly shot at civilians, razed villages in fashion reminiscent of Genghis Khan, shot cattle and dogs for fun, poisoned food stocks, and generally ravaged the countryside of South Vietnam." Yes, atrocities occurred, but they were extremely rare. It was not policy, it was not tolerated, and it was not acceptable to most American soldiers. There are far more examples of selfless sacrifice and efforts to help the people of Vietnam than are usually recounted.

FIREFIGHT: EXPERIENCE IN BATTLE

After a week in the bush Legg was getting used to his new life. He was always tired owing to the heat, humidity, stress, irregular sleep, poor chow, and endless "humping" up and down hills, wading through streams, "bustin' brush." Because he was a "cherry" he was thankful that he did not have to "walk point," the lead man looking for booby traps, enemy movement, with his M16 set on "rock and roll" – full-auto. He soon found that booby traps were not scattered at random through the jungle, but were found around firebases to catch patrols, on approaches to enemy base camps, and on trails around VC-controlled villages. Regardless, mines[9] and booby traps accounted for 32 percent of US casualties.

A LOH (pronounced "loach") light observation helicopter reported several men in green uniforms running into the jungle from a nearby "Ap" (village) as the battalion's Alpha Company approached from the west. Charlie Company, moving in from the east, halted while

A Huey drops off infantrymen as their company secures an artillery-blasted hilltop as a firebase. The second man carries a case of C-rats.

---

9 A mine often depicted in movies shows a soldier stepping on it, hearing a click, shouting "Mine!" and told that if he moves it will detonate. Such mines exist only in Hollywood.

the platoon leaders conferred with the CO. 3d Platoon and the company HQ continued east toward the village following a ridge. 1st Platoon moved down the ridge's north side to follow a stream toward the "vil," it being suspected that the fleeing enemy might use the densely vegetated ravine as an escape route. 2d Platoon would protect 1st Platoon's north flank by conducting a "cloverleaf" – a series of sweeps that would circle back to their point of origin – into the narrow belt of woods past the stream in event the enemy chose that route. They would also swing out into the broad elephant-grass field beyond the woods and check for possible escape trails. 1st Platoon moved down to the stream, establishing a blocking position, while 2d Platoon splashed through and began its looping search through the belt of trees. While the underbrush was less dense than in the wide ravine, visibility was limited and the going was slow. 1st Platoon continued down the stream toward the "vil." It was a seldom-seen situation in which the platoons spread out widely without being coiled together. The risk was acceptable, as it was only what was believed to be a small NVA foraging patrol that was being hunted. 2d Platoon followed a circuitous route through the trees to patrol out into the field and then circle back through the woods toward the ravine.

Reaching the wood line, the platoon paused to scan the broad expanse of elephant grass swaying in the breeze. It was impossible to tell if anyone was hidden amongst the dense, head-high grass. The platoon moved out, 26 men in single-file, silent, with Legg's squad in the lead. The platoon leader followed the lead squad and the platoon sergeant brought up the platoon's rear with the "tail-end Charlie" or "tail gunner." Shortly after entering the field the ground became soggy and wet, then the water deepened. They were in a long-abandoned rice paddy. With the point man pushing through grass, the column moved at a snail's pace. The "point" was rotated frequently relieving the exhausting effort. The squad leader followed behind the point with compass in hand and tried to maintain a pace count to estimate the distance traveled. Legg found himself behind the squad leader as the point rotated. He turned to Legg, "Take the point Cherry. Just stay cool, take it slow." Legg moved up, switching his selector to full-auto, a round already in the chamber. He pushed through the grass in calf-deep water unable to see anything around him and stumbled up a low grass-covered dyke. Some distance beyond the dyke he discovered a narrow open stream of muddied water, an irrigation ditch. He waved the squad leader up. Looking around, he muttered, "The water's muddy. Someone's been through here." He dropped back, motioning one of the grenadiers to take position beside him.

The platoon leader was moving up the line for a look-see. A ripping sound tore across the field, close. More rips and a grenade detonated as the platoon opened fire blindly into the grass on both sides of the column. With movement on both sides of him, Legg heard men splashing into the shallow ditch seeking what cover it offered. Legg slid over the low berm edging the ditch and heard bullets snapping over his head. Most of the troops were firing semi-auto, but straying rapid shots into the screening grass. The two M60s were hammering

VC Repatriation (surrender) leaflet aimed at US servicemen. Such propaganda attempts had virtually no effect.

A patrol returns to a firebase after a local security patrol. To protect firebases from surprise attacks, security patrols reconnoitered throughout the immediate area and observation posts were established. At night closer-in listening posts were manned and ambushes established on likely approach routes.

A firebase hacked out of the jungle was in a constant state of construction. Sandbags, empty ammunition boxes, and pallets were the basic construction materials for fighting positions, bunkers, and living quarters, called "hooches" regardless of the form they took. Here a battery of 105mm M102 howitzers is being emplaced.

short bursts punctuated by an occasional M79 thump and bangs as rounds detonated. Repeated AK-47 bursts ripped from both sides. On the far side of the ditch he heard movement and fired in that direction, surprising himself with a full-auto burst. The grenadier, who had his pistol out and had not fired the M79 yet, glared sharply at him, "Take it easy, man!" Legg switched to semi and triggered more rounds in the direction of the sound. His helmet was knocked over his eyes as Mojo slapped the back of his head while pushing past. "What ya doin, man? Keep cool!" Legg could hear a muted radio conversation behind him in the grass. Someone said, "Light fire team inbound." "Come on, Cherry!" Mojo motioned for Legg to join him down the ditch. Legg crawled awkwardly through the water on his knees, one hand holding his rifle out of the water.

The firing mostly died out with no visible targets. Yellow smoke coiled up out to the grass behind them and the faint beat of choppers could be heard. Legg could see an AH-1 Hueycobra gunship and an OH-6 LOH barreling in high over the field. Firing broke out with AKs ripping rounds through the grass, and M16s and M60s answered. It quickly increased to a steady roar, and it became impossible to distinguish individual shots and bursts. Legg sensed the NVA were making an effort to break for it before the helicopters arrived. Someone yelled "Beehive, beehive!" and a cluster of five red pop-up flare balls arched into the sky. Mojo grabbed Legg's left arm holding him out of the water and yanked on it, sending him face down into the mud. Puffs of smoke appeared behind the Cobra and long white streaks slanted toward the ground. The white trails terminated in gray puffs followed by a buzzing noise. Making a hard turn the Cobra ran back in from the opposite direction. More rockets leapt out followed by dull booms, dirty white smoke, and showering mud. Another hard turn and its mini-gun was buzzing out 4,000 rounds a minute, like ripping paper, with zipping noises scything through the grass. Small-arms fire died away. Most of the platoon was in the ditch, though some were securing the rear. The frontline was the direction in which one faced. Legg heard the radio crackle and the LT replied, "Thanks much, Blue Max. Out here."

Legg saw the platoon leader wave his arm, and the men were up, weapons at their hips. "Follow me," muttered Mojo cynically, repeating the Infantry motto, "Let's see what we got." Grenades sailed though the air and weapons rattled in short full-auto bursts as they pushed into the grass on line. A surprisingly short distance into the grass they came upon a large ragged, flattened and torn area. Three contorted bodies were lying in the muddy water. Legg's squad leader had him search one. The uniform was wet dark green and riddled with tiny holes, flechette darts poking from some. He gingerly pulled off the Chicom web gear and a small rucksack; it too was punctured by darts. He kept thinking, "I could end up like this." Others troopers snaked through the area and reported two more KIAs. Back on the dyke the medic, "Doc," was treating two wounded as the RTO reported "Dustoff," a medical evacuation (medevac) chopper, was inbound. Word was passed who the WIAs were and that they had minor wounds. Legg was squatting in the water and was surprised to learn that he had emptied four magazines; he did not remember changing them. They had just "zapped," "wasted," "hosed," "whacked" five young men, the enemy. Legg heard the squad leader say that the 2d Squad had found a blood trail of a wounded VC, "pink and foamy," indicating the man would not go far; he was bleeding out. No one suggested going in pursuit.

Legg suddenly felt a burning pain as he walked and discovered two small holes in his cargo pocket. Dropping his trousers he found a bullet graze across his thigh, on which Doc smeared betadine and taped on a gauze pad, cautioning him, "Keep it clean and watch for infection." Mojo slapped him on the arm as they shared a cigarette burning off leeches, "You done good Cherry. You got yaself a friggin' Purple Heart and CIB[10] on your first time bustin' brush and runnin' point." That was the last time Mojo or anyone called him "cherry".

THE REAL WORLD: AFTERMATH OF BATTLE

It was a long year for Legg. He did not know how many days he had spent in the boonies, or how many firefights and ambushes he had participated in. One day he was made responsible for a Cherry. The kid did OK; most did. A new LT took over and a month later the new platoon sergeant from another company replaced theirs after being wounded. Legg's squad leader ended up in the battalion HQ because they needed an assistant ops sergeant, and he could type. The new platoon leader instituted fire teams; Legg was selected as the Alpha Team leader, and eventually promoted to SP4. The new squad leader was a "Shake n' Bake" who did well, after following the platoon sergeant around for a couple of weeks before being given the squad. Mojo, still a PFC, reluctantly ran the squad until the Shake n' Bake took over, which was highly resented by Mojo. They once helped ARVN troops forcefully remove civilians from a village to be relocated to a New Life Hamlet and burned their abandoned homes. His squad shoved a scared NVA prisoner around after their machine gunner lost a leg to a grenade, but Legg never saw an atrocity. Mojo rotated home, leaving without saying a word to anyone. In his seventh month Legg went on R&R to Australia. He missed his opportunity for a three-day in-country R&R. Two months later he came down with dengue fever, also called "break-bone fever": aching joints accompanied by severe headaches and vomiting. Weak, he went back to his platoon after two weeks, but did light duty in the firebase for a week before going back to the bush. Old hands left and new faces arrived, constant turnover owing to the one-year rotation. Years later Legg could not remember many of them. Some he would never forget.

SP4 Legg sweated in the heat and humidity, shivered in the rain, choked in the dust, at times thought he would never be dry again, wanted for chow and water, suffered minor illnesses and diarrhea, endured all sorts of pests and boredom, stared into the jungle listening and waiting … on

A 105mm M102 howitzer is being prepared to be moved out by sling-loading it under a Chinook helicopter. This base is being abandoned and most of the positions and structures have been bulldozed down. VC scroungers would descend on the base to recover anything useful. The Americans might leave behind booby traps, saturate the area with tear gas powder, ambushes, and fire artillery randomly on the base.

A rifle platoon turns away from the blasting dust, gravel, and twigs thrown up by a landing Chinook that will transport them to their new area of operations (AO). An entire under-strength platoon could be transported in a Chinook.

10 The Combat Infantryman Badge was a coveted award eligible only to soldiers with an infantry MOS, assigned to infantry units below brigade-level, personally present and under fire and engaged in active ground combat for a period of at least 30 consecutive days in the combat zone.

countless nights, was scared spitless at times, laughed at pranks pulled by buddies, got drunk one night with the LT when they shared jokes about old girlfriends, thought endlessly about family and friends, was reamed out by the Top for something he did not remember doing, saw men die and others suffer horrendous wounds, wondered why a handsome NVA soldier died instead of himself, cried as he gave his remaining Cs to refugee kids on a muddy road, cursed other Vietnamese for not caring about the war, filled a million sandbags and burned a ton of shit, wondered what would happen next, and alternated between questioning and believing in why he was there.

A heavily loaded rifleman is assisted by two buddies up the side of a stream back. It was exhausting work, day after day, seemingly never ending.

Legg was pulled out of the field a month before his DEROS. He was assigned to a provisional security platoon and spent his final days pulling perimeter guard, filling sandbags, and other work details. While not a formal policy, many units felt a "short-timer" was less than effective in his final weeks, being preoccupied with thoughts of home and thus overly cautious. He was best employed elsewhere. A week, "six days and a wake-up," before his 365th day in country, Legg said what goodbyes he could; his old platoon was in the bush, already filling up with new faces. With a trophy SKS carbine[11] in hand, he flew to Phuoc Vinh, the CAV's new base 40 miles north of Saigon, on a work chopper where he turned in his rifle and battered LBE. A C-123 lifted him and other returnees to Bien Hoa Air Base and then a bus to the 90th Replacement Battalion at Long Binh Army Base outside of Saigon, a city few soldiers saw. He turned in most of his jungle fatigues, keeping one set, his boonie hat and boots. MPs searched his duffel bag for drugs and weapons. The returnees were bused to Ton Son Nhut Airport and boarded the "Freedom Bird" for home, the "real world." Once the airliner was airborne the captain announced to the cheering troops that they had left Vietnam airspace.

The next day they arrived in Oakland, CA (or Ft Lewis, WA), for out-processing at the US Army Personnel Center. Customs officers inspected duffel bags and the troops were issued a Public Health Service card, which they were asked to retain for two weeks, notifying doctors that the individual may have been exposed to plague, cholera, and other communicable diseases. Returning troops were kept segregated from those deploying to Vietnam. They were treated to a steak dinner with all the trimmings. Those declining the meal signed a form stating that it had been offered. Soldiers with less than five months remaining to their estimated time of separation (ETS) date were processed for discharge. A physical was given, paperwork for separation completed, a briefing given on veterans' benefits – the most important being the

A rifleman takes precautionary aim at an area that might conceal a lurking enemy. Note the bullet hole in the plastic forearm behind the foresight. The infantryman had a love-hate relationship with the M16A1 rifle, what he called the "black rifle" or the "plastic rifle." It had its flaws and benefits.

11 Soldiers could bring a single captured weapon home after approval by the unit intelligence officer. Only bolt-action or semi-automatic shoulder weapons or handguns were approved – no automatic or high explosive-firing weapons, no US or Allied weapons, no munitions.

GI Bill, which provided for a college education and low-interest home loans – and also a briefing on their remaining time on their six-year military obligation. They were happy to hear that they were in the Standby Reserve and not required to join a drilling Reserve or National Guard unit. Out-processing and discharge was accomplished in less than 24 hours. They were paid up to that day, to include any unused leave time. A new Army Green Class A uniform was issued and all necessary insignia provided for the trip home. The Army paid the airfare and booked the flight.

Some disgruntled soldiers immediately purchased civilian clothes and shed their uniforms. Most simply went home quietly. There was no fanfare, no parades, little in the way of a welcome home except from immediate family and friends. There are stories of soldiers being spit on and declared "baby killers." Such incidents occurred, but were extremely rare. Some Vietnam veterans proud of their service discovered that local veterans' groups did not always welcome them. Most friends did not want to hear about the war. Vets tended to keep it to themselves. Many of the wounded required post-service treatment for wounds or illnesses at Veterans Administration hospitals and had less than pleasant experiences. Many of the VA's deficiencies were eventually corrected. Controversies have lingered regarding soldiers contaminated with Agent Orange defoliant and resulting illnesses.[12] Much has been made of psychological problems suffered by some Vietnam veterans. While veterans have suffered from various difficulties, it is by no means widespread. Most veterans lead perfectly normal and productive lives and remain proud of their service.

> **Typical Decorations**
> A veteran infantryman, performing no particular acts of valor, though simply being an infantryman could be termed valorous, typically wore a number of decorations over his left breast pocket. From the wearer's right to left, top to bottom in order of precedence:
> Purple Heart – For wounds caused by enemy action.
> Army Commendation Medal – Awarded for overall service. Officers usually received the Bronze Star Medal*.
> National Defense Service Medal – For service in the US Armed Forces between 1 January 1961 and 14 August 1974.
> Vietnam Service Medal – For service in Vietnam between 3 July 1965 and 28 March 1973. Bronze service stars were worn for participation in designated campaigns.
> Vietnam Campaign Medal – Awarded to US armed forces by the government of Vietnam.
> The ribbons were topped by the Combat Infantryman Badge. Any special skill badges such as the Parachutist or Pathfinder Badge would be worn below the ribbons on the pocket flap. Gold-framed unit awards such as the Presidential Unit Citation, Valorous Unit Award, Meritorious Unit Commendation, Vietnamese Cross of Gallantry, and Vietnamese Civil Action Award might be worn above the right breast pocket.
> * The ACM and BS were also awarded for valor and identified by a bronze "V" device.

Results of a contact. Infantrymen load a wounded comrade into a medevac chopper. Dustoff chopper crews had a reputation for going into hot pick-up zones to medevac the wounded that regular assault helicopter crew would turn away from. They were far from being considered faint of heart.

COLLECTIONS, MUSEUMS, AND REENACTMENT

Numerous US Army museums display Vietnam War collections. These include the museums of the remaining active-duty divisions that served in Vietnam: 1st Infantry (Ft Riley, KS), 4th Infantry (Ft Hood, TX), 25th Infantry (Schofield Barracks, HI), 82d Airborne (Ft Bragg, NC), 101st Airborne (Ft Campbell, KY), 1st Cavalry Division (Ft Hood). The 5th, 9th,

---

12 It was officially designated "Herbicide Orange," identified by an orange band on drums. It is reported that the media coined the more sinister "Agent Orange" term. Other color-coded herbicides (purple, pink, blue, green, white) were also employed.

and AMERICAL Infantry Divisions are gone. Most Army posts have a Vietnam display in their museum or historical holding area. Posts with branch museums all have significant Vietnam displays. The National Infantry Museum at Ft Benning, GA, and the US Military Academy Museum at West Point, NY, possess excellent Vietnam collections. The National Vietnam War Museum site in Mineral Wells, TX (near Dallas), was dedicated in 2004, but will not open for some years yet.

Vietnam Campaign Participation Dates	
Campaign	**Inclusive Dates**
Advisory	March 15, 1962–March 7, 1965
Defense	March 8, 1965–December 24, 1965
Counteroffensive	December 25, 1965–June 30, 1966
Counteroffensive, Phase II	July 1, 1966–May 31, 1967
Counteroffensive, Phase III	June 1, 1967–January 29, 1968
Tet Counteroffensive	January 30, 1968–April 1, 1968
Counteroffensive, Phase IV	April 2, 1968–June 30, 1968
Counteroffensive, Phase V	July 1, 1968–November 1, 1968
Counteroffensive, Phase VI	November 2, 1968–February 22, 1969
Summer–Fall 1969	June 9, 1969–October 31, 1969
Winter–Spring 1970	November 1, 1969–April 30, 1970
Sanctuary Counteroffensive	May 1, 1970–June 30, 1970
Counteroffensive, Phase VII	July 1, 1970–June 30, 1971
Consolidation I	July 1, 1971–November 30, 1971
Consolidation II	December 1, 1971–March 29, 1972
Cease-fire	March 30, 1972–January 28, 1973

While many Vietnam veterans have no desire to see the country again, many do return with the cooperation of the Vietnamese government. They find a few propaganda-filled museums and shops selling reproduction items. Virtually nothing remains of American bases and installations. There are few signs of the war.

The collecting of Vietnam memorabilia, ranging from mementos, uniforms, equipment, and insignia, is a major field. Collectors are strongly urged to use caution and question the authenticity of any item presented as authentic Vietnam-era. This applies to items sold at militaria and gun shows, by private collectors, and especially on e-Bay, where fakes are frequently auctioned as authentic. Fakes are also produced in Vietnam and sold within and outside the country as authentic "Vietnam-made" items, but are post-war reproductions. Collectors are finding that actual Vietnam War items are becoming scarcer and more costly.

Vietnam reenactment groups flourish and are extremely popular in the United States, Britain, France, Japan, and elsewhere. There are even a few VC/NVA reenactment groups. Replica Vietnam War uniforms, equipment, and even rations are available to reenactors.

Vietnam is frequently portrayed in the movies, but it must be understood that these are the products of Hollywood. While many provide some glimpses of an infantryman's reality, for the most part they are misleading and inaccurate. The movies recommended by the author for their degree of accuracy are: *Go Tell the Spartans* (1978), *Hamburger Hill* (1987), *84 Charlie Mopic* (1989), and *We Were Soldiers* (2002).

A chaplain, what soldiers call a "sky pilot," conducts services in the field. Chaplains were a steadying influence, boosted morale, and helped instill confidence. The field ecclesiastical scarf is black with gold-embroidered US coat of arms and cross.

COLOR PLATE COMMENTARY

A: RECRUIT, FT POLK, LOUISIANA

PV1 Legg may have initially felt uncomfortable in his new uniform, but it was functional and practical: olive green (OG) shade 107 cotton sateen utility uniform, or simply "fatigues" (1 and 2). Fatigues were the routine hot and temperate uniform worn the world over, even in Vietnam, until jungle fatigues were introduced in 1963. The gold-on-black 'US ARMY' tape was worn until a black-on-OG tape was approved in 1968. The black-on-OG nametape had replaced the black-on-white version in 1966. The acting squad leader brassard consisted of a gold-yellow-on navy blue corporal chevron on a black armband.

PVT Legg also wears the M1 steel helmet. Ear protectors are carried in a plastic container by its chain through a jacket buttonhole. The back view displays the unpopular OG shade 106 field cap, or "baseball cap." He is armed with the 7.62mm M14 rifle. The M1956 load bearing equipment (LCE) consists of the utility belt, universal ammunition pouch, first aid case, canteen and carrier, and an M1961 combat pack, or "butt pack."

3.a. M1 steel helmet ("steel pot"). Basic trainees did not wear camouflage covers.

3.b. Laminated nylon helmet liner.

3.c. Helmet liner showing web suspension system.

4.a. Entrenching tool carrier with M6 bayonet-knife and M8A1 sheath.

4.b. M6 bayonet-knife (6.75-in. blade, 11.5-in. overall). The M16A1's M8 bayonet was almost identical.

4.c. Combination entrenching tool with pick.

5.a. Protective mask carrier carried on the left hip and strapped on beneath other web gear.

5.b. The M17 protective mask, or "gas mask."

6. The M1956 universal small arms ammunition pouch held two 20-round M14 magazines, four 20-round M16 magazines, four M2 carbine 30-round magazines, eight M1 rifle 8-round clips, three 40mm M79 grenades, 24 12-gauge shotgun shells, or two hand grenades plus grenade straps on the sides.

7. M1956 first aid case with old-type field dressing.

8. M1956 canteen carrier with 1-quart plastic canteen and canteen cup.

9. M1910 mess kit and utensils.

10. Poncho roll. In garrison training, when the butt pack was unnecessary, the poncho was carried on the back of the belt between the suspender straps.

B: VIET CONG VILLAGE, TIGERLAND

The simulated fortified VC villages of infantry training centers strove to orient infantrymen to the basics of surviving in Vietnam. Realism was compromised by Americans role-playing Vietnamese peasants and VC, the lack of women and children, smaller than real villages, pine trees, and below-freezing winter temperatures.

PV1 Legg (1) stands guard as his buddy (2) cautiously enters a hooch. A drill sergeant (3) looks on, wearing his characteristic Smoky Bear hat, Drill Sergeant Badge, Army Training Center crests, and the Fourth Army patch. The "hat, drill sergeant, male, enlisted," was influenced by its long use by Marine Corps' drill instructors. Drill corporals normally wore a glossy olive green helmet liner with a colored band indicating the training brigade, rank insignia on the front, and army training center and parent army decals on the sides. The Ft Polk village boasted a modest tunnel complex, but because of the high water table and rain it was often flooded. Lined with steel culvert pipe, compasses could not be used to practice mapping the system. It did provide a means of detecting tunnel entrances and air-vents and demonstrated the enemy's ability to pop-up behind soldiers. The villages were booby-trapped with simulated devices to instill a degree of caution.

Mild southern winters called for M1951 OG shade 107 field jackets with liners and sometimes heavier M1951 field trousers over fatigue trousers. Troops attending infantry AIT could be differentiated from basic trainees by camouflage helmet covers. Here M12 blank adapters are fitted to the M14 rifles.

C: BARRACKS LIFE, TIGERLAND

The half day's training on Saturdays was often dedicated to inspections. Trainees were provided mimeographed diagrams of the manner in which clothing was hung and equipment stowed in wall lockers, in footlockers, and laid out on the bunk or on a spread poncho before an erected pup tent for a "full field layout inspection." There was a good deal of harassment in the first inspections with drill sergeants flinging footlocker trays down the aisle, racking gear and even the mattress off the bunk with a sweep of the arm, and throwing neatly hung uniforms out of lockers whether the items were displayed correctly or not. This reinforced the need for attention to detail. By the fifth week of BCT things settled down, and trainees realized the real purpose of inspections was to ensure the serviceability and cleanness of

Up and away. Units of the 1st Cavalry Division were frequently relocated, not just tactically by helicopter, but operationally to other parts of Vietnam by C-130 transports. The division's lightweight equipment and airmobility mindset made it a useful fire brigade to be deployed rapidly where needed. The troops grabbed their rucks, duffel bags, and unit signs and went wherever necessary.

Arriving at their new base of operations, troops move off the runway to establish their new brigade base and would soon commence operations.

uniform items, equipment, and quarters. Inspections became more routine during AIT. That fifth week inspection was important for another reason: pass or failure determined whether or not one received his first off-post pass. Seldom-seen company officers conducted the later inspections, with a drill sergeant noting transgressions.

PV2 Legg (1) now wears infantry crossed rifles on his collar, since he is undertaking infantry AIT. He displays an Expert Badge with rifle and machine gun qualification bars, and a Marksman Badge with automatic rifle and pistol bars. The drill sergeant (3) also wears infantry distinctions in the form of robin's-egg-blue plastic discs behind his collar and hat insignia. Beneath the coveted Combat Infantryman's Badge are the typical ribbons of a soldier with over three years' service and a Vietnam tour (viewer's left-to-right): Army Commendation Medal, Good Conduct Medal, Vietnam Service Medal, National Defense Service Medal, and Vietnam Campaign Medal. On the right of his chest are the Presidential Unit Citation and Vietnamese Cross of Gallantry with Palm – unit awards. A company training officer (2) wears the service cap, more commonly known as the "bus driver" or "flying saucer" cap. The 2LT wears the Sharpshooter Badge for rifle and Marksman Badge for pistol.

D: INDIVIDUAL EQUIPMENT AND PLATOON WEAPONS

It was common for both subdued and full-color insignia to be worn on the same jungle fatigues. Armed with the XM16E1 rifle, troops soon found the nine 20-round magazines prescribed in the basic load insufficient. The lightweight rucksack, although developed for tropical (and arctic) use, was unpopular and soon fell from general use. The frame's wide lower portion meant that items could only be worn on the front of the pistol belt (1 and 2).

3. 40mm M79 grenade launcher.

4.a. 40mm ammunition was issued in six-round bandoliers.

4.b. A variety of 40mm ammunition was available (left-to-right): M406 HE, XM576E1 multiple projectile (27 x 33-cal 00 buckshot), and M583A1 white star parachute for illumination. A number of colored smoke signal cartridges similar in appearance to the white star parachute were used.

5. A few 66mm M72 light anti-tank weapons (LAW) were carried by platoons for use against snipers and bunkers. It is pictured in the extended firing mode. D2 depicts it in the closed carrying mode.

6. M49A1 trip flares were attached to barbed-wire pickets or stakes by a mounting bracket, or simply wired to a tree and rigged for activation by a tripwire. The magnesium flare ignited immediately, burning for 55–70 seconds at 50,000 candlepower, and illuminated up to a 300m radius.

7. Handheld ground signals, or "pop-ups," consisted of an aluminum launch-tube (7.a.) containing a rocket-propelled signal carrier (7.b.). They were carried removed from the steel packing tube (7.c.), the muzzle cap removed and slipped on to the opposite end, held at arm's length vertically, and the cap slapped with the palm of the other hand to fire a variety of colored flares and smoke signals to 600–700 feet:

M125 green, M158 red, and M159 white star cluster (five freefalling stars).

M195 green, M126 red, and M127 white star parachute (parachute-suspended flare).

M128 green, M129 red, and M194 yellow smoke parachute (parachute-suspended smoke).

8. Chemical burning-type grenades:

8.a. M7A2 tear gas to flush out tunnels and bunkers.

8.b. AN-M8 white smoke for screening.

8.c. AN-M14 incendiary for destroying equipment.

8.d. M18 colored smoke in green, red, yellow, and violet for air-to-ground signaling and marking positions.

9. The meal, combat, individual, or C-rations, was the most widely used field ration.

10. The lensatic compass, usually carried in a first aid pouch, was issued to platoon and squad leaders and platoon sergeants.

11. The plastic MX-911/U flashlight's screw-off bottom compartment contained an extra bulb and filters to reduce its light for night use.

12. M16-armed automatic riflemen were issued a cloth pin-type bipod in either a simple early-issue case or the XM3 case, which carried cleaning gear.

VC suspects are led to a helicopter for pick-up. The lack of a Vietnam national identity card was grounds for apprehension.

E: THE RIFLE PLATOON, THE GRUNT'S FAMILY

Whether standard, light, airborne, airmobile or mechanized, the rifle platoon was organized in essentially the same manner. Its 44 men were organized into a platoon headquarters with a platoon leader (LT), platoon sergeant (his position and rank), and an AN/PRC-25-equipped radio-telephone operator, all with M14s or M16A1s. An aidman and mortar forward observer were attached. The three 10-man rifle squads had a squad leader (staff sergeant) and two fire teams, each with a team leader (sergeant), grenadier, automatic rifleman, and one or two riflemen. Mechanized rifle squads also had a driver. All were armed with M14s or M16A1s, except grenadiers, who had M79 grenade launchers and M1911A1 pistols, and automatic riflemen, who had either M14E2 automatic rifles or M16A1s with bipod and were "authorized" to fire full-automatic. The 11-man weapons squad had a squad leader (staff sergeant) and two each machine gunners, assistant machine gunners, recoilless rifle gunners, assistant recoilless rifle gunners, and ammunition bearers. Squad armament was two M60 machine guns and two 90mm M67 recoilless rifles. Grenadiers, automatic riflemen, and gunners were SP4s while all others were PFCs.

The realities of Vietnam saw a different platoon organization. Manpower shortages, detached personnel, and a scarcity of NCOs typically saw platoons with 20–30 men organized into two or three squads and fire teams often abandoned. The weapons squad seldom existed since there was no need for antitank weapons: they and their ammunition were simply too heavy to carry. The two machine guns were either assigned to rifle squads or the platoon headquarters. Rifle squads were seven or eight men. Squad leaders were often sergeants or SP4s, while fire team leaders, if employed, were SP4s or PFCs. It was not uncommon for only two squads to be organized in order to

What were they thinking then? What will they most likely recall today?

provide a higher strength with 9–12 men, as depicted here. A two-man machine-gun crew is organic to both. There were usually two grenadiers per squad. Often when two squads were employed, and because of the inexperience of some squad leaders, the platoon leader and platoon sergeant would personally take charge of a squad when engaged. Medics became a platoon fixture, but mortar forward observers disappeared as artillery and attack helicopters became the primary fire support weapons.

F: FIREFIGHT – THE "SEVEN-MINUTE WAR"

The firefight was the most frequent type of engagement in Vietnam and typically brief – sometimes characterized as the "seven-minute war." Often they were chance contacts – meeting engagements. They might involve only a few sudden bursts of fire as two elements ran into one another and quickly broke contact, but they could become vicious close-range fights and escalate into major battles as both sides committed reinforcements.

This plate depicts two common aspects of a firefight: isolation and uncertainty. There was an extreme sense of individual isolation. The enemy was almost impossible to detect and it was sometimes difficult to determine from which direction fire was coming. Even in the comparatively open Mekong Delta with its sword-grass-covered plains, to soldiers hugging the mud, visibility was limited to a few meters. All that could be seen was the soldier on either side. Extreme uncertainty was encountered regardless of the initiative of leaders. Questions running through soldiers' minds might be, is it a quick and dirty fight with the enemy immediately breaking contact, have we walked into an ambush, are they maneuvering to surround us, are reinforcements rushing toward us this moment?

This patrol has marked its position with a yellow smoke grenade, extremely conspicuous against the sword grass, as a light fire team comprised of an AH-1G Hueycobra gunship and an OH-6A Cayuse light observation helicopter (LOH – pronounced "loach") dash in for support. Such teams were on standby to support patrols with 7.62mm minigun, 40mm automatic grenade launcher, and 2.75-in. rocket fire.

G: INDIVIDUAL AND PLATOON EQUIPMENT

Many soldiers stripped down to bare necessities to lighten their load, dispensing with LBE and attaching gear to rucksacks instead. SP4 Legg (1) carries a new nylon tropical rucksack designed for Vietnam. Canteens, grenades, and other gear, including a "pop-up" flare, are carried on the "ruck." M16A1 magazines are carried in seven-pocket bandoliers in which 5.56mm ammunition was issued with two 10-round stripper clips per pocket. He wears a towel around his neck, a "drive-on rag." A spring steel X-frame (2), which sometimes bowed in the wrong direction to dig into the soldier's back, supported the rucksack. A nylon poncho liner was an essential item, and, with an air mattress, served as bedding. The AN/PRC-25 radio and accessory bag (3) were carried by the platoon radio-telephone operator. The platoon and squad leaders and platoon sergeants may have used the "helmet radio," AN/PRR-9 receiver mounted on the helmet (4) and the handheld AN/PRT-4 transmitter for platoon communications. A new version of the 2-qt. canteen

(5) was easier to fill from a stream. The lightweight LRP ("lurp") ration (6) consisted of a dehydrated main course, dessert, and an accessory packet. Many platoon members carried an M18A1 Claymore mine (7) with 100ft of firing wire, an M57 firing device ("clacker"), and an M40 circuit test set (one with every six mines) in an M9 bandolier. Casualty-producing hand grenades (8) included:

8.a. M26A1 fragmentation remained in use through the war.

8.b. M57 fragmentation impact saw little use as it detonated if dropped or struck vegetation.

8.c. M67 fragmentation provided more effective casualty radius than the M26-series.

8.d. Mk 3A2 demolition or concussion grenade was effective for clearing bunkers.

8.e. M34 white phosphorus was a bursting-type grenade that rained WP particles down on troops in open positions.

The M9 protective mask (9) offered protection only from tear gas, but was lighter than the M17. The 7.62mm M60 machine gun (10) served as the platoon's primary heavy weapon. Ammunition was issued in 100-round assault bags, two bags per ammo can. A C-ration B unit long can was sometimes clipped in the ammunition box bracket to aid belt feed. The combination tool was necessary to clean the gas piston.

H: "DUSTOFF" – MEDEVAC

Casualties in Vietnam had a higher chance of surviving when compared to their World War II and Korean War counterparts. Besides advances in combat medicine, rapid evacuation by medical evacuation (medevac) helicopter helped greatly. Medevac chopper crews were renowned for their boldness, often flying into hot landing zones (LZ) under heavy fire that regular crews avoided. UH-1D medevac helicopters were unarmed, and the red cross markings seldom prevented the enemy from firing on them. Likewise medics seldom wore Geneva Convention armbands. "Dustoffs," the Army-wide call-sign of medevacs, transported some 120,000 casualties.

This 44th Medical Brigade Spec 5 medic wears standard aviator's clothing: SPH-4 flying helmet, K2B fire-resistant flight suit, air crewman body armor with add-on torso armor plate ("chicken plate"), and leather combat boots, as they were more fire-resistant than jungle boots.

A Dustoff Huey could carry three litters and two sitting wounded. The backpack-type M5 medical bag carried field dressings, bandages, tape, splints, blood-volume expander, saline solution, and IV kits. The smaller No. 3 medical instrument and supply set ("aid bag") was carried by medics with field dressings, airway, morphine, antiseptics, aspirin, and emergency instrument set with scalpels, forceps, clamps, bullet probe, and sutures. The standard 4 x 7-in. field dressing protects leg and chest wounds, the latter a sucking chest wound (punctured lung) made airtight by placing a split-open outer plastic dressing package beneath the dressing pad.

Highland Defense. **An exhausted machine gunner rests beside his M60 as his squad covers approaches a hastily established defensive position on the edge of a bomb-blasted area. Print by Frank M. Thomas, 1984.**

PART 2

GREEN BERET
IN VIETNAM
1957-73

GREEN BERET IN VIETNAM 1957–73

SPECIAL FORCES OVERVIEW

When Special Forces (SF) soldiers reflect upon their service with the US Army's complex and controversial involvement in Vietnam, they rarely relate similar experiences. Such men were asked to fulfil a wide variety of operations and missions – camp strike forces, mobile strike forces, mobile guerrilla forces, special reconnaissance projects, training missions, and headquarters duty – and each provided vastly different circumstances for SF soldiers.

The span of time was an equally important factor that affected the experiences of SF soldiers. Special Forces' involvement in Vietnam began in 1957 and ended in 1973. Even a difference of one year would result in contrasting perspectives, as the war was fought in a constantly changing environment. Terrain and weather conditions were similarly important. Vietnam offered varied geographic environments, ranging from chilly, forested mountains in the north, vast open plains in the central highlands, triple-canopy inland jungles, dense coastal swamps, and the inundated flood plains of the Mekong Delta. It was often said that Vietnam has three seasons; wet, dry, and dusty, which recur at approximately hourly intervals.

The effectiveness of an SF detachment was often determined by the personality of its members. While a certain degree of guidance was provided in the operation of A-camps and other SF activities, there was no official doctrine guiding day-to-day operations. In Vietnam, there was only "lore," and what was found to work best in a given situation. Expedients, substitutes, ingenious makeshift efforts, and resourcefulness were a matter of course. There were inevitably similarities between camps, but differences in routine were often vast.

This book will focus on the experiences of SF troops involved with camp strike forces. The more glamorous Special Forces missions, reconnaissance projects, and MIKE Forces for example, are more publicized in popular literature, but it was the A-camps that epitomized the heart and soul of Special Forces in Vietnam.

The camps, which were usually staffed by fewer than a dozen Americans in some of the most remote and inhospitable regions of Vietnam, were bases for indigenous, irregular counterinsurgency forces. They struggled to stifle the flow of

All SF troopers were required to specialize in a specific skill. Here communications NCOs practise encrypting and transmitting messages.

enemy forces and supplies from across the borders, and they secured isolated ethnic minority villages to prevent their exploitation by ruthless enemy forces. The A-camps experienced counterinsurgency at grassroots level and were involved in all aspects of counterguerrilla warfare; training, advising, and fighting with indigenous troops. To this end, they were also involved in the interrelated field of psychological operations (influencing the opinions, attitudes, and behavior of enemy forces, indigenous populations, friendly and military), civic action (improving local economic and social conditions), and intelligence collection (through reconnaissance, informers, and low-level agent nets in the camp's area).

Away from the battlefield, Special Forces gave medical, educational, agricultural, and housing construction assistance to the troops' families and local villagers. MEDCAP (MEDical/Civic Action Program) visits to local villages were routinely made.

SF training focused on the practical as well as the technical. Here a group of engineers attempt to construct a bridge with only hand tools. They would later destroy it as part of their demolitions training.

Image and reality

The popular image of Special Forces, which has unfortunately been influenced by the inane vision of John Rambo and other equally far-fetched motion picture characters, is far from reality. Such flamboyant, risk-taking characters would not have survived a single contact. The image of SF during the Vietnam era was also influenced by Robin Moore's fictionalization of some more "glamorous" exploits, *The Green Berets* (1964); John Wayne's motion picture of the same title (1968), and Staff Sergeant Berry Saddler's popular song, "The Ballad of the Green Berets" (1966). Rumors, assumptions, war stories, and the efforts of the John F. Kennedy Center for Special Warfare to promote its capabilities in countering communist-sponsored "people's wars" were just as much responsible for the popular image of Special Forces.[1]

SF students prepare to launch a 12ft semi-rigid assault boat. A 40hp outboard motor will be mounted on the transom. This type of training was often incorporated into hands-on exercises in the field rather than through formal instruction.

Soldiers invariably reflect the society that spawned them, and Special Forces soldiers demonstrated the highest values of American society. Most SF troopers were conservative by nature, but virtually apolitical.

A typical SF trooper, although most would resent such a generalization, was of higher than average intelligence (determined by extensive testing), no more physically fit than other paratroopers, generally moderate in temperament, and able to maintain a sense of humor (a critical requirement in Vietnam), which often leaned toward the dark side. There were heavy drinkers and teetotallers, hardcore lifers, rednecks, cowboys, intellectuals,

surfers, and motorcycle-gangers, to name a few. None were fanatical or ultra-right wing as often envisioned by a paranoid Hollywood.

There was a tendency to cut-up during training, and pranks were commonly inflicted on non-SF units and themselves without prejudice. However, SF was not a group of wild, rebellious misfits as portrayed in many motion pictures, although some senior commanders might argue otherwise. Regardless of personal attitudes, they were professional in appearance and actions. They were distinct individualists from a broad range of backgrounds with several things in common. Most were looking for something different and challenging, they wanted to prove themselves, and they were idealistic in a mildly patriotic, and at that time, unpopular way. Admittedly, most troopers distrusted overbearing, power-hungry, overly career-oriented officers.

Though it was not the goal of the selection process, troopers tended to have common attributes. Most were somewhat rebellious and independent, but still capable of working as members of a team; plus they tended to support the underdog, an invaluable attribute when it came to working with indigenous troops. They were all strongly anti-communist, though not because of indoctrination or political nurturing. All were triple volunteers, for the Army, Airborne, and Special Forces. They had to be at least 20 years old, have the same General Technical score (a form of IQ score) as required of officers, and have no police record. However, a surprising number had been in minor trouble with the law. A comparatively clean record was needed to obtain the required security clearance.

They represented all sectors of society, but most had middle-class backgrounds. No figures exist, but minorities were poorly represented. Blacks, Hispanics, Indians, and other minorities were found in numbers far below the Army-wide average. However, among the minorities accepted into SF, race discrimination was a rare complaint; one had only to prove oneself as an SF soldier and acceptance was complete. Religion was not a subject of discussion. One practised or did not practise as one saw fit.

A typical A-team's age spanned over 20 years, ranging from young SF soldiers on their first enlistment to a team sergeant who might be looking toward retirement. Military experiences were many and varied.

They worked hard and played with the same vigor. SF had its heavy drinkers, but a lower than average number of smokers at a time when smoking remained common (cigarettes were still included in C-rations). There were some genuine troublemakers, but they remained in SF because they could contribute. There were ongoing feuds between individuals, some resulting from real or perceived mistakes made in combat or even on training exercises, competition for promotion, women troubles (SF was said to have the highest divorce rate in the Army), and simple personality conflicts between strong-willed individualists.

A specialist 4 of the 5th SFGA headquarters endures the SF-run jump school at Dong Ba Thin where MIKE Force troops undertook jump school. The school was considerably tougher than Ft Benning, Georgia.

Special Forces was not a branch. No one was permanently assigned, although most NCOs served their entire careers in SF, with only occasional stints elsewhere. Officers were detached from combat arms branches to which they would return after an SF tour. Some returned to serve with SF, others did not. A small number of officers served much of their career with SF (limiting their future progression and assignments) and many of them were key in charting SF's course and development. But, it was the senior SF career NCOs who defined the organization's character.

SF resisted institutionalization and the formalities common elsewhere in the military. Such traditions as organization day, prop blast ceremonies, dinings-in, and NCO academies were shunned. The key social event for an SF unit was a family barbecue in the unit area or someone's home (a practice observed even in Vietnam, *sans* families). SF was basically comprised of men loyal to an operational concept: special warfare.

SF as an organization was not a model of military theory and practice. Many in SF only reluctantly admitted association to the US Army, insisting that their organization was US Special Forces (USSF) and not US Army Special Forces (USASF). When a 1,200-man SF group was required to attend, for example, a retirement ceremony at Ft Bragg, its five companies might make their way individually to the parade ground where the group would assemble as a body and depart in the same manner. Realistically, no attempt would be made to march the group on to the parade ground or conduct a pass in review; it had been tried and it seldom went smoothly. The "other Army" was too rigid, too regimented, and far too noisy. SF troopers were appalled at how conventional soldiers were treated by their officers, although their treatment was still high by any other army's standards. However, after the more relaxed attitudes of Special Forces, it seemed almost draconian. Within SF, even spec. 4s and buck sergeants were permitted a remarkable degree of latitude and responsibility.

The most significant attitude in SF was that everyone did whatever it took to accomplish the mission, regardless of their rank. Paratroopers of the 82d Airborne Division at Ft Bragg were stunned to see long-serving master sergeants and sergeants first class policing up pine cones in SF unit areas or shaking out parachutes alongside spec. 4s, because their A-team had been assigned the duty. That is one of the primary factors of SF effectiveness, and that is why SF buck sergeants with less than two years service were able to lead indigenous companies in Vietnam without supervision.

All of this resulted in a group of well-trained individualists welded into functional teams with the flexibility, ingenuity, imag-ination, experience, maturity, and desire to accomplish whatever mission they had been given. Teamwork was paramount, there is no "I" in "Team." The lack of a rigid doctrine[2]

A USSF trooper and CIDG Striker display their combat equipment. The Striker is armed with a .30cal M1A1 carbine with a folding stock while the SF soldier has a 5.56mm M16A1 rifle. He carries its 20-round magazines in a BAR belt.

allowed them the leeway to accomplish their tasks in unusual environments and circumstances, with austere support, low visibility, and limited political repercussions. A common attitude found among SF soldiers when given a task, be it a menial work detail or a mission to raise and train a village defense force, was, "Tell me what you want done and I'll do it, but don't tell me how to do it."

CHRONOLOGY

1950s

June 11, 1952 10th Special Forces Group (Airborne) (SFGA) activated at Ft Bragg, NC. This first SF unit deployed to Germany in 1953.

September 25, 1953 77th SFGA activated at Ft Bragg (redesignated 7th SFGA on May 20, 1960).

June 24, 1957 1st SFGA activated on Okinawa.

June 1957 14th SF Detachment begin training Vietnamese commandos.

November 1, 1957 Vietnamese 1st Observation Group formed as a special forces unit after initial training by USSF.

January 1959 North Vietnam (Socialist Republic of Vietnam – SRVN) issue a resolution that changes its "political struggle" in South Vietnam (Republic of Vietnam – RVN) to an "armed struggle."

May 1959 SRVN begins major improvements on the Ho Chi Minh Trail to supply its struggle in RVN.

1960

May Detachments from 1st and 7th SFGA begin rotating to RVN and three commando training centers are organized.

December 20 The National Liberation Front (NLF) is formed by SRVN and disguised as a communist RVN initiative. The Viet Cong (VC) is its military arm.

1961

January 28 President Kennedy approves a counterinsurgency plan requiring the RVN Government and armed forces to reform.

May Civilian Irregular Defense Group (CIDG) Program conceived as the Area Development Program and initiated by CIA. It is redesignated the CIDG in 1962.

September 21 5th SFGA activated at Ft Bragg to rotate detachments to RVN.

November 1 RVN 1st Observation Group redesignated 77th LLDB Group.

November Mountain Commando Program initiated by CIA; later redesignated Mountain Scout Program.

December 3 USSF begin training Montagnard self-defense forces; the Buon Enao experiment. Initiated by the Combined Studies Office, US Operations Mission in Vietnam.

1962

February 3 Rural pacification (strategic hamlet) program begins to relocate rural villagers to RVN Government-controlled areas.

February 6 Military Assistance Command, Vietnam (MACV) formed to control all US armed forces in RVN.

June Trailwatcher Program initiated by CIA; redesignated Border Surveillance Program in 1963.

November 8 US Army Special Forces, Vietnam, Provisional (USASFV) formed to control all in-country USSF operations; a miniature SF group.

Future interpreters fire for qualification with the .30cal M2 carbine while undergoing the eight-week Combat Interpreter Course, Nha Trang. The SF soldier in the center fires a .45cal M3A1 submachine gun.

1963

February 1 RVN 77th LLDB Group reorganized and 31st LLDB Group formed.

March 15 LLDB Command formed to control 31st and 77th LLDB Groups.

July 1 USASFV assumes support of the CIDG Program in Operation SWITCHBACK with LLDB in command.

October 26 CIA turns its Border Surveillance Program over to USASFV.

November 22 President John F. Kennedy is assassinated.

1964

January 16 MACV-SOG formed to conduct unconventional warfare operations in the RVN and adjacent countries.

April RVN forms Special Exploitation Service as its contribution to MACV-SOG.

May 15 Military Assistance Advisory Group, Vietnam disbanded.

May 15 Project LEAPING LENA established by USASFV for countrywide special reconnaissance operations.

June 20 Gen. William Westmoreland assumes command of MACV.

September 1 The 31st and 77th LLDB Groups redesignated 111th and 301st LLDB Groups respectively.

September 19 Montagnard uprising at four camps in the Ban Me Thuot area due to mistreatment by LLDB. A settlement is negotiated by USSF on September 28.

October 1 The 5th SFGA begins phased deployment to RVN and assumes control of all USSF operations in-country.

October Operation SWITCHBACK transition completed.

1965

March 8 First US Marine ground combat troops arrive in RVN.

April 6 US ground troops authorized to conduct offensive operations.

May 7 First US Army conventional ground combat troops arrive.

June Project LEAPING LENA redesignated Project DELTA (B-52).

June 15 First offensive ground action by conventional US troops.

July Mobile Strike (MIKE) Forces begin to be formed by 5th SFGA.

July 30 US Army, Vietnam (USARV) is formed to control Army forces, but 5th SFGA remains under MACV control.

1966

March 11 A Shau Strike Force Camp is overrun.

August Projects OMEGA (B-50) and SIGMA (B-56) formed by 5th SFGA for reconnaissance operations in II and III CTZs respectively.

September Mobile Guerrilla Forces begin to be formed by 5th SFGA.

September 15 MACV Recondo School formed by 5th SFGA at Nha Trang.

1967

June Project GAMMA (B-57) formed by 5th SFGA to collect intelligence on NVA bases in Cambodia.

September RVN Special Exploitation Service redesignated Strategic Technical Directorate (STD).

ABOVE **A sergeant first class instructs Montagnard self-defense force recruits on the disassembly of the .30cal M2 carbine. Two LLDB NCOs in "duck-hunter" camouflage assist him. Such instruction often had to be relayed through an English–Vietnamese interpreter before communication via a second interpreter who spoke the local dialect.**

BELOW **Newly assigned 5th SFGA troopers, who are attending the Combat Orientation Course, prepare to practise a break contract drill on Hon Tra Island off the coast from Na Trang. They have already purchased their tiger-stripe "boonie" hats, but will not be issued tiger-striped uniforms until assigned to their camps.**

October Mobile Guerrilla Forces absorbed into MIKE Forces.

November 1 Projects OMEGA and SIGMA transferred to MACV-SOG and Command and Control North, Central, and South formed.

1968

January 30 VC and NVA initiate the Tet Offensive, which ends on 26 Feb.

February 7 Lang Vei Strike Force Camp is overrun by NVA tanks.

March 31 US Government announces a de-escalation of its war effort.

May 12 Peace talks begin in Paris.

July 1 GEN Creighton Abrams assumes command of MACV.

1969

June 8 The US initiate the Vietnamization programme to turn the war effort completely over to RVN forces.

Late Camp Strike Forces begin to close or are converted to RF/PF.

1970

May Duc Hue and Tra Cu Camp Strike Forces and 3d MIKE Force engage NVA forces during the US incursion into Cambodia.

August – December Remaining Camp Strike Forces are converted to Border Rangers.

November 21 Son Tay Prison Camp raid in North Vietnam by SF task force.

December 31 CIDG Program is terminated and LLDB is dissolved the next day.

1971

March 1 US Army Individual Training Group (UITG) formed from Company A, 5th SFGA, to train Cambodian national troops.

March 3 The 5th SFGA is withdrawn from RVN. The 6th SFGA at Ft Bragg is redesignated the 5th SFGA.

1972

April 30 MACV-SOG disbanded and STD Advisory Team 158 formed.

May 15 UITG redesignated Forces Armée Nationale Khmer (FANK).

November 30 FANK disbanded.

1973

January 15 US announces halt of all offensive ground action.

March 12 STD Advisory Team 158 disbanded.

March 29 Final US troops are withdrawn from RVN and MACV is disbanded.

An SF NCO instructs a Montagnard Striker in close-reconnaissance techniques. Although SF provided training to the often-experienced Strikers, it was a two-way exchange. The SF learned much from the Strikers, particularly the Montagnards, who were totally attuned to their natural environment.

SPECIAL FORCES IN VIETNAM

The US Army's first SF unit was the 10th Special Forces Group (Airborne) (SFGA). Formed at Ft Bragg, NC, in June 1952, its original role was rather different to that of SF in Vietnam a decade later. The 10th SFGA was an attempt to create a formalized unit that was tasked with guerrilla or unconventional warfare (UW), evasion and escape, and resistance. Its mission was to infiltrate communist Eastern Europe, sending in teams that would contact, organize, train, and assist guerrilla forces in disrupting the rear areas of Soviet forces in the event of an invasion of Western Europe.

To accomplish this task, the 10th SFGA hand-picked soldiers with experience in World War Two special operations units, ethnic Eastern Europeans, and young, motivated paratroopers. They employed the training methods of the World War Two Office of Strategic Services' (OSS) Jedburg Teams and the organizational concept of OSS Operational Groups. The 10th SFGA deployed to Germany in November 1953 to be in place for the feared invasion. At the same time, a second group was formed, the 77th (redesignated 7th SFGA in May 1960), and tasked with worldwide missions. In June 1957 the 1st SFGA was activated on Okinawa to conduct missions in Asia.

President Kennedy's concern over the increase in communist-inspired "wars of liberation," led to the rapid expansion of SF. Since SF was trained to be guerrillas, what better force to charge with counterguerrilla warfare? Special Forces' role gradually shifted to assisting developing nations to combat the growing threat of "people's wars." The 5th SFGA was activated at Ft Bragg on September 21, 1961 specifically to support increasing commitments to Southeast Asia.

The expansion of SF had inherent difficulties. Standards, in regards to the previous service experience of recruits, were lowered to some degree and new personnel had to be "mass produced" by the new SF Training Group. SFTG was formed in 1963 along with the 3d, 6th, and 8th SFGAs, which were responsible for Africa, the Middle East, and Latin America respectively. To meet the growing need for SF troopers, first enlistment soldiers and second lieutenants were admitted for the first time.

Without the previous rigid selection criteria, the SF was now open to young, quality soldiers, who lacked experience, but who offered a high degree of enthusiasm. The expansion also brought substantial funding increases to support equipment development and acquisition, and individual and unit training.

In the early 1960s, seven Special Forces groups were conducting hundreds of mobile training team missions throughout the world to provide counterinsurgency training, civil affairs assistance, and instruction for foreign special operations units. Attention was increasingly focusing on the Republic of Vietnam and its rapidly growing insurgency.

To understand the SF soldier's Vietnam experience, a brief overview of SF organization, deployment, and development is first necessary. Special Forces' first experience in Vietnam took place in 1957, when a 77th SFGA

It is often said that one of the reasons for the success of Special Forces is that they trained and fought like the enemy. In the top photo VC guerrillas plan an attack on a government outpost. In the bottom photo an A-team training in the US plan an attack on an "enemy" government installation.

detachment provided training for a group of commandos, who would eventually provide the cadre for their own special forces. In May 1960 the 1st and 7th SFGAs began to send teams to assist with Vietnamese commando training.

In January 1960 President Kennedy had approved an all-encompassing counterinsurgency plan. In order to receive continued support, the Vietnamese Government and armed forces would undertake a broad range of reforms. In the meantime, the Central Intelligence Agency's US Programs Mission began developing several counterinsurgency programs among various ethnic minorities. These included the Civilian Irregular Defense Group (CIDG – referred to as "sidge") for village defense (May 1961); Mountain Commandos (November 1961 – later Mountain Scouts); and Trailwatchers (June 1962, later Border Surveillance). These paramilitary organizations were not part of the Army of the Republic of Vietnam (ARVN – referred to as "are-vin"). These programs, while administered by the CIA, were actually conducted by SF detachments.

ABOVE **The muzzle flash of a 4.2in. M30 mortar illuminates the interior of its pit. This particular example is larger than usually found. The exposed earth on the left side needs to be sandbagged before the wet season rains begin. Camp Thuong Duc, A-109, 1968.**

Vietnam's ethnic and religious minorities, who often resided in remote areas, were generally ignored or mistreated by the Saigon Government. Prejudice from Vietnamese was considered by many minorities to be as big a threat as that offered by the Viet Cong (VC), the military arm of Vietnam's communist National Liberation Front. Supported by communist North Vietnam, the VC were quick to exploit these neglected groups. The CIA, backed by Special Forces, intended to expand Vietnamese Government presence, provide a means for the minorities to defend themselves, and bring them into the national struggle.

Early 1962 saw SF begin the training of Montagnards at Buon Enao in the central highlands. This successful experiment would ultimately lead to scores of CIDG camps through-out Vietnam. In November 1962, the piecemeal dispatch of SF teams to Vietnam was formalized with the establishment of US Army Special Forces, Vietnam (Provisional)(USASFV); in effect a miniature SF group. Prior to this, teams were attached to the Counterinsurgency Support Office. By the next year, USASFV had grown to a controlling C-team in Nha Trang, four B-teams (one in each corps area[3]), and 36 A-teams. Over 50,000 CIDG and other paramilitary troops participated in the various programs. The SF teams were located in remote, fortified camps and conducted six-month temporary duty

BELOW **USSF and CIDG rush to off-load supplies from a UH-1H Huey atop Grand Sommit Mountain where Mission Support Site Da Hang was established in 1968. Such sites served as forward bases from which to launch operations.**

Close teamwork was necessary for effective operations and day-to-day running of the camp. Here the LLDB Camp Katum commander and the A-322 executive officer discuss known enemy dispositions via a combat interpreter.

(TDY) tours detached from the 1st, 5th, and 7th SFGAs. It was soon decided to concentrate the CIA's counterinsurgency programs under USASFV. Operation SWITCHBACK was initiated on July 1, 1963 to shift these programmes to USSF control. The transition was completed in October 1964.

In September 1964, USASFV was disbanded as the 5th SFGA relocated to Vietnam by phasing in its teams. The six-month tour became a thing of the past as individuals now conducted one-year tours. A team was assigned to a specific camp where it remained. As individuals completed their tours, their replacements arrived and it was not long before a continuous process of troopers departing and arriving became established. While the team cohesiveness of the old six-month tour offered distinct advantages, the new system ensured continuity of the advisory effort as there were always "old hands" in the teams, men who were familiar with the strike force and area of operations.

The primary missions of the camp strike forces were border security, infiltration trail interdiction, local village security, intelligence collection, and local civil action projects. Regardless of the various special projects and the strike force camps, the primary mission of the 5th Special Forces Group in Vietnam was to advise the Vietnamese Airborne Special Forces (Luc Luong Dac Biêt – LLDB)[4].

Special Forces organization

Special Forces unit organization was unique to the Army and, to the uninitiated, somewhat confusing. The primary unit to which SF soldiers identified was the Special Forces Group (Airborne). A group consisted of a Headquarters and Headquarters Company, a Signal Company, and four SF Companies (A–D). From 1963–65, some boasted an Aviation Company. A 250-man (approximately) company was divided into 16 SF operational detachments, or teams. Company headquarters (the C-team) was headed by a lieutenant-colonel while the three operational detachments (B-teams) were headed by majors (those in Vietnam were commanded by lieutenant-colonels from 1968). Both C- and B-teams had a complete staff, XO (executive officer), S-1 (personnel), S-2 (intelligence), S-3 (operations), S-4 (supply), and a communications officer. An S-5 (civil affairs) officer was added in Vietnam. Each officer had a senior NCO assistant, and both C- and B-teams possessed a sergeant-major. The B-team was additionally manned by the same NCO specialists as an A-team, increasing its capabilities. A C-team was manned by six officers and 12 NCOs; a B-team by six officers and 17 NCOs. There was also a company

Administrative Detachment, two officers and 13 cooks, clerks, and other support personnel.

The company's 12 A-teams (four per B-team) were the core element of Special Forces. There were two men in each specialty, allowing the team to be split into two elements. As within any military organization, the use of official terms was often the exception. The commonly used duty position titles are given in parentheses:[5]

From 1968 most A-teams in Vietnam were increased to 14 men and modified to more effectively accomplish the counterinsurgency role. A

Detachment Commander	Captain	Team Leader
Executive Officer	1st Lieut.	XO or jokingly, "Excess Officer"
Operations Sergeant	Master Sgt.	Team Sergeant
Heavy Weapons Leader	Sgt. 1st Cl.	Heavy Weapons Man
Intelligence Sergeant	Sgt. 1st Cl.	Intel Sergeant
Light Weapons Leader	Sgt. 1st Cl.	Light Weapons Man
Medical Specialist	Sgt. 1st Cl.	Senior or Team Medic
Radio Operator Supervisor	Sgt. 1st Cl.	Senior Radio Operator
Assistant Medical Specialist	Staff Sgt.	Junior Medic
Demolitions Sergeant	Staff Sgt.	Engineer Sgt.
Chief Radio Operator	Sgt.	Junior Radio Operator
Combat Demolitions Specialist	Spec. 5	Demo Man

1st lieutenant Civic Action/Psychological Operations Officer (CA/PO Officer – pronounced "kay-poe") and a specialist 5 CA/PO Specialist were added. The Demo Man was replaced by an Assistant Intelligence Sergeant. A-teams' rank structures were typically much lower than specified and usually understrength. The author, upon arrival at his team, found a full complement of officers, one master sergeant, two sergeants 1st class, one staff sergeant, and two sergeants. Shortages of medics and commo men were notoriously common.

The basic group structure was maintained by the 5th SFGA in Vietnam, but greatly modified and expanded. This flexibility to adapt to accommodate mission requirements is a keynote feature of SF organization.

By early 1968, the 5th SFGA's structure had stabilized, although minor changes continued to occur as camps opened and closed. The group maintained its Special Forces Operating Base (SFOB) at Nha Trang (II CTZ). The SFOB included the much expanded Group HQ and HQ Company, Company E (Signal) with detachments attached to C-teams, and the Logistical Support Center. Numerous Military Intelligence, Signal, and Engineer Detachments served with the SFOB and C-teams, with further attachments to the B-teams, which later increased to about 30 men. Nearby was the Vietnamese LLDB Command Headquarters.

Companies C, B, A, and D were responsible for USSF elements in I, II, III, and IV CTZs respectively. The company's C-teams were located near the Vietnamese Corps Headquarters and the parallel LLDB C-team. The C-team, while serving as a command and control headquarters for SF elements with the CTZ, mainly provided logistical support and liaison with US Army forces. The number of B-teams varied from the standard three to two or four. One B-team served as the MIKE Force command, while the others supported the A-teams at strike force camps. They were collocated with an LLDB B-team in a province capital. Both the B- and C-teams were augmented with intelligence and communications personnel.

Team numbering varied from group to group, but in Vietnam from 1965 it followed a simple system that identified the CTZ in which the team was located. The C-teams of Company C, B, A, and D were designated C-1, 2, 3, and 4 to match I, II, III, and IV CTZs; the system was, it must be said, a little confusing due to the order in which the companies had been assigned to corps areas. The companies, however, were seldom referred to as such, but simply as, for example, C-3. C-3's B-teams were B-32, 33, and 34. B-36 controlled the MIKE Force. Each B-team had four A-teams designated by three digit numbers, for example, B-33 controlled A-331 through 334.

Some eight B-teams, designated in the 50-series, were under 5th SFGA control. These supported the various special reconnaissance projects (B-50, 52, 53, 56, and 57), 5th MIKE Force (B-55), and LLDB Training Center (B-51).

CIDG Strikers distribute fresh rations that have been delivered by a C-7A Caribou transport to Camp Katum, 1969. Across the border in Cambodia was a VC mortar training school and Katum, nicknamed "Ka-boom," was the target. By 1968 the camp had received some 22,000 mortar rounds, forcing its conversion to a completely underground installation.

SPECIAL FORCES TRAINING

Enlistment, initial training, and SF recruitment

Most future SF troopers had enlisted in the regular Army at a time when it was more popular for young Americans to join the National Guard or gain an educational or conscientious objector deferment. Many were airborne qualified prior to volunteering for SF. The three-week Airborne Course, (Jump School), at Ft Benning, Georgia, demanded high physical and performance standards. Men had to complete five qualifying jumps, but it was neither as tough nor dangerous as often portrayed.

There were several ways that servicemen came to volunteer for SF. Some men, based on records screening, were approached by SF recruiting NCOs while attending Basic Combat Training or the Airborne Course. SF recruiters had no quota and they actually attempted to discourage prospective volunteers. Others volunteered after two or more years' service; many men from the 82d or 101st Airborne Divisions chose this route. Servicemen who had been exposed to SF in-country during a Vietnam tour, were another source of recruits. While most enlisted volunteers were infantrymen, they could possess any military occupation specialty (MOS). Unusual non-combatant MOSs were considered to provide SF troopers with a broader background when mixed with the predominating infantrymen.

The stipulation that enlisted men be triple volunteers – Army, Airborne, SF – like everything else in the Army, could be waived to accommodate qualified draftees. A soldier volunteering for the Army enlisted for three years and was designated Regular Army, his serial number prefixed by "RA." An inducted soldier, a draftee, was called to the colors for two years, his serial number was preceded by "US." In order to volunteer for SF, a draftee was required to extend his enlistment to three years or more and was redesignated "RA." A soldier was required to have at least 18 months remaining on his enlistment once he completed SF training. RA volunteers enlisting in the Army to attend specific training courses would not attend that training if they joined SF.

An SF engineer NCO discusses the construction of a below-ground bunker with a Striker, Cung Son, A-221, 1969. Between combat operations, A-team members spent long hours working with the Strikers on camp construction and endless refurbishing projects.

Junior officers often faced an uphill battle to enter SF. All units during the Vietnam War were critically short of officers. Commanders were reluctant to lose good officers to the "Snake Eaters" and sternly warned hopefuls that an SF tour could adversely affect their careers. SF officers could be of any combat arms branch: Infantry, Armor, Field and Air Defense Artillery, Engineer, and Military Police. Military Intelligence, Signal, Medical, Quartermaster officers and others could be assigned to SF to fill certain support functions, and not all attended the SF Officer Course. However, all were required to have completed their basic branch course before acceptance.

Both officers and enlisted men took the Army Physical Readiness Test (APRT), meeting airborne standards, and successfully completed the Combat Water Survival Test (CWST), a simple swimming test. Enlisted men had to additionally pass the mentally grueling Special Forces Selection Battery, which included personality, critical decision making, self-location (using a series of photos), and Morse code aptitude tests, which many men purposely failed in order to avoid a somewhat unpopular duty.

A common eight-week Basic Combat Training course was attended by all men entering the Army. It was conducted at one of 12 training centers (the number varied slightly over the war years) and provided a good foundation in basic military skills: physical fitness; dismounted drill; military customs and courtesies; bayonet and hand-to-hand combat; individual combat skills; first aid; and, most importantly, two weeks of rifle marksmanship. The use of grenades was the only other weapons training provided. "Basic" was followed by Advanced Individual Training (AIT) in one of scores of MOSs offered at the training centers or one of over 20 branch or specialty schools. AIT could last from eight weeks to many months depending on the MOS. Light Weapons Infantry AIT (MOS 11B) was eight weeks at one of seven infantry training centers. All except Ft Dix, NJ, were rated as "Vietnam oriented." Ft Dix was reserved for infantrymen slated for Germany, Korea, Alaska, and Panama. Infantry AIT covered squad tactics, combat and reconnaissance patrolling, land navigation, radio-telephone procedures, mine warfare, more physical fitness instruction, and three weeks of machine gun, automatic rifle, 40mm grenade launcher, and antitank weapons training. BCT and 11B AIT called for 10–14 hours a day, five days a week, with Saturdays dedicated to inspections and administration.

Special Forces training

Once accepted, the future SF trooper was sent to the US Army John F. Kennedy Center for Special Warfare (Airborne), which was identified by the awkward abbreviation of USAJFKCSW (ABN). The fact that it was the only organization within the Army that bore an individual's name was an indicator that it was different to anything experienced elsewhere in the Army. The SF student was expected to be on time for daily classes, but he was not marched there in formation. Once released from his training company's morning formation, he was on his own. After a week's processing, the student was assigned to one of the four training companies in Special Forces

Two SF engineer NCOs cut a length of detonating cord to prepare demolition materials in order to clear trees hampering the approach to Camp Duc Hue's A-325 airfield. One man carries an M1 rifle with an M2 flash hider.

Training Group (SFTG). Often he would have to wait several weeks before being assigned a class date. In the meantime he pulled KP (Kitchen Police), guard duty, and other work details to include roadside trash pick-up; it was a humbling experience. This was to take place between all phases of SF training. But one of the details was sought after, and proved to be of benefit to his training. Groups of Special Forces students awaiting their next phase were employed as "guerrillas" (Gs) to be trained by other students or "counter-guerrillas" (CGs) to act as an aggressor force in field exercises during the different training phases. It was considered a lot of fun to chase someone or even be chased through the woods for a week or two, especially when it spared one from KP, formations, and inspections.

Phase I of the Special Forces Tactics and Techniques Course was of only four weeks' duration. Students came from throughout the Army. Some had volunteered to flee boring Stateside assignments, others had completed an overseas tour and sported spec. 4 or sergeant stripes, a small handful had even been to Vietnam, but most were privates and PFCs with only Basic, AIT and Jump School under their belts. All were eager to meet the challenges of this new adventure.

The first class in Phase I was a math refresher, much to our student's surprise. But, the rest of the course concentrated on patrolling techniques, land navigation, basic survival, and methods of instruction. The teaching role assumed paramount importance. He found out that the Special

MEDCAP (Medical and Civil Affairs Program) was a standard mission for all SF camps. Local villagers would visit the strike camps and patrols would visit outlying villages in their tactical area of responsibility, thereby providing the only medical care the villagers had ever received.

Forces soldier was a teacher first and commando second. All of the hands-on instruction was given by NCOs, many with two or three tours in Vietnam behind them, and their years of practical experience were passed on to the student. The student himself taught progressively longer classes on a broad range of military subjects to his own group and was required to make his own training aids. The summation of the course was the Phase I Field Training Exercise (FTX), a week-long ordeal at Camp Mackall, southwest of Ft Bragg. After making a night jump into the dense pine forests, classes of 50 or more students conducted demanding, around the clock land navigation exercises, ambushes, reconnaissance patrols and raids, all with virtually no food and while enthusiastically hounded by the "CGs" – other students. Severely deprived of food and sleep the entire week, a grueling 20km-plus evasion and escape course followed. Upon completion of this phase he was awarded the green beret in a simple ceremony, but he was still a long way from being Special Forces qualified. The 1st Special Forces crest adorned his beret, but no unit flash was authorized.

Another break in training followed, bringing with it work details and speculation as to what SF MOS course he might draw during Phase II. An interview by an officer determined the soldier's MOS, but it was preceded by the warning, "Tell me which MOS you want and I'll tell you why you can't have it." All enlisted men were trained in one of five skills. Officers were trained separately in the 12-week Special Forces Officer Course (SFOC). Each of the MOS courses, except the medical, ended with a week-long FTX to practice new found skills. The officers undertook a two-week unconventional warfare FTX known as Exercise Gobbler Woods.

The ten-week Engineer Course (MOS 12B) covered conventional and unconventional (home-made) explosives (a week of each); demolition techniques; obstacles; light building and bridge construction; and engineer reconnaissance. The course's highlight was to build a bridge one week and blow it up the next. Most went on to heavy equipment operator training at Ft Belvior, Virginia, the Engineer School.

The eight-week Weapons Course was divided into light and heavy weapons phases. The five-week light weapons portion (MOS 11B) trained the student to operate and disassemble some 55 small arms. Timed disassembly and assembly tests were frequent. Current and obsolete US, Allied, and Communist Bloc weapons were studied along with basic small unit tactics. The two-week heavy weapons (MOS 11C) portion dealt with 57mm and 106mm recoilless rifles, the LAW and 3.5in. rocket launcher, and mortars, predominantly on the 60mm, 81mm, and 4.2in. mortars, as well as fire direction center operations. After a one-week tactical exercise and live firing of all weapons, graduates were awarded both MOSs.

In the 12-week Operations and Intelligence (O&I) Course (MOS 11F) for NCOs, students were required to be at least sergeants. They were taught the many aspects of mission planning, and unconventional warfare and special operations intelligence techniques. The skills learned ranged from photography, fingerprinting, and briefing procedures, to establishing agent nets.

The 16-week Communications Course (MOS 05B) covered operation of specialized radios and burst-transmission message devices, on- and off-line crypto-graphic systems, clandestine commo techniques, and special emphasis on manual Morse code. The SF standard was to send and receive 18 words per minute, the highest standard in the US armed forces, with the exception of nuclear submarine communicators, who operated at 20 wpm.

The CIDG crew of a newly issued 105mm M101A1 howitzer completes a training session under the guidance of A-245's weapons NCO. Many camps were provided with two of the howitzers as they were so remote that Allied artillery support was not always available. Dak Seang, 1969.

The extremely challenging 32-week Medical Course (MOS 91C) was conducted in four sub-phases. The first was an eight-week Special Forces Basic Aidman's Course (MOS 91A), which was modified from the regular course with more emphasis on tropical diseases and less on ward care. This was followed by attendance on the 12-week Clinical Specialist Course (MOS 91C) at Ft Sam Houston, Texas, the Army's Medical Training Center. From there, students spent six-weeks "internship" at an Army hospital working in emergency rooms and wards. They returned to Bragg for the most challenging portion of the course: the Medical Aid Procedures Course, which was unique to Special Forces medics and taught students skills normally reserved for physicians. The six weeks began with three weeks' clinical training followed by "Dog Lab," where each student received a dog that was treated the same as a human patient. After being cured of existing aliments, the "patient" was anesthetized and shot in a hind leg with a .22cal rifle, which was treated and another leg later amputated.[6] The graduates of this most demanding of Special Forces MOSs were highly respected by the other troops and Army surgeons. The civilian position of physician's assistant (PA) was originally created to utilize the skills of former SF medics.

An interesting aspect of the Training Group was that the students were intermixed within companies regardless of MOS and training phase. All the various MOSs might be represented within a single eight-man room. It was a situation that, when coupled with a variety of previous military training, led to a great deal of unofficial cross-fertilization of skills. The practice was, however, eliminated in late 1968 when students were concentrated into companies by phase and MOS. The change undoubtedly eased administration, but informal professional development suffered.

Now with a new MOS, the student was assigned to a group of students that possessed all SF MOSs to undertake Phase III. It was here that the student was taught the basics of unconventional warfare operations:

concepts, techniques, organization, mission planning, air support, low-level tradecraft, and more. He learned the nature of guerrillas, how to deal with them, how to organize them, and to motivate them to undertake missions that were beneficial to the military and political goals of the US and its allies, rather than the guerrilla's own, frequently short-sighted, aims. He was also taught how to demobilize a guerrilla force once a conflict was over.

The final two weeks of the six-week phase was spent in an unconventional warfare exercise. Students planned and prepared for the mission, then parachuted into Uwharrie National Forest northwest of Ft Bragg. Each student A-team linked up with its "guerrilla" force (made up of instructor-led SF students). The student A-teams organized and trained the "Gs," and then assisted them in the execution of raids, ambushes, and other missions while pursued by the "CGs," often provided by the 82d Airborne Division during this phase. The trust of the guerrilla leaders had to be gained but they often proved uncooperative and had to be persuaded to undertake some missions. Upon graduation from Phase III the student was now considered "flash-qualified" (authorized to sew his assigned group's flash on his beret) and had an "S" special skill identifier tacked on to the end of his MOS. Officers were designated by a "3" skill identifier. From 1969, the SF Qualification Course was rated as an NCO course, and graduating enlisted men were automatically promoted to sergeant (E5). Previously they had to work their way through the ranks.

The words of Berry Saddler's "Ballad of the Green Berets," which says: "One hundred men we'll test today, but only one will win the green beret," are not entirely accurate, but it was a demanding program with an extremely high attrition rate. Counting the pre-screening and selection battery tests, one out of 100 may well have been the end success rate.

The new Special Forces trooper was now assigned to an SF group, the 3d, 6th or 7th at Ft Bragg, 1st on Okinawa, 8th in Panama, or the 10th in Germany.[7] Small numbers were selected for assignment to the 46th SF Company in Thailand. Most of the graduating E4s and E5s were placed directly in E6 and E7 A-team positions. Many of those remaining at Bragg were eventually destined for Vietnam. The training actually never ended; it was continued in the groups by unit-level training, exercises, and attendance at specialized courses. Even when our trooper arrived in Vietnam, he undertook the two-week Combat Orientation Course at the Special-Forces-run MACV Recondo School. Contrary to popular perception, few of the new troopers were taught a foreign language or cross-trained in a second MOS. This was usually reserved for those who re-enlisted.

Besides medical treatment, MEDCAP missions also distributed food, clothes, tools, and agricultural materiel. Here A-246's civic action/psychological operations (CA/PO) officer distributes clothing to needy Montagnards near Camp Mang Buk.

The senior medic of A-334 and the LLDB team commander enter into a friendly competition with their favorite handguns, an M1911A1 pistol and an M1917 revolver, both .45cal, at Camp Tong Le Chon.

The new Special Forces troopers were by no means supermen, but they were trained to a high degree of proficiency, were extremely motivated, mentally and physically fit for the rigors ahead, and possessed an innate desire to accomplish the Special Forces motto, *De Oppresso Liber* (Free the Oppressed).

Deployment to Vietnam

The SF soldier selected for Vietnam duty was notified by the Department of the Army 120 days in advance by receipt of his alert orders. Those volunteering for Vietnam, a feat accomplished by a phone call to the Department of the Army's Special Assignments Section, often had a longer delay as they had to await vacancies in the next available allotment. In the meantime, the trooper undertook a pre-deployment physical, received numerous inoculations, took care of any dental work (none was available in Vietnam except for severe emergencies), completed a will, granted power of attorney to next of kin, and took a 30-day leave. His deployment orders directed that he report to either Ft Lewis, Washington, or Port of Embarkation, San Francisco, California. He spent a week there completing paperwork and received an issue of tropical uniforms.[8] Regular troops were required to possess at least one field cap (baseball cap), and if not in possession of one, they had to purchase one at Quartermaster Clothing Sales. SF soldiers were not required to have one; and they became a clothing item that no self-respecting trooper would be caught with. They did, however, rush to on-post dry cleaners to have name and "U.S. ARMY" tapes sewn on their new jungle fatigues at their own expense. Only the SF knew what unit they going to, and they had their "Lighting Bolt" patch and jumpwings sewn on. Between processing, the days were spent on post work details and the evenings at enlisted or NCO clubs. The flight to Vietnam was on a chartered commercial Boeing 707 with all the usual airline amenities, and it took the better part of a day.

Most SF troops processed through Ft Lewis arrived at Cam Ranh Bay in II CTZ and the 22d Replacement Battalion. Those from California arrived at Tan Son Nut Air Base in Saigon and went on to the 90th Replacement. More paperwork awaited them on arrival, including filling out next-of-kin notification cards. A soldier could specify that his next of kin not be notified if he was lightly wounded (most did this); regulations required that they be notified if seriously wounded, killed, or reported missing. Soldiers were also issued a Geneva Convention Card and MACV Ration Card (to control the purchase of electrical appliances, cameras, liquor, and cigarettes as a black market control measure). American dollars

In order for the Air Force to get accurate and timely weather information from the remote interior of Vietnam, many SF camps were provided with a weather kit and required to take thrice-daily readings on weather conditions and radio them in. While a source of jokes and a mild inconvenience, the reports were extremely valuable to the Air Force. A somewhat relaxed standard of footwear is seen at Camp Tra Bong, A-107.

were exchanged for Military Payment Certificates (MPCs), which were the standard medium of exchange in Vietnam. Our trooper brushed his teeth with a special one-time use fluoridated toothpaste, was cautioned on the danger of venereal diseases, and sternly briefed on the necessity of taking all of his daily and weekly anti-malaria pills. The conventional soldiers were assigned to units and after a few days were shipped out. The SF soldiers were even sooner flown to the SFOB at Nha Trang and began another round of paperwork.

Troops in Vietnam were paid in Military Payment Certificates. It was a violation of regulations to even possess US dollars or spend MPCs on the local economy. MPCs could be spent in post exchanges (PX), military clubs, Army post offices, and authorized Vietnamese concessionaires on bases (barbers, tailors, etc.) American car dealers also had salesmen on major rear bases. A soldier could select his car (the next year's model), arrange for payroll deductions, and pick up his new car when he returned to the States (if he were killed the payments made would be reimbursed to his next of kin). MPCs were to be exchanged for Vietnamese piasters at military pay offices and banks at a rate of US $1.00 = 115$ VN (115 piasters or 'Pees') in 1969. Troops were cautioned not to exchange dollars or MPCs for piasters on the black market, where they received a substantially better exchange rate, up to 200 percent. Most soldiers had a percentage of their pay deducted and banked in checking or savings accounts. The First National City and Chase Manhattan Banks had branch offices in Saigon offering 10 percent interest on savings accounts, higher than the Stateside standard. Money could also be sent home by postal money order obtained from Army post officers.

In 1969, an SF sergeant (E5) on his first tour had a monthly base pay of about $350 to which were added $65 hostile fire (combat) pay, $55 hazardous duty (jump) pay,[9] $77.10 subsistence allowance (rations not available pay), and $13 overseas allowance (no one could figure out what it was really for); all tax exempt in Vietnam. Letters home were free, but packages had to be paid for.

After processing through the 5th SFGA, the newly arrived SF trooper was attached to the Combat Orientation Course (COC or "Cock Course") under the tutelage of the MACV Recondo School, which was operated by the 5th SFGA. While awaiting the next course to begin, he was free to explore Nha Trang, to become familiar with Vietnamese culture, and to exchange the US dollars he had "forgotten" to declare for black market piasters. Restaurants, bars, steam baths, and tailor shops served as cultural

One of the precepts of SF is that everybody works together, pulling their load regardless of rank. That was extended to the CIDG, to serve as an example. SF troopers commonly worked alongside their Strikers sharing the same privations and labor. Here an A-326 sergeant first class at Camp Tra Cu leads a work detail to a site where a new weapons bunker will be constructed.

classrooms. Wherever he looked he saw the three most common features in Vietnam: sandbags, barbed wire, and motorbikes.

Upon completing the COC our trooper received his assignment and within 48 hours he was on his way to some far corner of Vietnam. His first stop would be the C-team, where a small group would spend a few days awaiting transport to their B-team. The trooper would meet the company commander and sergeant-major, receive a briefing from the S-2, S-3, and S-5 sections, and draw an M16A1 rifle. When he arrived at the B-team by helicopter or air transport, much the same process would be repeated and he would find out which camp he would be spending the next year at.

SPECIAL FORCES CAMP

No two Strike Force camps were alike, although there were many similarities. The early camps were somewhat crude, and living conditions spartan. Buildings were constructed of local logs and thatch, scrounged corrugated metal, scrap lumber, and ammo crates. Weak defenses consisted of a few machine-gun bunkers, light-mortar pits, a surrounding trench or berm (earth wall), punji stakes, some barbed wire, and occasionally a moat.

In the mid-1960s the camps began to be "hardened," after some remote camps were overrun, and were termed "fighting camps." Allocations of machine guns, mortars, and recoilless rifles were greatly increased. Trench-connected bunkered fighting positions were improved, and masses of barbed and concertina wire were made available. Other amenities began to appear, such as power generators, refrigerators (for medicine, fresh food, and beer), and movie projectors (for CIDG morale). The camp's perimeter was usually dictated by terrain, and it could be of almost any shape. The exact siting of a camp took into account soil conditions, drainage, location of villages, suitable airfield site, use of existing terrain features, and the location of dominating terrain features that would be of use to the enemy.

The camps were usually located in remote areas, often in regions where ARVN and US units seldom ventured. First-tier camps established on the Cambodian and Laotian borders were tasked with border surveillance and interdiction missions. Those in the second tier, further into the interior of Vietnam, were situated so as to interdict infiltration trails and conduct area combat reconnaissance. Many of the camps were also responsible for protecting nearby villages.

The camps were major construction projects taking months to build at a cost approaching $1 million. Army engineers and Navy construction battalions (Seabees) accomplished much of the major construction, with the CIDG undertaking lighter work, installing the barrier wire, building perimeter bunkers and mortar pits, filling thousands of sandbags, and even constructing their own quarters.

Touring a camp

The best way for a newly assigned A-team member to become familiar with a strike force camp was to follow an orientation tour conducted by an older hand. To this end, and because of his familiarity with it, the author's own camp (Chi Linh) is described below.

Chi Linh Camp was established in January 1967 as Camp Cau Song Be ("Song River Bridge"), but it was soon renamed to prevent confusion with B-34's Song Be Camp and because the bridge was blown by the VC. It was located about 11 miles southeast of An Loc, the capital of Binh Long Province and location of B-33. Located on the north side of Interprovincial Route 14 (closed due to the destruction of all bridges and culverts, thereby cutting off the camp from Chon Thanh the district capital to the west), it was 1.8 miles west of the Song Be River and 56 miles north of Saigon.

The camp was established by USSF Team A-333 and LLDB-team (*Toán*) A-162, to interdict part of an infiltration trail known as "Serge's Jungle Highway," an off-shoot of the Ho Chi Minh Trail running through Cambodia, 25 miles to the northwest. The camp had been built directly on the trail, resulting in a serious real-estate dispute, but once the camp was completed it was left in relative peace and the NVA re-routed the trail 3-4 miles east of the Song Be River in Phuoc Long Province. It remained the CSF's principal interdiction mission.

Chi Linh was an octagonal camp about 220yds across. It was built on flat ground in an area of gently rolling hills. The camp was surrounded by dense bamboo growth interspersed with small patches of hardwood timber and brush.

Chi Linh was securely surrounded by an impressive array of wire obstacles. Beginning at the outermost barrier and working inward through 110yds of obstacles, we find that there are five belts, and two types of wire. Standard military barbed wire, not unlike its civilian equivalent, was issued in spools. Concertina wire – spring steel wire – was wound in a coil 3ft in diameter, one coil giving a 50ft length when stretched out. Wire was supported by olive drab-painted U-shaped picket posts, which were issued in several lengths.

Between belts 2, 3, and 4 was "tanglefoot," a spider web arrangement of barbed wire strung at heights of 6in., 12in., and 18in. above the ground and secured to short pickets and barrier posts. Its purpose was to trip assaulting

ABOVE **An A-111 SF weapons NCO loads 23/4in. helicopter rockets into a makeshift rocket launcher mounted on a ¼ton trailer. It is just one of many examples of expedient weapons concocted at SF camps. Camp Plateau Gi, 1967.**

BELOW **An example of an earth berm on a camp perimeter. Besides providing defensive positions, this berm at Camp My An in the Mekong Delta also served to keep out flood waters during the wet season. The camp would literally become an island when the monsoon rains came. This perimeter machine-gun bunker was built high enough to stay above the water.**

troops and make it more difficult to low-crawl through. Belts 1, 2 and 3 and the tanglefoot had M49A1 tripflares emplaced.

Between belts 2 and 3 were emplaced M18A1 Claymore anti-personnel mines (see Plate D); about 600 guarded Chi Linh's wire. Some of these mines could be fired in banks of six from switchboards in the command bunker; the others were individually command-fired from perimeter machine-gun bunkers, where the firing devices were secured in clusters.

Belts 1 and 3 followed the eight-sided shape of the camp; the others traced a zig-zag pattern. The distance between the belts varied. The barriers were high in order to discourage the use of scaling ladders and bamboo mats. The greatest danger was posed by enemy sappers – specially trained solders whose task was to infiltrate through the wire, cutting a path and clearing mines and tripflares for the assault force. No height or thickness of barrier could stop them, and the only defense was constant vigilance. The quality of wire used in such a camp barrier system was phenomenal, requiring thousands of coils of concertina.

A sandbag parapet about 2ft high and 3½ft thick was constructed on the outer edge of the perimeter trench. It was capped with approximately 2in. of concrete, which was employed not for ballistic protection, but to prevent deterioration by weather and personnel. Individual firing positions – which were dug into the outer side of the 4ft-deep, 3½ft-wide trench – were cut into the parapet so that its top provided overhead cover, and each had a small firing port. There were about 30 such positions along each of the eight walls. Centered in each wall and at each corner were a total of 16 machine-gun bunkers. Each of these bunkers, which were constructed of concrete-capped sandbags,

Camp Lang Vei was fortunate enough to acquire a .50cal M55 quad machine gun. The camp was, however, frequently attacked by the NVA and in February 1968 it was overrun with the aid of PT-76 tanks. This picture of the USSF A-101 and LLDB team sergeants was taken in July 1967.

had a tripod-mounted .30cal M1919A6 machine gun, and three of them mounted two guns. A sandbagged guard post (complete with a corrugated steel roof) was perched atop each bunker.

Behind the perimeter trench were quarters for the 394 troops and almost an equal number of their family dependants. At some camps the dependants lived in a nearby village, requiring a permanent security force to guard them. The quarters were built of sandbagged walls with floors sunk about 2ft below ground level. Roofs were supported by timbers and covered with at least two layers of sandbags, topped with corrugated metal anchored with sandbags. Each of three CSF companies had a corrugated metal headquarters building. Other principal structures included a well-equipped dispensary, a vehicle maintenance facility, a schoolhouse for the Strikers' children, a camp store, the *Co Lac Bo* (combined recreation room and café), a tailor shop, and a barber shop. Most of these buildings were made from scrap wood with corrugated metal roofs.

A portion of the camp's northeast and east interior was occupied by an artillery platoon detached from the 5th ARVN Infantry Division. This platoon, with two 105mm M101A1 howitzers, was rotated every six months. Similar 105mm howitzers (often referred to simply as "one-oh-fives") were supplied to many camps in an effort to provide more widespread artillery coverage. Some camps' "one-oh-fives" were manned by specially trained Strikers.

At Chi Linh the howitzers were emplaced in heavily sandbagged positions with adjoining ammunition bunkers. The platoon had its own quarters, fire direction center, and supply room. The howitzers were of limited use for camp defense, due to their inability to deliver direct fire,

A CIDG 105mm howitzer crew demonstrate their crew drill to the 5th SFGA Command Readiness Team. The CRT visited each camp once or twice a year to evaluate its performance and combat readiness as well as make recommendations for improvements. To the right of the SF NCO are LLDB officers in olive- green and leaf-pattern uniforms.

and were used primarily to support CSF combat operations; their 12,000yd range covered most of the camp's TAOR - The Tactical Area of Responcibility was the permanent area assigned to a Strike Force camp for tactical operations. A Group directive specified that artillery be emplaced to fire directly into the wire with "beehive" rounds (flechet projectiles) if camp layout permitted it.

Dispersed at intervals around the troop area were nine 60mm M19 mortars. The interior of the above-ground pits was about 8ft across; the sandbag sides were 3ft high and 2ft thick. Each had an attached ammunition bunker. Visitors were surprised that any given mortar did not fire into the perimeter section closest to it, but instead was directed across the camp into a sector on the far side. This was because the pits on the side attacked might be under direct fire and the minimum range was 55yds. The mortar fire needed to be brought down close during an attack on the wire.

Additional fire support could be obtained from US fire support bases located to the north, south and west, in the form of 8in. and 155mm howitzers and 175mm guns. Close air support and flare ships could be on station from Ben Hoa Air Base in 20 minutes, and 1st Cavalry Division attack helicopters would follow shortly. A curtain of fire could be placed around the camp, but in such cases the VC/NVA, being the soldiers they were, could sometimes still get through.

An inner perimeter, capable of holding out even if the rest of the camp was overrun, was added to all camps that did not already have them in the mid-1960s. Chi Linh's was square in shape, with a slope-fronted, 5ft-high earth berm, which was about 8ft thick at its base. The inside was vertical and supported by corrugated metal or steel drums (with the ends removed, slit open and flattened) held in place by barbed wire posts. Numerous coils of concertina wire were strung on the berm's outer face.

Inside were the USSF and LLDB team houses and quarters, supply and arms rooms, interpreters' quarters, a wash house with showers, two main ammunition bunkers, underground communications and emergency medical bunkers, and two 10Kw power generators. The above-ground structures had either wood or corrugated metal sides and corrugated metal roofs. Earth-filled 55gal. drums protected the exterior of the team houses.

Emplaced into the perimeter were three 81mm M29 (see Plate E3) and one 4.2in. M30 mortars, in large sunken pits walled with concrete-capped sandbags. Inner perimeter machine-gun bunkers served a dual role. One was situated on each corner and midway on the walls (apart from the northeast wall and east corner, which had none), and each housed one or two M1919A6s. Some bunkers also mounted weapons on their roofs that were capable of firing into the camp's outer wire; these included three 57mm M18A1 recoilless rifles and one .50cal HB-M2 machine gun. Another .50cal was mounted on a 12ft tower near the northeast wall, which was referred to as the "CMH-Tower" (an allusion to the certainty of a posthumous Congressional Medal of Honor for anyone who tried to climb up during an attack).

There was only one entrance to the camp: a road running from the south wall to the airstrip. On the west side of the entrance road was the POL (petroleum, oil, lubricants) dump surrounded by upright

In 1969 many camps were provided with 106mm M40A1 recoilless rifles in light of the increased NVA armor threat, although some camps already possessed them. Besides its intended role, the "106" was effective for direct anti-personnel fire and was frequently used for long-range harassing fire. This rifle is located at Camp Ba Xoai, A-421. Behind it is a 5,000,000-candlepower exeon searchlight used to detect targets on the nearby Nui Cam Mountain.

earth-filled drums. A small guard shack stood near the outer barrier belt. Before sunset the entrance was secured by several sets of wood frame and barbed wire gates, plus half a dozen coils of concertina pulled across the road and rigged with Claymores and tripflares.

The most noticeable manmade feature outside the camp was a 3,500ft airstrip. The east–west runway was constructed directly on Route 14, which provided a substantial foundation. The packed laterite (a red, coarse, gravelly soil) was tested to a compactness of 94 percent of concrete and it could handle any aircraft up to and including C-130s. There were turnaround pads on the east and west sides of the camp, the latter doubling as a heli-pad. Across the runway was a small rifle range; near it was a demolitions pit where defective, dud, climate-deteriorated, and captured munitions were blown up. A village, Son La, stood just over $1\frac{1}{4}$ miles to the east. Its population was about 300 friendly Stieng Montagnards, and it was the only remaining populated place in Chi Linh's TAOR.

The foregoing is only an example of one type of camp. Construction materials varied, as did perimeter defenses and construction styles. In the mountainous I CTZ, camps were perched on hill tops or clung on mountain sides. Some camps built near the Cambodian border, across from NVA sanctuaries, were completely underground due to being used as mortar crew training targets. Floating camps, which were common in IV CTZ's inundated Mekong Delta, were constructed of bunkers and mortar position built up on mounds and floating buildings that would rest on the ground when the flood waters receded.

Camp life

Daily routine in most strike force camps was normally slow paced, even idyllic at times. There were of course many exceptions, such as in areas infested with the VC, or close to contested border areas, or when the tempo of local combat operations picked up. A company making contact in the field increased activity as reinforcements were launched, air and artillery strikes coordinated, medevacs requested, and ammunition resupplies loaded on borrowed helicopters. The apprehension in the camp could be felt as wives and children, Strikers, LLDB, and USSF alike grew concerned over family and friends.

In many camps, however, life was quiet and slow paced for long periods. Companies rotated on tactical operations, local security patrols were sent out, guards were mounted, and training occasionally undertaken. The dependants cooked, cleaned their quarters, washed clothes, and went on with daily life. The children went to the camp school and the SF medics treated everyone's illnesses and injuries.

Work details were daily events and took up much of the Strikers' time in camp: filling sandbags, rebuilding and improving bunkers and other

fortifications, clearing weeds from the wire, trash collection, water trailer runs to a nearby stream, pumping water from the camp well and filling 55gal. drums throughout the camp, and so forth. All of the SF soldiers had their own pet projects they concentrated on. Improving camp defenses and the life of the Strikers, their families, and local villagers' lot were the main focuses.

The work day began at 0600 hours with company role call and work detail assignments. The SF soldier on the last radio watch awoke his team-mates. Radio watch was a two-hour shift conducted by all team members regardless of rank and was maintained 24 hours a day. An AN/VRC-47, located in the team house, monitored two channels, one on the B-team net along with the three other A-teams, and the tactical net on which the camp's company in the field communicated. Breakfast was served to all present team members by the hired cooks and they soon dispersed to discharge their duties.

Special Forces were not issued government rations, but each trooper received a monthly subsistence allowance. The food was actually scrounged or traded from US units at bases, with frozen and canned food (B-rations) acquired by team members making monthly trips to these bases. A ¼-ton jeep and trailer was borrowed from C-team in which to make the rounds. The scrounged food was stored in refrigerators and freezers provided for this purpose at the C-team and flown out to the camp the next day by an Air Force CV-2 Caribou transport. The camps had a few refrigerators and chest-type freezers. Since tiger-stripe uniforms and Montagnard crossbows were much-sought-after bartering goods, the teams usually ate well, though there were times of shortages. The lack of government rations also applied to field rations.

The background of this well-built CIDG-manned 105mm howitzer position provides an excellent example of the general appearance of a typical CIDG camp, here Camp Bu Dop, A-341. Camps were a mix of new construction and rundown structures, some of crude appearance. The gun position's sides are revetted by olive-drab steel airfield planking. The World War-Two-style pierced landing matting was also used.

Engineers and weapons men oversaw (and participated in) the construction and repair of buildings, bunkers, and defenses. They also conducted tactical and weapons training, and oversaw the maintenance of crew-served weapons. The medics ran sick call for the Strikers and dependants, conducted MEDCAPs to nearby villages, trained CIDG medics, and spent a great deal of time on camp sanitation matters. The commo men hid away in their air-conditioned communications bunker, from where they repaired radios, processed messages received by courier from higher headquarters, and constantly tinkered with camp radio antennas, internal telephone systems, the power network, and generators. Everyone was involved in training from time to time and all shared the never ending paperwork.

The team was assisted in its duties by a number of civilian employees paid for through a special fund. These included a couple of cooks, mechanics to maintain vehicles and generators, a school teacher, an armorer, and a nurse or two. In an effort to provide some degree of employment for camp dependants, the team paid out of their own pockets for housekeepers, assistant cooks, and laundresses.

There were few A-teams that did not possess several pets, which, in Vietnam, ranged from scarce cats to pythons. Dogs were universally the favorite and were considered part of the team. In the background is Camp Thuong Duc's, A-109, concrete-capped commo bunker. The layer of concrete, which is probably 2in. thick, served to protect the sandbag bunker from the elements rather than add additional protection.

Combat interpreters, three or four per camp, were also civilian employees, but were paid for from other special funds. Close friendships frequently developed between team members and interpreters who were usually considered part of the team. A good interpreter, proficient in English, capable of maintaining good relations with the LLDB, and effective in the field was worth his weight in gold. He would have to be protected from pirating by another team, especially if living conditions were better at another camp and the threat from the local VC not as great. Camps in highly contested areas had a difficult time attracting interpreters.

Relations with the LLDB counterpart team varied greatly, ranging from a close-working relationship to open hostility. Fortunately, the latter case was rare. While the LLDB had complete authority over the CIDG and the Americans were only advisors, working relationships evolved and varied greatly from camp to camp. The LLDB tended to oversee day-to-day camp administration, while the Americans controlled combat operations to a large degree. The Americans could easily manage events in the strike force, as they controlled funding, rations, supplies, and materials.

Work and training were halted at 1100 hours when "pok time" (*ngu trua*) was taken during the heat of the day. Lunch for the SF troops was sandwiches and a soft drink. Work resumed at 1300 hours and went on until 1700 hours. Dinner was simple and might be followed by a couple of beers or soft drinks while watching the sunset from atop bunkers. Two or three nights a week the Americans and LLDB would watch 16mm movies in the US team house; war movies and westerns were always popular with both Americans and Strikers. There was a television set in the US and LLDB team houses and at least one in each company area. In all but the most remote areas, the Armed Forces Television Network and a couple of Vietnamese stations could be picked up with elaborate antenna arrays erected by the commo men.

SF NCO and Strikers replace a bunker destroyed in an attack, Camp Dac Hue, A-325. Distorted airfield landing planks and timbers from the destroyed bunker are in the foreground. Some of those materials will be reused in the new bunker. Olive-drab U-shaped barbed wire pickets brace the new sandbag walls.

Dances and firelight dinner parties (*bua chen*), which are best described as food orgies, were occasionally conducted by the Strikers and happily attended by the USSF and LLDB. Most of the SF troopers became involved to some degree in the daily life of Strikers and their families by teaching in the school, providing English lessons, helping to improve living conditions on their own time, and aiding the medics in everything from suturing minor cuts to delivering babies. One rule was strictly adhered to, no relations with local women … ever.

Twice a week the "work chopper" (Whisky Charley) would arrive at the camp, dropping off mail, movies (rotated between camps), and official correspondence. In-coming replacements, those going on R & R or returning, those making visits to the B- and C-teams, and those finishing their tours all traveled via the Whisky Charley. It would make two trips on the day it came, going between the B-team and all A-team camps before returning to the C-team.

Rations, ammunition, and spare parts arrived by C-130 or CV-2 transports. The few camps without an airstrip were resupplied by overland convoys or even air drop (the motion picture *Dumbo Drop* was loosely based on fact). Once a month the camp's payroll was delivered. A pay officer from the C-team paid the Americans in MPC and the CIDG payroll was delivered to the team commander. A pay formation was held and the Strikers were paid in piasters by the team commander, not the LLDB.

Local diversions were few. Invariably there was a basketball net, and volley ball and soccer matches were played with the Strikers (the play was rough and rules were lax, being referred to as "jungle rules"). Poker, the card game of choice, and reading were the main off-duty interests. Every US soldier in Vietnam was authorized a five-day out-of-country rest and recreation leave[10] (non-chargeable to his annual 30 days' leave) plus an in-country three-day R & R at Vung Tau (III CTZ) or China Beach in Da Nang (I CTZ). Bangkok and Sydney were the most popular R & R

93

A USSF officer inspects the Danish Madsen 9mm M/50 submachine guns of a platoon of Rhade Montagnard Mountain Scouts. Some in the left-rear are armed with .30cal M1903 rifles. With their weapons concealed in back-pack baskets they would scout mountain trails posing as food gathers to report VC activities. Note the officer's World-War-Two-era jungle boots.

centers among SF, although many married men often met their wives in Hawaii. Few SF bothered with the in-country R & R, having occasional opportunity to let off stream at the modest B- or C-team clubs.

WEAPONS OF THE SPECIAL FORCES SOLDIER

Special Forces and the CIDG used a wide range of weapons dating from before World War Two to the latest available. Most of the older weapons initially issued to the CIDG were obtained from Army and CIA contingency stocks. SF and CIDG missions demanded weapons suitable for light-infantry operations, reconnaissance, and camp defense in widely different types of terrain. Reliability, simple operation, and light weight were the main prerequisites. The latter was a major issue due to the small stature of Asians and the demands of jungle, swamp, and mountain warfare.

The use of exotic weapons (for example, foreign submachine guns, shotguns, etc.) must be mentioned. Simply put, they were not widely used for a variety of reasons foremost of which, was ammunition and magazine compatibility. It was impractical, and dangerous, to use a weapon that used ammunition and magazines different from the remainder of the unit. It was just as impractical for hastily assembled helicopter resupply loads to include different calibers of ammunition. It was common practice for the enemy to fire on any weapon that sounded different or at an individual armed differently. One's own troops might even fire on a different-sounding weapon.

SF troopers tended to be inventive, and unauthorized weapon modifications and bizarre experiments with munitions were common. Group frequently issued directives forbidding such grassroots research and development, usually after an accident or reported safety violation, which tended to be extreme. SF "R & D" led to .30cal quad-mounted

Special Forces Training Group, Phase I field
training exercise, Camp Mackall, NC

Special Forces clothing and insignia in Vietnam

Claymore ambush

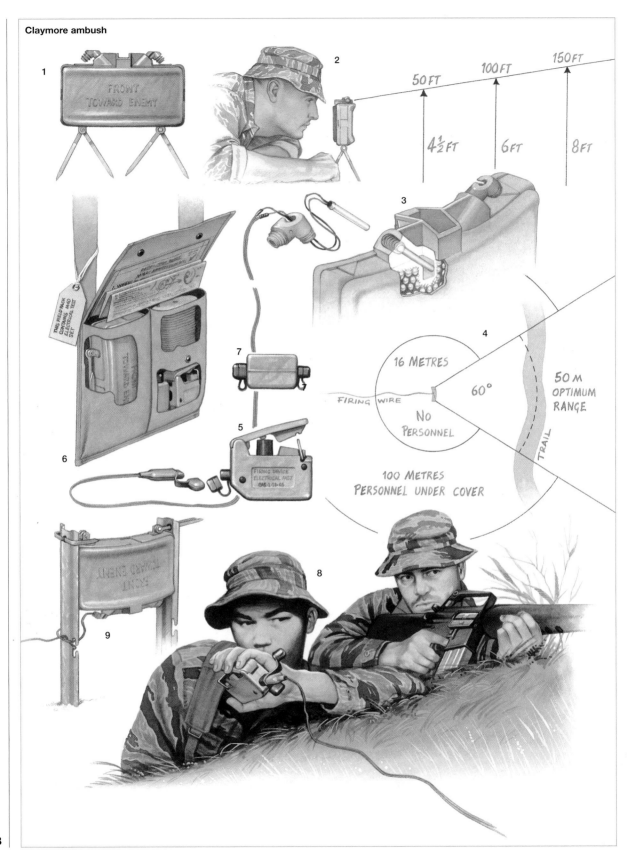

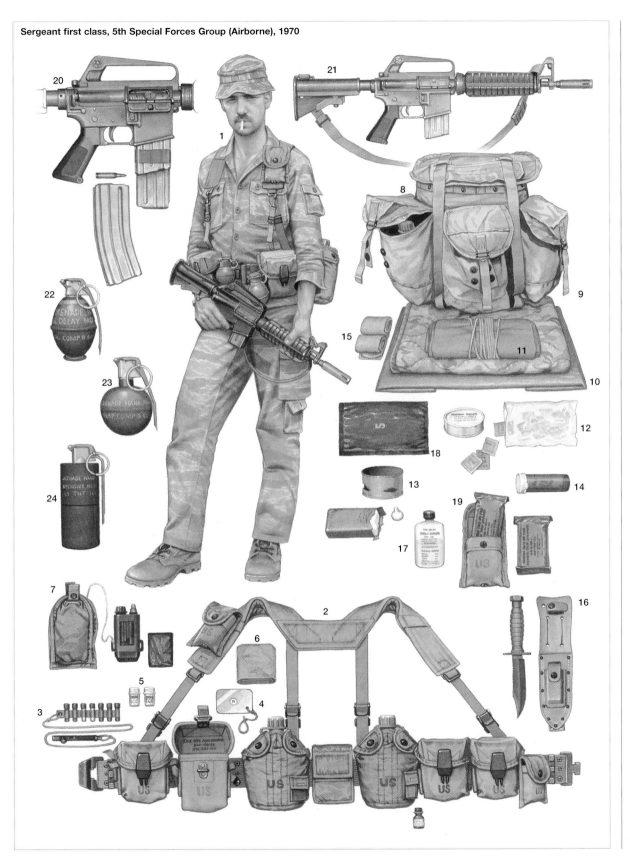

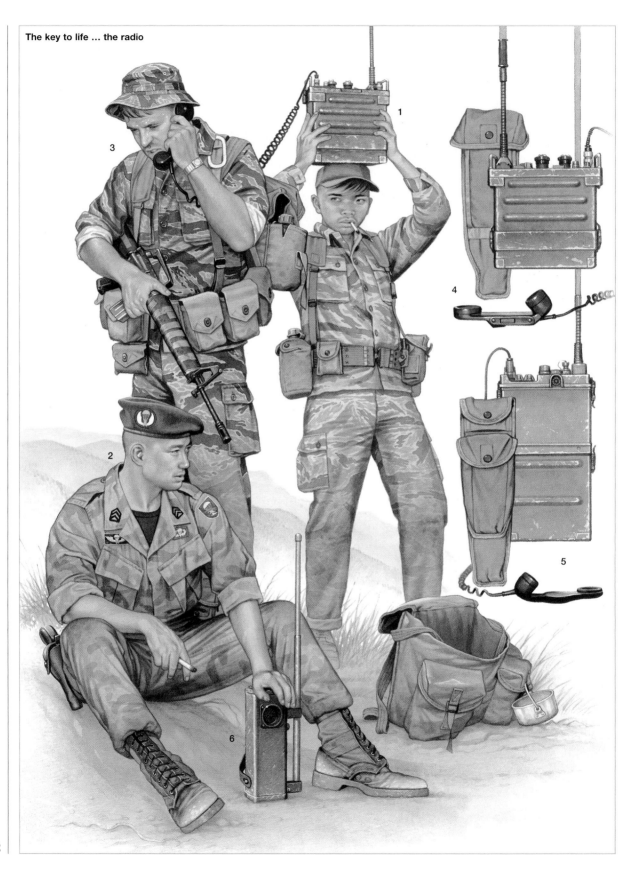

The key to life ... the radio

1

3

4

2

5

6

machine guns, ground-launched 2.75in. helicopter rockets, small arms with cut-down barrels and stocks, and all sorts of devilish demolitions and booby traps.

Individual weapons

The .30cal M1903A3 rifle was adopted in 1942 to speed production over earlier models. The '03 Springfield, held in reserve stocks for just such a contingency, was issued to Montagnard self-defense forces in the early 1960s. However, although "Yards" (nickname for the *Mao* tribal groups) are larger than Vietnamese, the 8.69lb,[11] five-shot, bolt-action rifle's recoil was excessive and it was soon replaced by more handy carbines.

The semi-automatic, 9.5lb .30cal M1 rifle, while inflicting less recoil than the '03, was heavier and difficult for Vietnamese to handle. The eight-shot M1 Garand saw limited use in strike forces. Some use was made of M1C and M1D sniper rifles, which were standard M1 rifles fitted with a telescope mount, 2.2x M84 telescope, leather cheek-rest laced to the stock, and M2 cone-shaped or T37 prong-type flash hider.

The .30cal M2 carbine was adopted in 1945 and intended as a more compact weapon than a rifle, but more substantial than a pistol. It was a lightweight, 5.5lb, selective-fire weapon and had a 30-round "banana clip" magazine. A few examples had the barrel cut down almost to the forearm and the butt stock cut off to a pistol grip. The M2 was declared the CIDG's standard shoulder weapon in 1962. Semi-automatic M1 carbines were also used, with both 15- and 30-round magazines. The cone-shaped M3 flash hider was seldom available. While the carbine's lighter weight and high rate of fire made it an excellent weapon for small-statured Asians, these guns lacked sufficient hitting power and penetration, and they were eventually outclassed by the AK-47 assault rifle.

The .45cal M3A1 submachine gun (SMG) initially saw wide issue to the Mountain Commandos and Trailwatchers, often with the cone-shaped T34 flash hider attached. It was felt that its high rate of fire, knockdown power, and compactness would be of benefit. However, the "grease gun" proved to be a disappointment due to its inaccuracy at even short ranges and its heavy weight (8lbs); each loaded 30-round magazine added 2¼lbs. Very small numbers of even heavier Thompson .45cal M1A1 SMGs were issued. The 10lb 7oz Tommy gun used both 20- and 30-round box magazines, the latter being more common.

Small numbers of foreign 9mm submachine guns were provided by the CIA in the early days. These included the German MP.40 SMG (incorrectly called the Schmeisser) and the Swedish Carl Gustav m/45b SMG (commonly known as the "Swedish K"). Even more widely used was the Danish Manden M/50 SMG. The MP.40 and M/50 used 32-round magazines while the m/45b had a 36-round magazine.

Led by a USSF NCO, CIDG Strikers launch an attack from a 1,000lb bomb-crater to assault across a shallow river. I CTZ, 1968.

The selective-fire 5.56mm XM16 rifle was adopted by SF in 1962 to replace the M2 carbine. The "black magic" had significant teething problems, but these were eventually resolved, and the XM16E1 was standardized as the M16A1 rifle on February 28, 1967. Improvements included a bolt forward assist device, better-designed bolt and buffer, chrome-plated chamber, and improved flash hider. Related improvements included changing the cartridge's propellant and refining cleaning and lubricating procedures. The M16A1 was first issued to CIDG units in the spring of 1969, replacing M1 rifles, M2 carbines, BARs, and various submachine guns. The M16A1 weighed just under 6lb 5oz and had a 20-round magazine.

ABOVE **An SF officer and his radio operator conduct a last minute "commo check" on an AN/PRC-77 radio prior to departing on a helicopter assault, Dong Tre, A-222, 1969.**

The 5.56mm XM177, XM177E1, and XM177E2 SMGs were highly modified versions of the M16 rifle with a shortened barrel and forearm, large flash hider (serving as a counterbalance, it was not a suppresser), and telescoping stock. The Air Force's XM177 had a 10in. barrel and lacked a bolt forward assist, while the Army's E1 added a bolt assist. Both were issued in 1966. The more widely used E2 had an 111/2in. barrel and was introduced in 1967. Commonly known by their commercial designation, CAR-15 (Colt Automatic Carbine), all three were used by recon teams and MIKE Forces, but a few found their way to A-camps. A 30-round magazine was available, but shortages often forced the use of 20-round ones.

The 40mm M79 grenade launcher saw widespread use, adding greatly to small unit firepower (see Plate F for characteristics). Limited use was made of 12-gauge pump and automatic (actually semi-auto) shotguns. The Army had a number of standard adapted commercial models in the inventory, all with 20in. cylinder bore barrels and 6-round tubular magazines. Among these were the Winchester Model 1200; Remington Models 11-48*, 31 and 870; Savage Model 720C*; Stevens Model 620A; and Ithaca Model 37 shotguns (*semi-auto). The idea of using shotguns in jungle combat is outwardly appealing due to their apparent devastating firepower and ability to sweep underbrush with 00 buckshot at a high rate. The reality, however, is that buckshot has only limited penetration through dense vegetation (even less in bamboo) and once emptied, can only be reloaded one round at a time.

BELOW **Rhade Montagnard Strikers from the Camp Buon Blech, A-238, cross a log bridge as some fill their canteens. A .30cal M1918A2 BAR is seen in the foreground as it's hoisted high to keep it dry. On this operation the 582d CIDG Company killed 64 VC.**

Each SF soldier was authorized a Colt .45cal M1911A1 pistol, according to tables of organization and equipment, but few were actually on-hand, and they were seldom carried in the field. The CIA issued a small number of Belgian-made 9mm Browning Hi-Power M1935 pistols in the early days, along with some German 9mm Luger P.08 and Walther P.38 pistols, most of which returned home with veterans. A wide variety of privately purchased handguns could be encountered in Vietnam, most of which were brought into the country by SF troopers against regulations, and sold or given to fellow team members when they departed. In this manner, such guns were handed down for years. The most common calibers were .45cal and 9mm pistols and .38 Special and .357 Magnum revolvers.

After days and sometimes weeks in the jungle SF NCOs tended to present a ragged appearance. Nonetheless, contrary to conventional wisdom, it did not hinder their combat capabilities.

The .30cal M1918A2 Browning automatic rifle, was intended to provide the rifle squad's base for fire. At 19lbs 6oz, it was difficult for most Asians to handle. The bipod-equipped BAR had selective slow and high rates of fire and a 20-round magazine.

Crew-served weapons

The air-cooled Browning .30cal M1919A6 light machine gun was issued on the basis of two per CIDG company (Camp Strike and MIKE Forces). They were also the principal machine gun mounted in camp defensive bunkers. The 31lb M1919A4 light machine gun was also used for this purpose. The 32lb 8oz M1919A6 had a lighter barrel than the A4, included a modified muzzle-bearing fitted with flash hider, bipod, carrying handle, and detachable stamped-steel shoulder stock. It could be mounted on a 14lb M2 tripod, on which the A4 was used. They were fed by a disintegrating link belt issued in 250-round cans.

Small numbers of 7.62mm M60 machine guns were issued to CIDG companies in lieu of the M1919A6. The M60 was a lighter weapon and was more easily handled by Asians, who called it the "number sixty." M1919A6s remained in camp bunkers. The 23lb 1oz M60, usually used on its bipod, could also be mounted on a 15lb M122 tripod. The weapon had selective fire and a quick-change barrel. It was fed by a disintegrating link belt issued in 100-round fabric assault packs (two to a can).

Camps usually had one to four Browning .50cal HB-M2 machine guns (HB = heavy barrel) mounted atop towers or in key bunkers. It was overkill if used to repel ground attacks,[12] but was excellent for suppressing enemy weapon positions and long-range fires on suspected positions. It weighed 84lbs; its M3 tripod added 44lbs. The "fiftycal" used disintegrating link belts issued in 100-round cans. M60s, M1919A4/A6s, and HB-M2s were fully automatic only, but their 450–550 rounds-per-minute cyclic rate permitted single shots with ease.

Two 60mm M19 mortars were issued to each CIDG company and reinforced camp defensive fires. Three, four, or more 81mm M29 mortars were emplaced in most camps as key defensive weapons (see Plate E for both mortars' characteristics). The World-War-Two-vintage 81mm M1 mortar saw use in the early days and was still found in some camps until the US withdrawal in 1973. It weighed 136lbs with its M1 mount and had a maximum effective range of 3,290yds[13] and a minimum of 100yds.

One or more 4.2in. M30 mortars were issued to many camps. Camps with no 105mm howitzers could have up to four "four-duces" (107mm). The massive rifled 672¼lb mortar had a maximum effective range of 5,500yds. Its minimum range was 800yds, making it of marginal use in camp defense, except for firing illumination. It was mainly used to provide fire support to combat patrols and to suppress enemy positions if under siege.

A common scene that transcends the ages of warfare: a group of men clustered around a map or crude sketch in the dirt. CIDG platoon leaders in spotted "duck-hunter" camouflage brief SF A-413 NCOs on their patrol routes, Camp Binh Thanh Thon, 1967.

Man-portable antitank weapons were employed mainly for direct fire support and as antipersonnel weapons for camp defense, rather than for their intended use. The Korean-War-era 3½in. M20A1B1 rocket launcher saw limited use in the early days as a fire support weapon in the field. The 13lb "bazooka" had a 270yd effective range against point targets and 900yds for area targets with its 9lb M28A2 high explosive anti-tank (HEAT) and M30 WP rockets. The "three-point-five's" aluminium tube could be broken down into two sections for carrying.

Many camps had one to three Korean-War-era 57mm M18A1 recoilless rifles, which were no longer used by the conventional Army. The 44lb weapon could be fired from the shoulder, its bipod, or a 53lb 2oz M1917A1 tripod (as used with the .30cal M1917A1 water-cooled machine gun). Ammunition included M306A1 HE, M307A1 HEAT, M308A1 WP, and T25E5 canister (154 or 176 stacked, cylindrical steel slugs). It had a maximum effective range of around 1,000yds from the shoulder and 1,800yds from the tripod with an M86F telescope. It was mainly used as an anti-personnel weapon (HE and canister, the latter with a 180yd maximum effective range); the HEAT round penetrated less than one inch of armor.

The 66mm M72 and M72A1 light antitank weapons were single-shot, disposable rocket launchers introduced in the early 1960s. The LAW's HEAT rocket had a maximum effective range of 251yds. The 5lb 3oz weapon was mainly used to knock out bunkers, but was also an excellent anti-sniper weapon when fired into a tree. It was prone to misfire due to moisture infiltrating the firing system, and it frequently failed to detonate unless it struck a solid, near-vertical surface. Firing a LAW at a bamboo hut resulted in a puff of dirty gray smoke and a hole a few inches in diameter through both walls.

A few camps, especially those on the Laotian and Cambodian borders after Lang Vei was overrun in February 1968 and Ben Het was attacked by NVA PT-76 tanks in March 1969, received one or two 106mm M40A1 recoilless rifles. It was on a dismountable M79 tripod aboard an M825 weapons carrier (a modified ¼-ton M151A1 truck, or jeep). When a "one-oh-six" was issued, it was stipulated that the 460lb rifle had to remain mounted on the jeep, as it was feared by Group that some A-teams might requisition the weapon only to selfishly procure an additional scarce jeep. It mounted a .50cal M8C spotting rifle, using a shorter cartridge than the .50cal machine gun. The weapon had a 2,200yd range with HEAT, WP, high explosive plastic-tracer (HEP-T) (for both anti-personnel and AT use), and anti-personnel-tracer (AP-T) (flechette – 1¼in. darts). It could knock out any tank in the NVA inventory.

A small number of camps were issued a pair of towed 105mm M101A1 howitzers (designated M2A1 prior to 1962) in mid-1969 to improve their fire support capabilities. The "one-oh-five" had a range of 6.8 miles with HE, HEP-T, HEAT, WP, AP-T, and illumination. Many camps already had an attached ARVN artillery platoon with either two 105mm M101A1 or 155mm M114A1 howitzers.

LIFE IN THE FIELD

Combat operations conducted in the camp's TAOR were of limited

The commander of A-301, Camp Long Hai, moves with the reaction force company to check out an abandoned coastal resort. This camp spent part of its career as the III CTZ CIDG training center.

duration and scale. They focused on area denial and interdiction of enemy forces. The lightly armed Strikers were not intended for long-duration, high-tempo operations against major enemy units; their operations tended to be simple in both plan and goals. Most engagements were small, chance encounter firefights and ambushes fought against small Local Force VC elements. The Strikers and VC were fairly evenly matched, except that the Strikers were normally in company strength and they could call for artillery, attack helicopters, and air strikes, which suddenly made an action rather one-sided and the result inevitable.

Many of the tactics and techniques used by both sides were similar. SF soldiers tend to read history, especially at the tactical level, more than their conventional counterparts, borrowing techniques from past guerrilla wars. They seldom closely imitated tactics outlined by the "Ft Benning School for Boys" – Officer Candidate School.

Vicious battles with Main Force VC and NVA units increasingly took place as the war escalated. By 1968, Vietnam was not a guerrilla war, but a mid-intensity conflict with large, conventional maneuver forces being employed by both sides.

For the most part, however, strike force operations were at the low end of the tactical spectrum. Operations were generally around five days in duration, with one company kept in the field at all times. The combat reconnaissance platoon would run similar length operations every couple of weeks or might work in conjunction with a company. The companies usually walked into and out of their AOs (the Area of Operations was a temporarily assigned area in which units conducted combat operations) but helicopters were sometimes provided. In such cases, a company going into the field could be inserted by helicopter in the morning and the same choppers would pick up the in-coming company from a different area within the TAOR.

Two Americans and one or two LLDB would accompany each operation. A single interpreter and two radio-telephone operators (RTO)[14] would be detailed to them while the LLDB would have his own RTO. The operation itself consisted of simply conducting sweeps through areas suspected of containing VC. In dense forests and steep terrain, the company would move in a column, with appropriate outer security, a "long green line." In areas with light underbrush an "open box" would be formed, with one platoon on line across the front and the others in columns on the flanks (sides) of the box. Local villages would be checked along with known trails and possible water points. In many instances the Strikers were native to the area they operated in and visits to villages became homecoming affairs. Information on local VC activities was freely provided by the villagers. Day and night ambushes would be established on likely enemy routes.

Each of the companies' three platoons had two or three 40mm M79 grenade launchers with 30 rounds apiece. Though a weapons platoon

Working out of a forward support base established at Sa Huynh, a 1st MIKE Force NCO searches the entrance of a VC tunnel. He is armed with a 5.56mm XM177E2 submachine gun and carries its 20-round magazines in a BAR belt.

was authorized to have two 60mm mortars and M60 machine guns, the authorization existed only on paper. The two M60s, with each gun's 800 rounds distributed between riflemen, were simply attached to the lead platoons, while the mortars remained in camp as they were too heavy to take to the field. In any case, artillery could be called as needed along with air strikes. While few frag grenades were carried, they were dangerous in the dense forest; lots of colored smoke grenades were hung on rucksacks for air-to-ground marking so that helicopter gunships and strike fighters could identify friendly positions. Claymores were liberally distributed for ambushes and night defense.

The company would begin moving at day break, usually with little if anything in the way of breakfast. It would move until about 1100 hours, then halt for a couple of hours for "pok time" and lunch. It would continue moving until an hour or so before sunset, break for dinner, and then move until last light, at which time it would occupy its night position, called the RON (Remain Over Night). Security and ambushes would be put out, guards mounted, and usually the night was spent in relative peace. The VC, contrary to popular belief, did not stealthily sneak through the jungles endlessly. Indeed, they feared the night and moved off of trails only out of necessity, often using flashlights. Nevertheless, the VC were excellent fighters and a challenging foe due

On the edge of a bamboo forest, a patrol from Camp Tong La Chon, A-334, halts to send in one of its periodic location reports to the camp. Map grid coordinate locations were normally sent via a simple shackle code, for example, the designated ten-letter code for a particular operation might be "BLACKNIGHT" (no two letters the same) with the letters representing 1 through 9 plus 0. The patrol's six-digit grid coordinate location would be reported by substituting the corresponding letters:
BLACKNIGHT
1234567890
Therefore if the coordinate is 894726 it is 'shackled' as GHCILN.

to motivation, practical training, and local knowledge. The Americans reported into the camp by radio in the morning, during pok time, at 1500 hours, and after occupying the RON. All in all it was fairly routine and even boring work. The occasional contacts were, of course, memorable and were usually nasty, for one side or the other. The VC and NVA simply did not take CIDG prisoners, but USSF prisoners were sought, though few were captured.

The gear carried by an SF trooper in the field varied by preference, but a typical rucksack load follows (see Plate G - item 8). A poncho liner was placed in the indigenous ("indig") rucksack where it would act as a pad between the gear and the bearer's back. On either side were pockets for 1qt canteens. A third pocket was centered on the back. In this was placed a plastic bag containing extra field dressings, gauze rolls, adhesive tape, antiseptic, morphine, Compazine and ephedrine syrettes, sterile packets of pre-threaded sutures, and a bottle of assorted pills. A can containing serum albumin, a blood expander, and an intravenous injection set was also carried. While the team medics had trained a couple of Strikers in each company in basic medic skills, it was the Americans who provided real emergency treatment in the field. All SF troopers received additional training from their team medics.

The usual rations were Packet, Indigenous Ration (PIR), one meal per day for the operation's planned five days, plus one spare, just in case. An equal number of cans of mackerel and cereal bars were packed. Included too was a plastic bag of coffee, sugar, cream, cocoa, chewing gum, toilet paper, and a couple of plastic spoons, all hoarded from the LRP and C-rations that occasionally came the team's way. Bottles of antimalarial pills and halazone (water purification) tablets were included.

Another plastic bag contained an empty C-rat can with slits cut in the side, a tube of matches, and half an M112 demolition charge – ¾lb of C4 plastic explosive. A jawbreaker-sized ball of C4 would be placed in the silted can and lit. It burned like a small blowtorch and would bring a canteen cup of water to boil in a few minutes. It was safe enough, as long as one did not inhale the pungent fumes (causing brain damage) or attempt to stamp out the burning glob of C4, which would detonate. The boiling water was then added to the PIR instant rice. While the rice was heating up and expanding in its tube-like plastic bag, a can of mackerel would be heated. The canteen cup, now filled with more water, would have a packet of pre-sweetened Koolaid poured in. After only a cereal bar and a cup of lukewarm coffee for breakfast and no lunch, the rice and mackerel never seemed to heat fast enough for the much-anticipated single meal of the day.

Still another plastic bag held a pair of socks and OG undershirt and boxer undershorts. The latter item was not intended as underwear, but as an outer garment. Tiger-stripes were of comparatively flimsy construction and it was common for the crotch to rip out when crawling up stream banks or over fallen trees. The boxer shorts were simply pulled over the trousers as a quick fix.

A tightly rolled nylon indig hammock, with an 18in. extension sewn to one end to accommodate an American, was shoved in. An indig poncho, also with an 18in. extension, with the hood removed and its opening covered with a patch, was placed on top. This was used as a fly pitched over the hammock rather than as a rain garment. Two white-star

parachute pop-up flares, for self-illumination, were shoved into the sides along with a penlight and Air Force survival knife. Most troopers did not look at this excellent knife as a weapon, but a tool, and carried it where it would not be lost. M18 smoke grenades, one each in red, yellow, and violet, were attached to web loops on the rucksack's back.

The small rucksack weighed less than 30lbs. However, unlike many US infantrymen, who often fastened all their gear to their rucksack or carried only limited items on their web gear, SF tended to load their harnesses down. A description of typical web gear is provided in Plate G2.

A field bivouac simply entailed selecting two suitable trees and stringing the hammock between them. If it looked like rain the poncho was erected as a simple fly. The web gear and rucksack were stowed under the hammock. The RTO turned over the radio, also placed under the hammock, and the trooper slept (fully clothed) with the handset tucked beside his ear. The poncho was needed only during the dry season with its comparatively cool nights and an issue sweater was comfortable in the northern mountains. Insect repellent was used rather than a bulky mosquito net regardless of the density and aggressiveness of these insects.

A typically uniformed SF trooper about to depart on a patrol. Note the can of serum albumin behind his neck, the M18 colored smoke grenade, and the olive-drab tape applied to the handguard of his M16A1 rifle to break up its solid black appearance, which otherwise tended to stand out.

Returning home

With his year in Vietnam coming to an end and the SF soldier looking forward to DEROS (Date Eligible for Return from Overseas), he frequently endured conflicting emotions. The desire for home, family, and friends was of course overwhelming, but many felt they were leaving an important part of themselves behind. It is a curious paradox in the soldier's heart that makes one yearn for the camaraderie, adventure, and excitement experienced, regardless of the dangers, strife, and boredom. Curious too are the feelings of closeness to those, in this case the stalwart Strikers, who have been a care and often a trouble. The thought of leaving those forlorn soldiers and their families brought as much sorrow to many as the thought of going home did joy. While the job had its perils, challenges, and demands, most SF soldiers viewed camp strike force duty with a strong fondness. Most of all, they would never forget their fellow team members and the Strikers.

NOTES

1. In the mid-1960s the Centre for Special Warfare received a public relations award normally given to Wall Street advertising agencies, a testament to the effectiveness of SF psychological operations.
2. The sum of SF "doctrine" was held in two small field manuals: FM 31-20, *Special Forces Operational Techniques* (some methods for doing things) and FM 31-21, *Special Forces Operations* (generally what to do on different kinds of missions).
3. South Vietnam was divided into four Corps Tactical Zones (CTZ) for regional command and control. These were ARVN commands, but were used by US forces because of their convenient designation of areas of the country and US unit boundaries were overlaid on them.
4. Due to space limitations, the LLDB cannot be fully addressed. Readers are referred to Elite 29, *Vietnam Airborne*.
5. While titles and ranks have changed, today's A-team maintains the same structure of two NCOs in each specialty. Today's SF also has its own MOS career field (18-series).
6. While SF medics were nicknamed "dog-killers," the dogs were humanely treated and anesthetized throughout the process. If one died through neglect or error, the student was terminated from the course. Animal rights groups eventually forced the use of goats, for whatever difference that made.
7. Each group was assigned an area of responsibility: 1st– Asia and Pacific, 3d– Africa, 6th– Middle East, 7th– worldwide reserve (which offered the advantage of training from Alaska to the Caribbean), 8th– Latin America, 10th– Europe.
8. Three sets of tropical combat uniforms ("jungle fatigues"), two pairs of tropical combat boots ("jungle boots"), five sets of olive-green undershirts and undershorts (white were still issued Stateside), and two OG towels.
9. Officers received $110. Unless assigned to a MIKE Force or the LLDB Training Center, which operated the MIKE Force jump school, SF troopers seldom had the opportunity to jump in Vietnam. Jumps were few and far between for even the MIKE Forces. However, all parachute-qualified personnel assigned to SF and airborne units in Vietnam continued to receive jump pay due to non-availability of aircraft and parachutes.
10. Bangkok, Thailand; Honolulu, Hawaii; Manila, Philippines; Sydney, Australia; Hong Kong; Singapore; Tokyo; Taipei, Taiwan; or Kuala Lumpur, Malaysia.
11. All weights are for unloaded weapons.
12. The myth that it is illegal to fire the .50-caliber at personnel is completely unfounded.
13. Weapons adopted after the late 1950s used meters on sight range scales and firing tables, and mils in deflection and elevation scales to comply with NATO standards. Earlier weapons used yards and degrees
14. RTO was in essence a traditional term as the use of field telephones was almost unheard of.

GLOSSARY

The Vietnam War arguably produced more slang terms and acronyms than any American conflict. Only those terms generally unique to SF are described here. Regretfully, space does not permit the inclusion of the complete rich vocabulary of Vietnamese-English slang with which SF and Strikers routinely communicated. Popular pronunciations are given in quotation marks within parentheses.

A-camp: CIDG Strike Force Camp.

A-team: SF operational detachment A; the basic SF operational element.

Bac-si: Vietnamese for doctor. Common term for an SF medic.

B-team: SF operational detachment B. An SF command and control element controlling four or more A-teams.

Cambods: Ethnic Cambodians, or Khmers, or *Khamer-Serei* born and raised in Vietnam. Often served in Camp Strike and MIKE Forces.

Camp Strike Force (CSF): A battalion-size CIDG unit manning an A-camp.

CA/PO ("Kay-Pole"): Civil Affairs and Psychological Operations (Psyops).

CRP: Combat Reconnaissance Platoon. One or two were assigned to a Camp Strike Force.

CIDG ("Sidge"): Civilian Irregular Defense Group; refers to either the organization or its individual members.

COC: Combat Orientation Course, also known as "Cock Course."

C-team: SF operational detachment C. An SF company headquarters usually controlling three or four B-teams.

CTZ: Corps Tactical Zone. Commonly called I ("Eye"), II (Two), III (Three), and IV (Four) Corps.

Dai-'Uy ("Die-wee"): Vietnamese for captain. Common term used by A-team members for their detachment commander.

Duck hunter suit: Early commercial spotted-pattern camouflage uniform. Also known as the leopard suit, but this was a little-used term.

Group: 5th Special Forces Group (Airborne) (5th SFGA). Frequently preceded by colorful expletives.

Indig: Indigenous (native) troops or equipment items made specifically for indig troops (indig gear).

JFK Center: US Army John F. Kennedy Center for Special Warfare (Airborne) (USAJFKCSWA) at Ft Bragg, NC. Redesignated US Army JFK Center for Military Assistance (USAJFKCMA) in late 1968. Also simply "Center."

KKK: The Khrum Kampuchea Khmer ("Crom Cam-pa-che-ah Camer") was a militant political organization that sought to regain control of Lower Cambodia, i.e. the Mekong Delta, from Vietnam after the war.

Little People: Somewhat patronizing term used by SF when referring to indigenous troops; however, not as derogatory as the more common terms used by many Americans.

LL: Contraction of LLDB. Also Lima Lima.

In the field it was not uncommon to eat only one meal a day. The priority was to travel as light as possible. Since a typical operation lasted five days, SF troopers were conditioned to deal with such reduced rations before they lost efficiency because of the light diet.

LLDB *(Luc-luong Dac-Biêt)*: Vietnamese Airborne Special Forces.

MIKE Force: Mobile Strike Force. Also MSF.

MACV-SOG ("Mac-vee sog"): Military Assistance Command, Vietnam-Studies and Observation Group.

Nungs: Ethnic Chinese-Vietnamese often serving in MIKE Forces.

PIR: Packet, Indigenous Rations.

Projects: Special reconnaissance projects: DELTA, GAMMA, SIGMA, and OMEGA.

Recondo School: MACV Recondo School operated by 5th SFGA for US and Free World forces reconnaissance personnel at Nha Trang.

RON: Remain Over Night. Refers to both the act and location of a unit's position at night; RON position.

SFOB: Special Forces Operating Base, the 5th SFGA headquarters at Nha Trang.

Striker: CIDG soldier.

TAOR: Tactical Area of Responsibility. The designated surrounding area for which a camp strike force was responsible.

Tiger-stripes: Striped camouflage pattern uniform.

Training Group: Special Forces Training Group (Airborne) (SFTG) at Ft Bragg, NC.

Trung-Si ("Trung-see"): Vietnamese for sergeant. Common general term for an SF NCO.

VOCO: Verbal Order of Commanding Officer. The authority by which an SF soldier traveled about in Vietnam. When signing in at transient billet, he would enter this in the Authority column.

Yards: Derived from the French word for mountaineers, *Montagnards*. It was used to describe mountain tribesmen serving in many Camp Strike and MIKE Forces. The Mao tribal groups.

X-Ray: Radio code word for the LLDB.

A-404 operated the 4th MIKE Force's Airboat Company. This was an extremely valuable means of transportation in the water-logged Mekong Delta. A .30cal M1919A6 machine gun is mounted in the boat's bow. Approaching Air Cat boats could be heard from a considerable distance, but it was virtually impossible for the VC to tell how far away they were, or even the direction from which they were approaching, until it was too late.

COLOR PLATE COMMENTARY

PLATE A: SPECIAL FORCES TRAINING GROUP, PHASE I FIELD TRAINING EXERCISE, CAMP MACKALL, NC

Each of the three phases of Special Forces training concluded with a field training exercise (FTX), in which the students practised their newly learned skills under realistic and trying conditions. The instructors, who were all Vietnam veterans, strived to make the FTXs challenging and grueling. The week-long Phase I FTX was designed to allow the practice of reconnaissance and combat patrolling, land navigation, and survival skills. The tasks included: day and night ambushes on foot troops and vehicle convoys; a night attack on a well-defended Special Forces camp, effectively trading places with the Viet Cong; and an all-night cross-country exfiltration course.

However, the FTX's main purpose was to eliminate students who lacked the strength of will to succeed. By following round-the-clock patrols and compass courses, while all the time dogged by counterguerrilla forces and with negligible sleep or rations, the students experienced the guerrilla's hunted existence. When one mission was completed the operation order for the next was issued and minimal planning and rehearsal time was permitted. Rations were not an issue, for example the author's class of 60 students shared a single live goat and a handful of rice midway through the FTX. It was the only meal provided. Students and their gear were searched for contraband rations and candy bars prior to a night parachute jump into Camp Mackall.

No special uniforms or equipment were used by SF students. Standard Stateside-issue OG 107 fatigues, M1964 field jackets, M1951 patrol caps, and leather combat boots were worn. Standard infantry M1956 load-bearing equipment (LBE) was used, but two canteens were issued, bayonets were not carried, and the small combat, or "butt," pack was not issued. In its place was the lightweight nylon rucksack with aluminum frame. The rucksack, which was little used in Vietnam, was usually fastened to the lower portion of the frame, but could be attached to the upper. The mountain sleeping bag, usually stuffed in a waterproof clothing bag or wrapped in a poncho, was normally strapped to the upper frame. Instead of a shelter half, or "pup tent," issued to conventional troops, two ponchos were issued to SF soldiers allowing two men to build a substantial shelter. Entrenching tools, if carried, were fastened to the rucksack's frame upside-down. A radio, such as an AN/PRC-25, could be fastened to the upper portion of the rucksack's frame. Little was carried in the pack: minimal toilet items, several spare pairs of socks, the ponchos, and, under normal circumstances, rations. Mess kits were never carried. Students also placed their M1C parachutist's steel helmet in the pack once they had jumped in. In a real operation it would have been buried along with the parachute.

While M16 rifles and M60 machine guns were available, SF students carried 7.62mm M14 rifles and .30cal M1919A6 machine guns, for the simple reason that they were heavier. The M1919A6 was widely used for camp defense in Vietnam.

PLATE B: STAFF SERGEANT, US ARMY SPECIAL FORCES, VIETNAM, 1963

While the tropical combat uniform ("jungle fatigues"), which was adopted in 1963, was worn within camps, during combat operations SF troopers wore the same camouflage uniforms as the Strikers. From the late 1950s to the early 1960s,

ABOVE **An arms catche recovered by the 1st MIKE Force in the Song The Valley, 1969. It includes scores of Communist, French, and US-made small arms and over 40 crew-served weapons. Most of the stacked arms are 7.62mm SKS carbines.**

LEFT **Members of the 47th MIKE Force Company, 4th Mobile Strike Force pose with weapons recovered from an enemy arms catche near Ba Xoai, 1968. Captured weapons include 7.62mm SGM machine guns and 7.62mm RPD light machine guns.**

LEFT **Members of the 3d MIKE Force examine part of an arms cache recovered during fighting northeast of Saigon in early 1969. The water-cooled machine guns are German World War One 7.92mm MG.08s. Some of the NCOs wear the MIKE Force's red, white, and blue scarves.**

BELOW **Strikers and an SF NCO examine a 12.7mm DShKM-1938 machine gun that has been blown off a PT-76 tank in the background. It was one of two that were knocked out by US M48A3 tanks when they attacked Camp Ben Het, A-244, April 1969.**

American-made spotted "duck-hunter" uniforms were purchased by the CIA for use by Strikers or from various Asian countries under Mutual Defense Assistance Program (MDAP) funding. Uniforms were also made locally by Vietnamese tailors. The duck-hunter patterns, intended for marshlands, were ineffective in dense jungles that lacked dappled sunlight; however, they did well in the Mekong Delta. No rank or unit insignia were worn on these uniforms. The Vietnamese referred to them as *Beo-Gâ'm* (leopard) pattern. The tiger-stripe "boonie hat" was the most commonly seen headgear, although duck-hunter pattern field caps were also used.

1: This staff sergeant, attached to US Army Special Forces, Vietnam, on temporary duty from the 1st Special Forces Group, wears mostly standard M1956 LBE with an indigenous rucksack. World-War-Two and Korean-War-era web gear was also widely used. The early tropical combat boots ("jungle boots") varied in pattern as they were test items.

2: The 5.56mm XM16 rifle was adopted by SF in 1962, but many SF troopers favored M2 carbines (see below).

3: Troopers often chose to carry M2 carbines to ensure ammunition compatibility with the troops they advised.

4: The .45cal M3A1 submachine gun (also known as the "grease gun") was almost universally fitted with a T34 flash hider. It was a weapon, like those illustrated in Plate B (items 5 and 6) that were issued to Strikers from CIA stocks in the early days of America's involvement in Vietnam.

5: "Swedish K" 9mm m/45b with a six-magazine pouch.

6: Danish Madsen 9mm M/50 submachine gun.

7: The indigenous rucksack was copied from a captured NVA model by the CIA's Counterinsurgency Support Office (CISO) and manufactured in Taiwan, Okinawa, and South Korea for less than US $3.00 each. Most examples were made from gray-green waterproofed canvas, but some were of untreated OD (olive-drab) canvas.

8: Plastic canteens had not yet widely replaced the metal model. A canteen cup and a Korean War-era M1910 carrier are depicted.

9: The lensatic compass was often carried in an M1943 first aid pouch, but M1956 pouches were also used.

10: The field dressing was carried in an M1956 OG (olive-green) first aid pouch.

11: The combat, individual, or C ration ("C rats"), weighed almost 2lbs and provided a complete high-calorie meal. It comprised of meat unit, canned fruit or desert, a B unit with crackers, spread or chocolate drink mix and cookies, and an accessory packet with matches, cigarettes, toilet paper, instant coffee, salt, sugar, cream packets, and chewing gum.

12: Madsen submachine magazine pouch.

13: World-War-Two-era hand grenades were still in use early in the war and included Mk 2A1 fragmentation ("pineapple") grenades with packing container, as well as the examples illustrated in Plate B (items 14 and 15).

14: M15 white phosphorus ("Willy Pete") grenade.

15: M18 colored smoke hand grenades (red, yellow, green, violet – indicated by the color of the top). The M18 was used throughout the war, but this one bears early color coding.

PLATE C: SPECIAL FORCES CLOTHING AND INSIGNIA IN VIETNAM

1: The green beret, or officially, "beret, man's, wool, rifle green, army shade 297," was as much an organizational insignia as a uniform item. The battle to legitimize the wearing of the beret began in 1954 and lasted until it was finally authorized in 1961 (and it is a story that is well documented in other sources). During the Vietnam War, it was the only beret authorized by Army regulations, regardless of others worn by certain units. Upon completion of Phase I training the beret was awarded in a simple ceremony. The students arrived wearing baseball caps with their berets in their trouser pockets. After a short speech by the chief instructor alluding to the honor of wearing the beret and the trials yet to come, the order, "Don, berets," was given, with someone in the formation muttering, "Who's Don Barays?"

2: The 5th Special Forces Group (Airborne) flash was worn over the left eye. The same flash had previously been worn by US Army Special Forces, Vietnam, from 1963 until late 1964, when the 5th SFGA arrived to replace the USASF. The 5th SFGA had previously worn a white-bordered black flash. All SF units wore the 1st Special Forces crest, although officers wore their rank in its place.

3: One of the first purchases made by the SF trooper after arriving in Vietnam was a tiger-stripe "boonie hat" from a Da Nang tailor shop. Designs and patterns varied and it would become a cherished memento.

4: More commonly known as "jungle fatigues," the tropical combat uniform was the principal duty uniform worn by all US forces in Vietnam. Development of prototype uniforms took place in the early 1950s, but it was not until October 1962 that the Army specified the need for such a uniform. Standard cotton OG 107 fatigues were worn in Vietnam prior to the issue of jungle fatigues. The tropical uniform's design was based on the M1942 parachutist's suit. It was extremely functional, lightweight, fast drying, and one of the most popular field uniforms adopted. Made of shade 107 olive-green (OG) fabric, its color provided effective concealment in Vietnam. The uniform was standardized on June 20, 1963 and issue soon began to troops in Vietnam. It was made of wind-resistant cotton poplin and featured shoulder loops, side-adjusting tabs on the coat, anti-gas flaps inside the trousers' fly and coat front opening, and exposed pocket flap buttons (the August 1964 specification had concealed pocket flap buttons). The name and "U.S. ARMY" tapes were sewn on either horizontally (as here) or parallel with the slanted pocket top; it was a decision left up to the unit or even individuals. The LLDB patch was worn on the left breast pocket to indicate USSF's advisory capacity to that organization. LLDB jumpwings were honorarith awarded to all USSF personnel. The horizontal manner of tape display was standardized in February 1968. Black-on-white name tapes were used until 1965, when black-on-OG were authorized in Vietnam. Gold-on-black "U.S. ARMY" tapes were used until replaced by black-on-OG in 1966 in Vietnam. Full-color unit insignia and skill badges remained in common use, even though subdued black-on-OG insignia were authorized in July 1966. Due to continued shortages, it was not until 1970 that subdued insignia completely replaced full-color. This sergeant wears the Combat Infantryman and Parachutist Badges. A mystery to many troops was a small pocket inside the trousers left cargo pocket. It was usually used to carry a wallet or cigarettes in a plastic bag, but it had been intended for a never-issued survival kit.

5: The December 1966 specification class 1 tropical combat uniform deleted the shoulder loops, side tabs, and anti-gas flaps. Except for some early versions still made of cotton poplin, this issue was fabricated of rip-stop cotton poplin (class 2 uniforms were made of four-color woodlands camouflage fabric and were little used by USSF). Subdued insignia had largely replaced the full-color, although both types could be worn mixed on the same uniform due to availability. Black metal pin-on collar rank insignia were authorized for wear in Vietnam in July 1967, to be followed by the rest of the Army the next year. In October 1969, it was directed that name and "U.S. ARMY" tapes be sewn on parallel with the slanted pockets to make them fully visible along with any skill badges. This sergeant first class wears the Combat Medic and Master Parachutist Badges. The LLDB patch was often worn in a clear plastic hanger.

6: The "tiger-stripe" uniform has come to be identified as *the* Vietnam camouflage pattern. From 1962, it was the standard CIDG uniform. The origins of its design are unknown, but it is believed to have been developed in an Asian country – Thailand is the best guess – and recommended by US advisors. Besides CIDG use, it was widely employed by US and other Free World reconnaissance units. However, its first use was by the Vietnamese Marines, who referred to it as the "sea wave-pattern." It proved to be an extremely effective pattern and coloration for most areas of Vietnam. Some examples were manufactured in Vietnam, but most were acquired through

In one of the most vicious battles experienced by **MIKE Forces, two battalions of the 4th and 5th MIKE Forces cleared the Seven Mountains in the Mekong Delta in March 1969. To support the operation a special weapons platoon was formed from 5th SFGA headquarters volunteers to man 106mm recoilless rifles, .50cal machine guns, and flamethrowers. This picture illustrates the rugged, boulder-strewn terrain.**

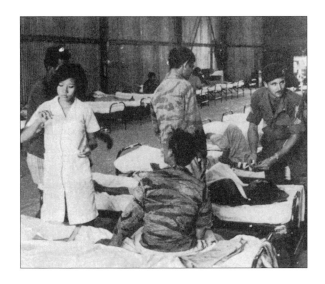

LEFT **A temporary hospital established to support a MIKE Force operation is manned by CIDG nurses, medics, and technicians, all trained by USSF medics and backed by five American surgeons.**

BELOW **CIDG Strikers seriously wounded in combat were rehabilitated and taught new job skills before they were discharged. This prepared them for civilian life, increased the Strikers' confidence in USSF, and reduced the burden on the Vietnamese welfare program. Unfortunately, seriously disabled former CIDG today do not receive aid from the communist government of Vietnam, as they were employees of the US Government and not Vietnam.**

MDAP off-shore procurement purchases from Thailand, Taiwan, Okinawa, and South Korea. Consequently, color, pattern, fabric, and design differences varied greatly. In the several issues the author's camp received, no two sets of shirts and trousers matched. It was not uncommon for "tigers," "duck-hunter," and OG uniform components to be mixed by Strikers. MDAP procured "tiger-stripes" in size ranges appropriate for Asians and Americans. USSF, like their Strikers, wore no insignia on "tigers" in the field. It was important that troopers were as indistinguishable as possible, regardless of the difference in size between them and their Strikers.

7: Besides the black, square, open-face buckle and tip, the issue trouser belt was worn with a heavier brass version as well as the rectangular, solid-faced brass buckle and tip as worn with service uniforms.

8: OG 107 undershirts and OG 109 boxer undershorts began to be issued in early 1966. Prior to 1966, white underwear was often dyed green by individuals before deployment.

9: OG 408 cushion-sole boot socks began to replace the black shade 51 version in 1968.

10: Based on the 1943 combat boot, limited issues were made of M1945 tropical combat boots found in depots. The development of the modern tropical combat boot, or "jungle boot," began in 1955 with various test models issued to USSF and advisors in Vietnam in the early 1960s. Standard black all-leather combat boots were worn by those not issued test boots.

11: Most test boots had cotton canvas or nylon uppers with Vibram soles. Various different materials were used in other components.

12: A standardized jungle boot was not adopted until January 1965. The model chosen contained a punji stake-resistant insole. From May 1966 the jungle boot was improved by adding a two-piece, steel spike protective insole. It was also made with better materials, had nylon reinforcing webbing on the sides, and the "Panama sole," which was more effective in shedding mud. Vibram-soled boots were issued into 1969, however.

13: US Special Forces shoulder sleeve insignia, full-color and subdued.

14: LLDB insignia.

PLATE D: CLAYMORE AMBUSH

1: Besides endless patrols through jungles, hills, and swamps in search of an elusive enemy, the ambush was a principal offensive tactic employed by Special Forces. Established on trails suspected to be in use by the enemy, the key to success was firepower. A high volume of aimed rifle fire, machine guns, and 40mm grenade launchers provided the required firepower. However, it was the Claymore M18A1 antipersonnel mine (seen here) that proved to be most devastating in an ambush. Unlike conventional mines, the Claymore was emplaced above ground and was not activated by stepping on it. A curved, rectangular fiberglass box contained 704 $\frac{7}{32}$in. diameter steel ball bearings embedded in a plastic matrix and backed by 1½lbs of C4 plastic explosive. The Claymore was emplaced on two pairs of folding metal legs outside the kill zone to cover a 60-degree fan.

2: The Claymore was aimed (the front was marked "FRONT TOWARD ENEMY") by means of an integral sight at a point about 8ft off the ground some 150ft away.

3: A detonator was inserted in one of the Claymore's two cap wells and the 100ft electrical firing wire was run to a protected firing position.

4: There was a great deal of blast and secondary fragmentation to the rear and sides, 110yds and more. With multiple Claymores covering the kill zone in overlapping

LEFT **The MIKE Forces fought many extremely brutal battles, often suffering terrible casualties. Here walking wounded of the 3d MIKE Force are guided towards one of three CH-47 helicopters necessary to evacuate just the walking wounded near Puc Phong, 1969.**

BELOW **SF NCOs and a Striker carry a wounded Striker from a medical evacuation (medevac) helicopter into Camp Mai Loc, the northernmost CIDG camp in Vietnam. A-101, 1969.**

fans, it was essential that consideration be given to the positioning of friendly troops.

5: An M57 firing device was fitted to the firer's end of the wire after the mine had been emplaced and concealed. Known as a "clacker," the firing device looked like a staple gun and generated an electrical current when punched to immediately detonate the mine.

6: Each mine was issued in a canvas, two-pocket carrying bag packed six to a box. In the bag was a plastic spool with the firing wire and detonator and a firing device.

7: An M40 test set was issued with every six mines to check the continuity of the electrical firing system. A pinhole light indicated a good circuit.

8: There were two tricks that contributed to a successful Claymore ambush that were not taught in training centers. The detonation of a Claymore was frequently used as the signal to initiate an ambush along with opening fire with a rifle or machine gun. When the ambush force leader initiated the ambush, he would also shout "Fire!" to ensure the ambush was executed even in the event of the Claymore or rifle failing. Fractions of a second counted. Sometimes the clacker would not generate sufficient current to detonate the Claymore with that first frantic punch. Claymore firers learned to repeatedly punch the firing device until the mine detonated and not just punch it once, then hesitate or assume the detonator was a dud. In an ambush hesitation can be fatal.

Claymores could also be rigged with a tripwire for an "automatic ambush," or several mines could be linked together by lengths of instantaneous detonating cord. Command-firing one Claymore would instantaneously detonate all of the mines linked to the det cord. Sometimes automatic ambushes, or "mousetraps," with several trip-wired Claymores linked by detonating cord were left at a key point such as a known enemy stream crossing. Patrols would occasionally check the site for results.

Scores and even hundreds of Claymores were used to protect Special Forces camps with belts of mines often emplaced for command-detonation en masse; it was a tactic known as a "wave-breaker." Mines emplaced in the perimeter wire had to be secured in order to prevent sappers from removing them or turning them around to face the camp's perimeter.

9: One of many techniques saw the Claymore inserted upside down in the "U" channels of two 32in. barbed wire pickets and wrapped with barbed wire. Claymores were also emplaced around the perimeter of Strike Force company or reconnaissance team night locations. Compromised reconnaissance teams being pursued by the enemy might leave a trip-wired Claymore or one with a time delay fuse to provide the pursuers with an excuse to quit.

Yet another use for Claymores came by adapting their 1½lbs of C4. With a ten-second time fuse fitted in the cap well, a Claymore could be used as a "satchel charge" to blow bunkers by shoving it through the firing port. The body could be broken open and the C4 packed into a notch cut in a tree. Using the firing wire and clacker to detonate the C4, a tree could be removed allowing an otherwise open clearing to be used as a helicopter landing zone.

PLATE E: MORTAR TRAINING

Mortars were one of the principal weapons for camp defense. It was the job of the A-Team's weapons specialists to train the Strike Force mortar sections and the other team members in their use. Few Americans were sufficiently proficient in Vietnamese to directly present instruction on such a subject.

SF troopers were frequently accused of "going native" by their conventional counterparts. While there were instances of individuals going to extremes, it was actually part of the job. To win the loyalty of remote ethnic groups with a long history of mistreatment by the government, traders, and just about everyone else, SF had to demonstrate that they understood and sympathized with their situation.

A Vietnamese interpreter proficient in weapons terminology was employed. Often when training Montagnards or other ethnic minorities, the instruction had to be relayed through a Vietnamese interpreter to a second interpreter who spoke the local dialect. To make matters worse, many Montagnard dialects had no appropriate technical words or even words for numbers. It was necessary, therefore, to teach not only a technical vocabulary but also basic concepts, such as numbers, degrees, and units of measurement. Nevertheless, classes were informal with a certain amount of humor allowed to keep the interest of the students. It was also not uncommon for family members to sit in as a simple diversion from daily camp routine.

Two 60mm mortars were authorized for the mortar section of camp and MIKE Force companies' weapons platoons. They seldom accompanied units to the field due to their weight, ammunition weight, and the quick responsiveness of supporting artillery, attack helicopters, and close air support.

1: When taken to the field, the M4 sight, M5 bipod, and baseplate were often dispensed with and replaced with a spade-type M1 baseplate, enabling the weapon to be fired in the handheld mode. These mortars were more often retained in camp for defense and emplaced in sandbagged positions.

The M19, dating from 1945, could be drop- or trigger-fired (the World War Two M2, still occasionally encountered, lacked the trigger-fire mode). The 45lb 3oz M19 had a maximum effective range of 2,000yds and a minimum range of 50yds. Their employment was simplistic, with no use made of a fire direction center. Striker crews were trained simply to point the weapon in the direction of the attack, set a given elevation, and begin dropping rounds into the wire, occasionally adding an "illum" to light up the perimeter.

2: The 81mm M29 mortar's "threaded" tube served to aid its cooling and reinforcement, allowing longer range charges (the World War Two M1 mortar had a smooth tube). The M29E1, later redesignated M29A1, was identical, but had a chrome-plated bore to prolong barrel life. The 93lb 8oz drop-fired mortar included an M53 sight, M23A1 bipod, and M3 lightweight Canadian baseplate. The M29 "eighty-one's" maximum effective range was 3,990yds with a minimum range of 76yds.

Both 60mm and 81mm mortar rounds were of the traditional fin-stabilized, tear-drop design.

Four types of 60mm rounds were available: M49A2 HE; M50 improved HE; M302A1 WP smoke; and M83A3 illumination.

Three series of ammunition were available for the 81mm. The World-War-Two-Korean-War-era series included: M43 light HE; M56 heavy HE; M57 WP; and M301A2 illumination. Modernized rounds adopted in the early 1950s included: M362 HE and M370 WP. Improved rounds, introduced in the early 1960s, included: M374 HE and M375 WP (M301A2 illum remained standard). Besides having longer range, to take advantage of the M29 mortar's reinforced tube, the HE and WP rounds of the two improved series were ballistically matched, precluding the need to readjust the sight for different rounds. While similar in appearance to the M362/M370, the M374/M375 had a higher filler capacity, resulting in a considerably larger casualty radius.

PLATE F: FIRE FIGHT

In the dense jungles over rolling terrain, visibility was limited and sound was muffled. The opportunity for chance contact between two forces was great, especially since both were moving, their own quiet noises covering that of the enemy. Fire fights were often initiated at ranges of less than 30yds, frequently less than 10yds. Quick reaction was crucial, not only to personal survival but also to the domination of the fight by fire and maneuver. The side that succeeded in getting the most men, especially those with machine guns and grenade launchers, into position to open fire and begin flanking the enemy, was generally the victor.

The side that failed to dominate began to suffer casualties. Realizing that they were being outflanked by enemy elements extending to their right or left, their effort shifted from gaining fire superiority to disengaging and withdrawing in bounds with elements covering each other. Chance fire fights were brief, often called the "15-minute war," and casualties were light. Most were suffered in the first few seconds. The Strikers did, however, enjoy the advantage of access to the USSF NCOs and their radios. Artillery fire could be called for and delivered in less than ten minutes. Attack helicopters, or even jet fighters, could be on-station within 20 minutes. Unless they had a superior force to the CIDG, the VC would attempt to break contact if they could not crack the Strikers within the first few minutes

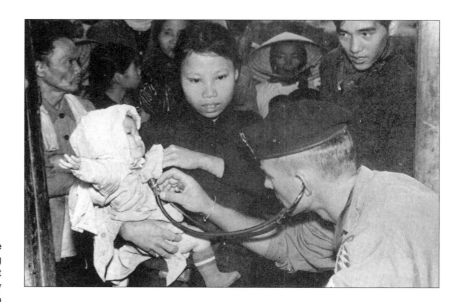

Camp Thuong Duc, A-109, was established in northern South Vietnam to provide a secure haven for Vietnamese refugees fleeing VC-controlled areas. Within months the camp was aiding some 8,000 refugees and its strike force kept the VC at a distance. What struck the refugees the most was the medical care given them by the SF, which ranged from treating common colds to assisting at child birth. Such basic care was denied them by the VC.

of the fight. Their other choice was to "hug" the Strikers, getting in as close as possible to prevent the CIDG from using artillery and air strikes. If they failed to overwhelm the Strikers they could become trapped as helicopter-borne reinforcements were lifted in behind them. If either side could quickly get reinforcements into the area, fire fights could turn into pitched battles.

Probably no other infantry weapon symbolizes the Vietnam War more than the "blooper" or "thumper." Adopted in 1958, the 40mm M79 grenade launcher was lightweight, compact, simple, rugged, and delivered a tremendous amount of firepower for its size. This one has the later fibreglass stock, which was designed to prevent splitting and warping in the tropics. The M79 was intended to replace rifle grenades and fill the range gap between hand grenades and mortars. The single-shot, break-open, breech-loading weapon weighed only 6lbs and was 29in. long. CIDG rifle squads were authorized one, but there were seldom enough to arm all squads. High explosive (HE) rounds were the most commonly used, but others were available including buckshot-loaded multiple projectile, tear gas, and a wide variety of colored smoke and flare rounds for signaling. The 1972 manual listed 35 approved rounds.

HE rounds had an impact fuse and contained a golf ball-size, spherical fragmentation charge with a 5½yd casualty radius. Its maximum effective range against area targets was 382yds and 164yds for point targets. Early M381 HE rounds' fuse armed at 2–3yds, but this could cause friendly casualties due to close-in tree-strikes or accidental firing. Later M406 HE rounds armed at 15–30yds. It would not detonate on impact at closer ranges, but was as deadly as a high-velocity brick when it hit an individual.

Ammunition could be carried in bandoleers (three rounds in each of two pockets, 12 bandoleers to a shipping case), either slung over the shoulder or with the straps cut off and hung in clusters on the rucksack. They were also carried in universal ammunition pouches (three rounds), canteen covers (six to seven rounds), or Claymore bags.

PLATE G: SERGEANT FIRST CLASS, 5TH SPECIAL FORCES GROUP (AIRBORNE), 1970

Since the early 1960s a great deal of equipment had been developed for use in Vietnam. Equipment had to be tough to

survive the alternating wet and dry, hot tropical climate, and the treatment that was inflicted upon it. Virtually everything changed, from the designs of weapons to how ammunition and first aid supplies were packaged. Special clothing was developed and nylon, today the universal material of web gear, came into use.

Tiger-striped camouflage uniforms were still standard issue for Special Forces, but the quality of their fabric had improved somewhat. The outward appearance of an SF trooper (1) had changed little, but he was better armed and equipped.

2: There was no standard arrangement of web gear used by SF, even within a given A-team. Its configuration depended on availability, mission requirements, duties, weapons, terrain conditions, but mostly, individual preference. World-War-Two and Korean-War-era web gear, and late war nylon equipment was used by some, but the M1956 LBE saw the widest use. This example was used by an SF soldier, advising a CIDG Camp Strike Force, late in the war, and it was made up of: M1956 suspenders; nylon individual equipment belt with quick-release buckle; three nylon M16 ammunition pouches, each holding four 20-round

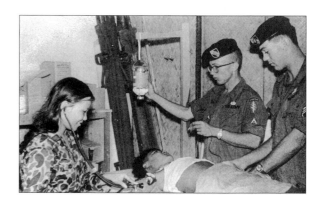

A-412 medics at Camp Kinh Quan II connect an intravenous drip to a Vietnamese boy wounded by VC action. The assisting nurse wears a "duck-hunter" uniform.

M16A1 magazines; an M1956 universal small arms ammunition case for air/ground marking aids; Gyro Jet M186 "pen flare" projector with seven flares (**3**); signal mirror (**4**); mini smoke grenades (**5**); VS-17 marker panel section (day glow orange and pink) (**6**); two LC-1 nylon canteen covers (with pocket for water purification tablets) with 1qt plastic canteens, operational packet of a tropical survival kit (with its contents customized), two nylon first aid pouches (one for field dressings, one for lensatic compass).

The diverse aids for air-to-ground signaling were important for survival. From the air the jungle appeared as a rolling green sea with few terrain features for reference. A small group of camouflaged men was extremely difficult to pin-point. A variety of means were used to attract attention. One of the most effective, day or night, was the SDU-5/E strobe light (**7**) usually carried in a nylon case on the suspender's shoulder. It is fitted with a blue filter to prevent air crews from mistaking its fraction of a second flashes for muzzle flashes. It could be seen for up to ten miles and did not destroy night vision. A plastic flash guard, which was stowed by sliding it over the light's body, prevented its detection from the ground. The light could also be shielded by flashing it through the barrel of an opened M79 grenade launcher.

The "indig" rucksack was widely used by SF troopers, but from late 1968 the Army's nylon tropical rucksack (**8**) was

acquired by some. Its design was influenced by the "indig" rucksack, but it was made of OG 106 nylon, had a spring steel frame, and numerous modern improvements. An SF trooper's rucksack held only a minimum of necessities: US poncho liner (**9**); "indig" poncho (**10**) modified as a hammock fly (18in. extension added, hood removed and patched over); "indig" hammock (18in. extension added) (**11**); condiment bag (**12**); makeshift C-ration can stove and C4 plastic explosive for cooking fuel (**13**); pill bottle (**14**); spare socks (**15**); Air Force survival knife (**16**); insect repellent (**17**); early type, 2qt bladder canteen packed in the top (**18**), and 1qt canteens in the side pockets (rations not depicted).

The Packet, Indigenous Ration (PIR) (**19**) is the popular Menu #5, shrimp-mushrooms. Other meals were

123

a "sawdust-filled" sausage, beef (which left an oil slick after prolonged boiling), "boot heel" mutton, and dried fish-squid; it was like chewing a mouthful of rubber bands all day long. PIRs included a bag of instant rice and small packets of dried vegetables, candied fruit pieces, dried hot peppers, tea, salt, and a vitamin pill. Canned mackerel was a common supplement mixed with the PIR rice.

20: The 5.56mm M16A1 rifle was issued to the MIKE Forces in early 1969 and to the Camp Strike Forces in the spring. MIKE Forces and reconnaissance projects used the 5.56mm XM177E2 submachine gun (**21**). The 20-round magazine was still common, but 30-round magazines were making an appearance too. Priority for the scarce 30-round magazine went to reconnaissance projects. Sometimes a pair of 20-round magazines were taped together allowing rapid magazine change.

Hand grenades too had been improved. The M26A1 fragmentation or "lemon grenade" (**22**) was the most widely used. The similar M61 had an additional safety clip to secure the lever. The M67 fragmentation or "baseball grenade" (**23**) provided even more effective and uniform fragmentation. The Mk3A2 offensive or "concussion grenade" (**24**) relied on its ½lb of TNT for blast effect to neutralize bunkers.

PLATE H: THE KEY TO LIFE ... THE RADIO

1: Each USSF trooper was closely followed by his assigned RTO (radio-telephone operator). Not only did he "hump" the radio for his American, but brewed morning coffee for both of them and handled other minor chores. He received a "gratuity payment" for his services in the form of a couple of highly valued M112 C4 demolition blocks. The RTO shared his good fortune with his buddies by purchasing cooking fuel.

2: A Striker RTO, seldom weighing more than 110lbs, carried little more than the radio and spare batteries, often, not even a rifle. His buddies carried his rations and bedroll. Batteries, however, were a nagging problem. Usually one a day was required per radio. Units moved with the radios habitually turned off to conserve the heavy batteries. Note the World War Two Browning automatic rifle (BAR) belt carried by the USSF troop. Four 20-round M16A1 magazines could be carried in its six pockets, although some pockets would hold grenades, air-to-ground marker aids, and field dressings. In the field the Vietnamese Special Forces (**3**) strove to look as much like Strikers as possible; their capture was virtually a death sentence. This LLDB master sergeant wears the distinctive camouflage uniform adopted in the early 1960s, as was common practice by elite ARVN forces. Worn in camp, they were manufactured in both fatigue and jungle uniform styles.

In the early days patrols maintained communications with their base camp with the AN/PRC-10 manpack radio (**4**), which was inelegantly known as the "Prick-10" – an acronym used with all AN/PRC-series radios. This 26lb FM radio, adopted at the end of the Korean War, was heavy for its 3–5-mile range. It also required annoying manual calibration and consumed its heavy batteries at a high rate. Provided with a web carrying harness, it was more frequently carried in a rucksack. The CW-216(*)/PR accessory bag was seldom carried in the field; the extra components were simply stuck in the rucksack.

The AN/PRC-10 radio was replaced by the transistorized AN/PRC-25 (**5**) by 1968. This 24lb 7oz FM radio had an 5-mile planning range, was simpler to operate, more reliable, and offered 920 channels as opposed to 170. Rock-and-roll radio stations in Saigon could sometimes be picked up. The AN/PRC-77 was externally identical, but could be fitted with an AN/KY-57 secure voice device (cryptographic scrambler). The "Key-57" was only used on A-camp base radios for communications with the B-team and was never taken to the field to prevent its capture. The camp often seemed to be out of radio range. The simple expedient of lifting the radio over one's head would sometimes provide that extra click of range.

6: Hallicrafters HT-1 walkie-talkies were widely issued to Strike Forces down to platoon-level for inter-company communications. Procured through the CIA from commercial sources, they had a range of less than 1¼ miles and operated on eight D-cell flashlight batteries. Operating instructions were printed in English and Vietnamese. They were also fitted with a self-destruct button that would burnout their circuits to prevent their use by the enemy. However, this button was often disconnected after curious Strikers caused havoc by playing with it.

SF NCOs of A-221, depart Camp Cung Son for the last time after it was converted to a Regional Force battalion as part of the phaseout of the CIDG, March 1969. Taped to the back of the suspenders' yoke of the lead man is a serum albumin can, an intravenous blood expander that saved many lives.

PART 3

US MARINE RIFLEMAN
IN VIETNAM
1965-73

US MARINE RIFLEMAN IN VIETNAM 1965–73

INTRODUCTION

The Corps and the War

Portrayed in this title are US Marine riflemen as they "locate, close with, and destroy the enemy by fire and maneuver, or repel the enemy's assaults by fire and close combat." We follow fictional fire-team members through enlistment, training, battle, and return during the war's climax. This is a representative account, if not a specific one, to answer the veteran's touchstone questions: "Who were you with?" and "When were you there?" It is about men in combat against the enemies of their country and tells in part the story of the 1st Company, 1st Battalion, 9th Regiment of Marines during a mobile operation in the western highlands on the border of Vietnam and Laos in early 1969.

Since November 10, 1775 the American Marines have viewed themselves as light infantry, complete with green uniforms, black accoutrements and, for a time, a hunting-horn emblem (a French horn rather than a German bugle). In various forms the Marines served in most of the declared and undeclared US conflicts "from the halls of Montezuma to the shores of Tripoli." Two brigades served in Europe in World War One and six divisions, along with aviation and supporting troops, battled in the Pacific during World War Two. A national defense act in 1947 established the modern Marine Corps: three amphibious divisions, three aircraft wings and a reserve. This settled the Corps' position within the defense structure at a fixed minimum size. Major bases were at Quantico, Virginia; Camp Lejeune, North Carolina; Camp Pendleton, California; and throughout the Pacific region. Headquarters were in Arlington, Virginia, outside Washington D.C.

Starting in 1950, Marines served in Korea, Indo-China, Lebanon, Cuba, Laos, Haiti, and the Dominican Republic. The Cold War turned into an era of numerous "hot" conflicts that

The Drill Instructor was the non-commissioned officer charged with the conversion of civilians into enlisted Marines at the recruit depots, the boot camps in South Carolina on the East Coast and California on the West Coast. The old-fashioned campaign hat was symbolic of the position. (USNI)

With drill, weapons training, and uniform inspections came a requirement for cleanliness and order that saw frequent "field days" by recruits to keep barracks free from dirt and dust. Worn is the scarlet and gold athletic uniform referred to as the "Mickey Mouse" outfit. (DOD)

stopped short of general or even limited war. After the withdrawal of France from Indo-China and the partition of Vietnam into north and south pending elections, the Americans moved to help the Republic of South Vietnam against the People's Republic of Vietnam in the north. The civil war that ensued had international implications that involved several world powers and their clients.

By 1960, the date on the Vietnam Campaign Medal, a state of armed conflict existed between the two Vietnams and their allies. Marine advisors were present in South Vietnam and the first tactical units sent were Marine helicopter squadrons in 1962. The landing of the 9th Marine Expeditionary Brigade at Da Nang in March 1965 ensured large-scale Marine Corps involvement.

When the commitment in Southeast Asia began, the US Marines were well trained, organized and equipped for orthodox operations. They were confronted in South Vietnam by what Marine Gen. Lewis W. Walt characterized as a "strange war, strange strategy." The conflict displayed a full spectrum of violence, from individual terrorism and guerrilla fighting to conventional land combat with extensive sea and air components. All of this was within the context of diplomatic and domestic politics of the various parties in Vietnam at the time.

The US Marines mainly operated in I Corps, the northernmost of the South Vietnamese regions bordering Laos, North Vietnam and the South China Sea. From the west, valleys and ridges served as infiltration routes for Communists attacking coastal population zones, and these same hinterlands served as enemy rear and staging areas.

In 1965 the Marines organized the coastal enclaves and took an expanding "oil spot" approach to operations from Da Nang and Chu Lai. By 1967 North Vietnamese build-ups along the demilitarized zone (DMZ) were met by Marines in a defensive posture that carried through until 1968, with decisive confrontations at Khe Sanh, Dong Ha and Hue City. By mid-1968 allied forces held, and Marines used a mobile approach to "search and destroy" Communist forces. This continued into 1969. The Marines began to leave that year as the South Vietnamese assumed a larger role in the fighting and most US units were gone by July 1971. Fighting continued until the eventual defeat of the South Vietnamese by the North and the subsequent change of regional order in 1975. The conflict, the longest in the history of the Corps, exacted a high cost, with more than 14,800 Marines killed and 88,000 wounded. It is against a background of two decades of war that this account should be viewed.

CHRONOLOGY

1961	Direct US military aid to South Vietnam begins.
1964	US warships attacked in the Gulf of Tonkin. President Lyndon Johnson calls for action.
1965	US bases attacked in South Vietnam. Tactical bombing of North Vietnam begins, and US Marines land, along with army units.
1966	Strategic bombing of North Vietnam begins and US ground forces continue to build up, including Marines at Da Nang and Chu Lai.
1967	Heavy fighting by army near Saigon and Marines move to defend the demilitarized zone.

1968

January–April	Defense of Khe Sanh by Marines. Tet offensive launched throughout South Vietnam, with fighting in Saigon and Hue.
March–May	Bombing restricted by Americans, with renewed attacks and negotiation offers by the Communists.
November	Bombing halt in North Vietnam. Richard Nixon elected president.

1969

January	Truce negotiations begin in Paris. US forces in Vietnam at a peak of 542,400.
July	Planned withdrawal of US troops begins.
November	Massive anti-war demonstrations in America.

1970

March	US and South Vietnamese invade Cambodia.
May	Violent anti-war demonstrations in America.
June–July	Withdrawals from Cambodia.
December	Congress repeals Tonkin Gulf resolutions.

1971

February –March	South Vietnamese invade Laos. US force reductions continue.
July	Last Marine combat units depart.

1972

March	North Vietnamese invade South Vietnam, bombing of North Vietnam resumes and Americans support returns.
May	North Vietnam ports mined and bombing increased.
August	Last US combat forces depart South Vietnam, leaving 43,000 support personnel.

1973

January	Peace agreement signed between US and North Vietnam.
March	Remaining US forces depart South Vietnam.

ENLISTMENT

The Human Factor

An estimated 500,000 Marines served in Vietnam from 1962 through to 1975. In 1968 Marines numbered 85,881, from more than 501,000 Americans under the Military Advisory Command Vietnam. By then, those joining the armed forces or conscripted by selective

Physical fitness formed a part of the program designed to rapidly build up recruits through exercise and nutrition. The instructor on the right looks for an aggressive attitude. The recruits wear combat boots, utility trousers, and gray sweat shirts. (USNI)

Privates Benotz, Valdez, and Murphy learned the spirit of the bayonet was to "Kill, Kill, Kill" as recruits demonstrate with M14 rifles and bayonets. Pugnacity was demanded during bayonet training both as a drill and during "pugil stick" bouts with padded "rifles" and protective equipment. (USNI)

service knew the prospect of combat was not a matter of if, but when. The Commandant of the Marine Corps at the time, Gen. Leonard F. Chapman, stated that there were three kinds of Marines: "those in Vietnam, those who had just come back from Vietnam, and those who were getting ready to go to Vietnam."

The average Marine was an 18- or 19-year-old male with a high school education, from an urban working class or rural small town background, and of an economic and racial mix that was more varied than American society as a whole. Motivation for enlistment was patriotism, self-advancement, personal reasons, and the looming prospect of being drafted (about 20,000 Marines were conscripted during the war).

Members of the high school Class of 1968 not deferred from the draft often ended up with local recruiters who used fabled sales techniques, guaranteeing that "The Marine Corps Builds Men." This might be bolstered by family histories of military service and Hollywood images from *The Sands of Iwo Jima* or *Victory at Sea* for background. However, this was tempered by graphic television images and combat veterans returning – wounded and dead – from the conflict.

One new recruit was Joe Benotz, whose failure to manage car payments, a girlfriend , and college classes found him walking into the Marine Corps store front in Watertown, New York, and signing up to be one of America's finest. The Marines offered a two-year enlistment with the same obligations as the draft, and Benotz felt that "if you were going to have to fight, then you might as well be trained by the best." This entailed a quick four months of preparation, usually followed by a Vietnam tour. Whatever the recruit's reasons for joining up, the Marine Corps Recruit Depot (MCRD) quickly made logic irrelevant with the shock of the "boot camp" and the overriding rigors of day-to-day service.

TRAINING

Recruit Depot and Infantry Training Regiment

San Diego, California, and Parris Island, South Carolina, were the processing centers for civilians seeking entry into the Corps' ranks. Recruit depots were to "receive, degrade, sanitize, immunize, clothe, equip, train, pain, scold, mold, sand, and polish" according to former Commandant Gen. David M. Shoup. Recruits were trained by methods that bear little comparison with any other profession, avocation, or sport: they had to learn to leave a place of comparative safety, on order, and to go towards an armed enemy "whose purpose in life is to kill you." This was imparted with the fundamentals of drill, physical training, and marksmanship. The 10 weeks allocated to initial training were divided rigidly into Receiving, Forming, and Phases I, II and III.

Regardless of the initial terms of entry or final assignment, all enlisted Marines went through this training process (and officers endured their own version of it at Quantico, Virginia). Training was administered by enlisted drill instructors, whose creed stated: "I will train them to the best of my ability. I will develop them into smartly disciplined, physically fit, basically trained Marines, thoroughly indoctrinated in love of corps and country." This was sublimated to: "Be damned sure no man's ghost returns to ask 'If your training program had only done its job.'"

Journalist William Mares, a reservist, wrote that by late 1968 the Marine Corps had had to adjust to replace the dead, wounded and discharged of the ranks. It had been forced "to reduce the length of training, increase the input of recruits and lower the mental and physical standards for enlistment." He concluded that these changes "put increased pressure on the teacher-priest-guard-father-mother hen most responsible for training the recruits – the DIs." This pressure was passed on to the "Boots," who struggled to shed their civilian background faced with their new realities. "No one forced you to join. If you don't like it, then tough shit."

Pat Murphy, from Philadelphia, got the first view of his home for the next weeks through the greasy window of a bus in the middle of the night. What impressions he had were soon disrupted by a disembodied shout that emptied the bus with: "My name is Staff Sergeant Brown and I am a member of the finest fighting outfit in the world! You scum-bags have ten seconds to get off this bus, NOW!" Murphy and 38 others fought their way out the door and on to yellow footprints painted on the pavement. The shouting and

Limited field training was conducted as part of the recruit process, primarily in the form of conditioning hikes with packs and rifles. This drill instructor carries the M41 pack with blanket roll to set the example for his heavily laden charges at left. (USNI)

ABOVE LEFT **After graduation from boot camp, Marines assigned to the infantry went on to training for the various specialties from rifleman to crew-served weapons. In this case an instructor lectures on the use of the 60mm mortar to students wearing helmets with camouflage covers. They wear M62 utility uniforms. (DOD)**

ABOVE RIGHT **Pre-deployment training used jungle lane firing exercises, village search and clearing drills, and orientation to the weapons that would be encountered in Vietnam from captured stocks. These Marines handle the Communist-bloc hardware they might find in combat. (DOD)**

prodding by khaki-clad instructors in "Smokey-the-Bear" hats became familiar in the weeks to follow.

Receiving and forming was designed to process the incoming recruits rapidly into 75-man training platoons, under the supervision of a senior drill instructor and two assistant drill instructors as part of a four platoon "series." All were crammed into open "squad bays" in old brick barracks or even older prefabricated huts. The recruits' personal space centered on a bed or "rack," a foot locker, and a wall locker.

A "PX" (post exchange) issue included the essentials of bucket, brushes, towel, soap, razor, toothbrush, toothpaste, Brasso metal polish, Kiwi shoe polish, physical training clothing, consumable sundries, and a *Guidebook for Marines* to cover any information the instructors might miss. Recruits also received clothing and equipment to be used and looked after. This included some 37 different pieces of uniform and clothing for dress, service, and utility uniforms.

Individual combat equipment was known by Vietnam-era Marines as "782" gear. Fielded as Marine Corps M1941 individual combat equipment, the sturdy construction of canvas, webbing and brass fittings was almost indestructible. The marching, field marching, transport and field transport packs were memorized and assembled at boot camp, if nowhere else.

To make recruits more responsive to schedules, methods, and expectations it was necessary to disorient them. This was done by stripping them of clothing, possessions, hair, and any false dignity they might have. Drill, speech, bodily functions and even personal hygiene was accomplished "by the numbers" in an instructor-approved fashion. No area of human existence was too personal to be regulated. Compliance with the Marine Corps way was the only way: "a place for everything and everything in its place." Infractions were punished with warnings, physical exercise and group ridicule. If physical abuse was not

NAME (Last, First, Middle Initial)						GRADE		SSN	

ORGANIZATION							DATE		

INDIVIDUAL EQUIPMENT			QTY	INIT	ITEM	QTY	INIT	ITEM	
QTY	INIT	ITEM			KNIFE, HUNTING 7" W/SHEATH				
		BAG, WATERPROOF CLOTHING			LINE, TENT, COTTON				
		BAYONET W/SCABBARD			LINER, COAT, MAN'S FIELD				
		BELT, CARTRIDGE OR PISTOL			LINER, PONCHO				
		BLANKET, BED			LINER, STEEL HELMET				
		CANTEEN			MATTRESS, PNEUMATIC				
		CASE, FIRST AID W/PACKET			POCKET, AMMUNITION MAGAZINE CAL. 45				
		COAT, MAN'S FIELD			POCKET, AMMUNITION POUCH M				
		COVER, CANTEEN			POLE, TENT SHELTERHALF			GARRISON EQUIPMENT	
		COVER, HELMET, CAMOUFLAGE			PONCHO			BUNK, STEEL	
		CUP, CANTEEN			SLEEPING BAG, MOUNTAIN, W/CASE			COVER, MATTRESS, COTTON	
		HAT AND MOSQUITO NET			STRAP, BLANKET ROLL			HOLDER, ID CARD, BUNK	
		HAVERSACK			SUSPENDERS, BELT, MCP, PR.			LOCKER, STEEL	
		HELMET STEEL			TENT, SHELTERHALF			MATTRESS, COTTON	
		HOLSTER, PISTOL CAL 45			PAN, MESS KIT W/COVER			PILLOW, BED	
		HOLSTER, REVOLVER CAL 38			PIN, TENT, SHELTERHALF			PILLOWCASE	
		HOOD FIELD JACKET						SHEET, BED	
		INTRENCHING TOOL W/CARRIER						TRUNK, LOCKER, PLYWOOD, W/TRAY	
		KNAPSACK, MCP							
		KNIFE, FORK, SPOON, FIELD MESS							

MEMORANDUM RECEIPT FOR INDIVIDUAL/GARRISON EQUIPMENT (4430)
NAVMC 10577 (REV   ) SN 0000-00-006-0903 U/I SE

SIGN HERE ➤   I certify that I have the above articles of government property.

NAME (Last, First, Middle Initial)		GRADE	SSN

Individual Equipment Receipt, the Vietnam-era version of the fabled "Form 782" that gave the name "782 Gear" to personal equipment used by Marines. This included everything needed in the field or barracks while assigned a specific unit.

condoned, it certainly existed, and recruits either functioned or failed under pressure.

Marines had to learn three things: a proper respect for lawful authority (how to obey orders); how to take care of themselves (maintenance of clothing, equipment and health) ; and how to live with fellow Marines (teamwork). The underlying theory was that the sooner these fundamentals were learned the better, for the longer they took to grasp, the more traumatic an experience it would be. The three weeks of Phase I included drill, calisthenics, memorizing orders, trying to wear

Squad tents used as living quarters in a base camp in Vietnam, often with plywood flooring and wooden hardback frames. A Marine examines animal traps used as booby-traps by the Communists. He wears theater-issued jungle utilities with M62 cover. (USNI)

The field mess; Marines go through the scullery to wash and disinfect utensils in garbage cans of water heated by immersion burners. Sanitation was a concern, particularly in base areas that depended upon primitive measures to prevent disease or vermin from spreading. Rain suits were worn in the wet weather. (USNI)

the uniform and equipment, and cleaning and carrying an eight-and-a-half-pound M14 service rifle. Days began and ended with physical training by the numbers of the "daily seven." Marine historian and depot alumni Dr. V. Keith Fleming recalled: "Drill instructors ceaselessly stalk about the platoon, their anger ready to boil over as they scream and shout at the young privates."

The recruits, many of whom were far from their familiar neighborhood for the first time, learned about their instructors and each other, and learned to depend upon others from diverse backgrounds. The goal was to understand the importance of collective discipline. They also learned hygiene, weapons, customs and courtesies, first aid and packs, through lectures, demonstrations and practical application.

Most of the training was reinforced on an informal level by the ever-present drill instructors, and competition with other platoons measured individual and collective performance. Proper "motivation" was considered as important as actual knowledge or proficiency.

The three weeks of Phase II were devoted to using the rifle on a known distance range. This meant an intensive focus on a skill that distinguished Marines: the use of small arms in battle. With war in progress, recruits dedicated marksmanship training "to the VC, to give them a better chance to die" for their country (Mares). Together with their whole platoon, Murphy and Benotz recited MajGen W. H. Rupertus' creed, *My Rifle*: "This is my rifle. There are many like it, but this one is mine. My rifle is my best friend. It is my life. I must master it as I must master my life. My rifle, without me is useless. Without my rifle, I am useless!"

The tasks of nomenclature, marksmanship theory, snapping in drills and the qualification course were designed to enable Marines to hit the target at 200, 300 and 500 yards, and so turn them into marksmen, sharpshooters and expert riflemen. Success for "dingers" was offset by the failure of others, the "unqs," for not qualifying. Familiarization with the pistol was taught in passing. Phase II ended with a week of "mess and maintenance" duties that had the recruits work in the dining hall to feed other recruits – including women Marines sometimes.

133

Civic action maintained good relations with the Vietnamese civilians in the populated base areas. A medical corpsman takes advantage of purified water supplies to allow local children to bath as a treatment of endemic skin conditions. (DOD)

Phase III primed the recruits for graduation and assignment – drill, examinations and swimming instruction (Marines were a seagoing service). Physical training focused on the readiness test, conditioning runs and hikes, and hand-to-hand combat. There would be an overnight in the field, a military field meet, a drill competition, and maybe a platoon party to mark the end of training. Daily inspection ensured that the early lessons were not forgotten and that the proper esprit was being exhibited. The recruits who had not made it that far disappeared to motivation platoons, special training, series recycle, or medical discharges.

In the series Mares followed, of 300 that started, about 240 graduated. Those that did not were enough in number to make those that remained feel like survivors entitled to be called Marines. Murphy and Benotz's drill instructor's parting words were: "Work as hard as you can. Don't suck ass. Be yourself. You are an ambassador of the United States and the Marine Corps. Good luck."

A short graduation parade and recognition of platoon and series "Honor Men" marked the completion of this rite-of-passage, with a pass-in-review to the sounds of John Philip Sousa's *Semper Fidelis*. Parents, girlfriends and others attended, and the new Marines were given a few hours off before they had to return to the barracks for the assignment of "military occupational specialties" (MOSS) and further training at other locations. High school graduates went to aviation or communications schools; the less gifted went to service support assignments ("Why die? Go supply!"), and those in between went to the combat arms. For half of the recruit platoon this meant the Infantry Training Regiments (ITRs) at Camp Pendleton or Lejeune. While tradition demanded that "every Marine is a rifleman," in practice only those assigned Occupational Field 03 were "school trained" for this. The goal of the ITR was to produce riflemen, machine-gunners, mortar men, assault men, and anti-tank assault men for Fleet Marine Force Pacific or Atlantic in just four weeks. There followed a year of combat for most, although a select few were picked for barracks, ship, and embassy duties.

Infantry training was less intense and without the full-time presence of drill instructors; the infantry students were able to flex their newfound freedom and their paychecks. Pay-day was bi-monthly, in cash, although a private's $1,383.40 annual pay did not go very far. Deductions were made for taxes, insurance, charities and lost equipment. Extra allowances were given for meals, dependants, and uniforms, and they had to put aside enough to pay for haircuts, starch, and boot polish.

Though it was still before dawn, the Quonset hut was sweltering as Juan Valdez woke to the sounds of his bunkmate barfing in the lower rack. The last bus from town was not the "vomit comet" for nothing, he thought. Southern California was his home, and it did not hold the same fascination for him that it did for the others in his training platoon. Patrick Murphy had come back to the San Onofre area with a hangover and a bloody tattoo that proclaimed "Death Before Dishonor" on his right arm. This might be worth a run to the top of the hill known as "Old Smokey" and back if an instructor noticed it.

Replacement battalion was followed by familiarization with the M16 rifle, instruction in the Marine's role in Vietnam, personal experience from small unit leaders, and something called "civic action." Valdez recalled that their troop handler, a veteran of Hue City, had been asked what happened in an ambush. "You die!" had been the monosyllabic reply. This same sergeant also spent extra time showing them how to clean the unfamiliar M16 and then sent them to buy paint brushes and commercial lubricant for this purpose. "If it's not clean enough to eat from, you're gonna die."

Vietnamese civilians provided services, like this "papa-san" barber with hand clippers and single hair style – "high and tight." This did not encourage business from younger Marines, especially when prejudiced that Vietnamese might cut their throat if given a chance. Base workers were the most familiar Vietnamese encountered. (MCHC)

Being run through "Asian" villages and jungle lanes in California's arid climate is an incongruity not always appreciated. Historian and 9th Marines commander in Vietnam, BrigGen Edwin H. Simmons described one of these exercises. The demonstration "follows a simple predictable scenario… a Marine force encircles the village, forming the cordon for the cordon-and-search operation to come. A helicopter flies overhead, making a loudspeaker broadcast and dropping leaflets… One by one the VC are eliminated." All this was play-acting, without the ever-present wood smoke, cooking smells, and farm animals, and the tension caused by restricted movement and visibility. For the privates it must have seemed like "a walk in the sun." Training was completed in time for Christmas and New Year's leave; then the Marines went on to first duty stations in January 1969 – with Vietnam being the destination for Privates Benotz, Valdez, and Murphy. They were leaving the Age of Aquarius for the world of the Universal Soldier.

Marines served a 13-month Vietnam tour, and when ordered overseas were limited to a summer khaki uniform and an "overnight" or "AWOL" (for absent without leave) bag of 25 pounds. Exceptions were those who were deployed as units by ship or plane, who already had field uniforms and equipment. Departure by commercial airlines was from Travis and Norton Air Force Bases in California to Okinawa, near Japan. On Okinawa, personnel were processed through Camp Hague and then on to Vietnam, where they were issued with the necessary clothing and equipment at the unit level. Throughout the stay "in country" the unit replaced items as required, sometimes by the reissue of salvaged gear. Marines left a sea bag (and a footlocker for officers and staff non-commissioned officers) in the rear with excess uniforms and belongings. In most cases these were not seen again until the Marines were "rotated" back to the United States.

EVERYDAY LIFE IN VIETNAM

In the Rear with the Gear

The III Marine Amphibious Force was the senior Marine and American command in I Corps. Assigned to it were elements of the 1st and 3rd Marine Divisions, the 1st Marine Aircraft Wing and the Force Logistic Command. Allied forces in I Corps had four tasks to accomplish: defend critical bases and airfields; destroy Communist combat forces; eliminate Communist subversive infrastructure; and conduct civic action to support the government of South Vietnam. This was in an area covering 10,700 square miles, including the coastal enclaves of Phu Bai, Da Nang and Chu Lai. It encompassed a population of 2,755,800 in five provinces, six cities and 549 major villages.

Benatz, Murphy, and Valdez arrived at the end of the replacement pipeline on the same commercial airline – Freedom Bird – that was used for those departing at the end of their tour. From Da Nang they were sent to Dong Ha Combat Base and 3rd Marine Division, for eventual assignment to the 9th Marines at Vandegrift Combat Base – a grueling aircraft and truck trip to the first battalion's first company, "Alpha 1/9." The sprawling tent-city was hot and dirty, and smelled "like shit."

Sports passed the time in the rear, albeit in primitive form such as this football game at the 3rd Marine Division's Dong Ha Combat Base. This "Dust Bowl" inter-battalion classic was played with a day's practice and won 12–0. (DOD)

Entertainment was provided by the United Services Organization, most of which by traveling troupes of performers as opposed to the more publicized Christmas shows. In this case by University of Texas students on an improvised stage behind a metal Butler building. (MCHC)

The lads were processed into the company by the executive officer, 1st Lt Lee R. Herron, and the first sergeant, and then assigned to 2nd Lt George M. Malone's platoon. They learned the company commander was a "mustang" officer commissioned from the ranks, who had served in force recon and with the Vietnamese Marines. The battalion was in the field, and replacements were put on working parties to maintain the base, burning trash and latrines, and any other duties the battalion police sergeant could dream up.

Base camps had grown inside the barbed wire into fortified garrison towns. Screened Southeast Asian huts replaced tents; tarmac covered the red mud; and the food was good. General Simmons observed there were "post exchanges, chapels, clubs stratified by rank, and plentiful electricity for radios, television, refrigeration and even air conditioning." "Little Americas" were created within base areas despite the military necessity of the deployment, a trend that became more pronounced as the war became routine. The difference between the front and the rear in terms of creature comforts was significant, and this led to some incongruous efforts to supply luxury items. Even outposts or fire support bases could have picnic-style meals helicoptered in. Shipboard living for Marines with the amphibious Special Landing Force (SLF) was an improvement too, since they were dry and well fed by the US Navy.

Marines looked forward to a six-day rest and recreation leave (R&R, also known as I&I – intercourse and intoxication) halfway through their tour, to Hawaii, Hong Kong, the Philippines, Taiwan, Japan, or Australia. There was also "In-country R&R," which sent units to China Beach in Da Nang for sleep, sun, surf, and beer-bust style barbecues. "One good deal after another," commented the wags, who suspected the aviation and support personnel always lived like this.

Replacements heard rumors about the local Vietnamese putting glass in drinks, having razors in orifices, and something called "black syph." The wartime personal response program sought to instill the rapport Marines needed to win "hearts and minds" or at least prevent abuses that would drive Vietnamese civilians to the other side (an American program and not a South Vietnamese effort). It posed the question, "So why are you here?" A scholar, Christian G. Appy, assumed that Joe, Juan, and Pat either took the war on its own terms, blocked from their minds the purpose or value of it, or gave "as little of themselves to the war as possible." Little time for introspection existed once in country and the average riflemen viewed civic action as somewhat hypocritical: "Let me win your hearts and minds or I'll burn your damn huts down." Where the 9th Marines were along the DMZ found few civilians left to deal with anyway.

Administrative moves within Vietnam were by motor transport. A convoy of five-ton cargo trucks churns through a bypass on Route 9 between the Dong Ha Combat Base and the Vandegrift Combat Base, a trip made daily to run supplies from division to regiment in the northern sector of I Corps. (DOD)

ORGANIZATION FOR COMBAT

Striking Ninth and Walking Dead

Under MajGen Raymond G. Davis, the 3rd Marine Division had been carrying out mobile operations against North Vietnamese units using superior firepower and helicopter mobility since the middle of 1968. It controlled three infantry regiments and several support or service units which together made up a complete combined-arms team, including field artillery, armor, reconnaissance, engineers, communications, motor transport, medical, maintenance and supply.

Among Davis' regiments was the 9th Marines, one of the Marine Corps "work-horse" regiments from World War One, through World War Two and the subsequent Cold War. The 9th Marines and its battalions were deployed to Vietnam in March 1965 and remained until 1969 – "first in, first out." Along with a record of heavy combat, it had pioneered the "county fair" approach to civic action.

Three infantry battalions and a headquarters company made up the 9th Marines Regiment. The first battalion gained notoriety as the subject of a lurid account of the burning of Cam Ne village in 1965 and as the unit Dr. Bernard B. Fall was killed with on the "Street Without Joy." The battalion's nickname, "The Walking Dead," was earned through bloody fights with the North Vietnamese along the demilitarized zone under conventional

Key locations in I Corps, South Vietnam (USMC)

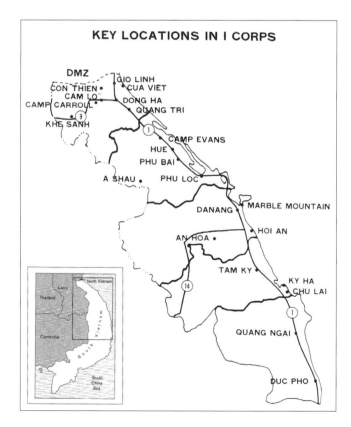

KEY LOCATIONS IN I CORPS

More urgent resupply was made by helicopters, to include water, ammunition, and rations. Normally made once a day or so, returning aircraft would also take back injured personnel and empty water containers for the next trip. These often pinpointed Marine locations and drew enemy fire. (DOD)

warfare conditions, notably during Operation Buffalo in 1967. These savage engagements continued through 1968 as the Marines fought along the DMZ and around Khe Sanh Combat Base.

Their grim reputation was earned, as rock-and-roll reporter Michael Herr commented, because the belief that "one Marine was better than ten Slopes saw Marine squads fed against known NVA platoons, platoons against companies, and on and on…" Herr wrote that Marine riflemen "got savaged a lot and softened a lot, their secret brutalized them and darkened them and very often it made them beautiful. It took no age, seasoning, or education to make them know exactly where true violence resided." They were the killers, and 1/9's reputation, Herr felt, was the kind that "takes hold most deeply among the men of the outfit itself."

Each 1,193-man infantry battalion had four 216-man rifle companies lettered "A"–"D" in the 1st battalion, "E"–"H" in the 2nd battalion, and "I"–"M" in the 3rd battalion ("J" was not used). Each battalion had its own heavy weapons support, the headquarters and service company 81mm mortars and 106mm recoilless rifles. In practice, battalions – and even companies – were used in mixed task forces.

Marine Rifle Company Organization (USMC)

RIFLE COMPANY (RIFLE CO) INFANTRY BATTALION

T/O M-1013 Rev 2 6Jun67
T/O M-1013

Primary mission: To locate, close with and destroy the enemy by fire and maneuver or to repel his assault by fire and close combat

Major items of equipment:
6 Machine Gun 7.62mm M60
9 Grenade Launcher, M79
6 Rocket Launcher, 3.5, M20A1
3 Infantry Mortar 60mm

RIFLE CO			
USMC		USN	
OFF	ENL	OFF	ENL
6	210	0	0

CO HQ		WPNS PLAT		RIFLE PLAT	
2-7	0-0	1-65	0-0	1-46	0-0

A rifle company had a total of 210 men and six officers. The company was divided into three rifle platoons, each of about 46 men and one lieutenant; a slightly larger weapons platoon, also with one lieutenant; and a headquarters. The headquarters consisted of the captain in command of the company and those who helped him direct it in training and in battle – a lieutenant executive officer, a first sergeant, a gunnery sergeant, an armorer, a supply sergeant and administrative clerks.

Support for the three rifle platoons was from a weapons platoon which had three sections besides its small headquarters group (in which were the platoon leader, platoon sergeant, and a small number of others). The three sections were: the 60mm mortar section, with three M19 mortars and crews; an M60 machine-gun section, with three two-gun squads and crews; and an assault section of three squads of two teams each (by 1969 the M20 rocket launcher had usually been replaced by the M72 light-anti-armor-weapon, or LAAW).

The three rifle platoons were each led by a lieutenant who had a staff sergeant as his second-in-command. In each platoon there were three rifle squads and a small command group – the platoon leader, a platoon sergeant, a right guide, a radio operator, and a medical corpsman. Each of the rifle squads was led by a sergeant, and these 14 men usually had among them 13 M16 rifles and one M79 grenade-launcher. All these Marines carried a number of hand-grenades and most had bayonets to put on their rifles; some had knives. A fire-team of four men was the basic unit, with a team leader (the senior man), an automatic rifleman (next senior and designated to use automatic fire), and two riflemen (a scout and an assistant automatic rifleman). The actual number of personnel present was often below that authorized, with the ebb and flow of manpower demands.

Day-to-day activities involved seeking enemy soldiers, supplies, and bunkers in sweeps of the Demilitarized Zone. Night began a constant vigil against North Vietnamese attacks after numbing daytime exertion, alternating ambushes and patrols. (DOD)

CAMPAIGN LIFE IN VIETNAM

In the Boondocks

While a member of a Corps that stressed air-ground task forces and combined arms teams, it was still the infantry that bore the brunt of the daily burden of combat, in conditions that placed them on a relatively equitable footing in a fire-fight with a deadly enemy; after a while in the bush, their attitudes and mannerisms changed from the more civilized ones of the rear echelon.

General Simmons wrote that the realities of war for Marine riflemen were "heat, wetness, malaria, leeches, repetitive patrols, ambushes, sapper attacks, and antipersonnel mines." The infantry's experience of combat was qualitatively and quantitatively different to that of support and service personnel, even though their modern warfare was very much a team effort. Newsman George Casey reported that the average Grunt accepted "the facts of rotting wrist watch bands, a "Dear John" letter, reconstituted milk, canned meat, three salt tablets a day, last choice of C rations, and warm beer." One Marine reconnaissance unit veteran commented that at least he rotated patrols and had time in between to rest and relax before going out again; but in the infantry "you went out and stayed out."

The return to Vandegrift base of the rest of Alpha Company did not ease the burden on new replacements who were generally overlooked. First platoon had a lot of Southerners, as well as some Midwesterners, none of whom were very forthcoming. Squad leader Sgt Leroy Black, of Detroit, Michigan, turned Benotz, Valdez, and Murphy over to their fire-team leader, Cpl Mike Smith of Topeka, Kansas. The taciturn Black was on a second combat tour, while Smith was six months into his assignment. What Smith and Black thought was guarded by realities they faced.

One day the platoon guide took Valdez, Benotz, and Murphy to pick up rations and ammunition. Valdez asked: "Sarge, what gives with the squad? No-one will talk to us." Perhaps because Valdez was the quietest of the three, the sergeant responded: "It's like this: they knew the guys you replaced and they don't know you. You might foul up and get them killed or they'll foul up and get you killed – so they won't get too close."

Unknown to our "chosen" men, but of major importance all the same, in January 1969 the III MAF and I Corps commands were concerned about expanded enemy activity in the Annamite mountain range, where Communist forces from Laos were moving along Routes 922 in Laos and 548 in South Vietnam, leading to Hue, Da Nang, and the populated coastal plain. Troop and supply concentrations were evident in Base Area 611 astride the international border. Recent increases in antiaircraft defenses had indicated that the NVA had something to protect. This was to be the origin of the operation codenamed "Dewey Canyon" that took "our men" into combat for the first time.

Sergeant Black simplified tactics for old and new "hands" as they prepared to move to the field: "Keep your head out of your ass and pay

Commanding the 3d Marine Division from 1968 to 1969 was MajGen Raymond G. Davis. A veteran of World War Two and Korea, where he earned a Medal of Honor, Davis used his battalions to search and destroy the enemy forces in 1 Corps. (DOD)

The 9th Marine Regiment was commanded by Col Robert H. Barrow, another veteran of World War Two and Korea, and later Commandant of the Marine Corps. He took three battalions in the most successful regimental-size operation of the war, code-named "Dewey Canyon." (DOD)

141

attention to what is going on. Keep your eyes on your team leaders and me – you watch me and follow what I do pronto. When I get down, you drop; when I shoot, you open fire; when I run, you haul ass – no more no less. If you new guys screw up, you won't last – forget all that John Wayne stuff over here. If you shoot, shoot to kill, stay alert and you might stay alive – if not, sorry about that."

UNIFORMS, EQUIPMENT, WEAPONS

Tools of the Trade

Appearance

Though American combat uniforms in Vietnam looked the same, the alert observer can detect differences between soldiers and Marines. This is explained by procurement, supply practices and local conditions, and varied according to individual or unit preference, authorization of weapons, unit missions and the type of organization (combat, support, or service). Once overseas, the Marines were often far from their depots in the United States and had to adapt to whatever materiel was at hand. Marines also had an affectation for "salty" clothing and equipment – they preferred older items to newer things to convey an image of experience. The supply system was not consistent enough to allow completely uniform appearance, so despite regulation, variety flourished.

Individual or "tribal" markings were seen in beards, bracelets, necklaces, helmet graffiti, tattoos, and even flags. The longer a unit remained in the field, the "grungier" they would look, as uniforms and equipment took on the faded hue of the dust in the local area.

Alpha Company, 9th Marines was led by 1st Lt Wesley L. Fox during Operation "Dewey Canyon." Lieutenant Fox fought his company against an enemy bunker complex and earned a Medal of Honor. The fire team in this narrative was in Alpha's first platoon. (DOD)

Personnel displayed a characteristic "farmer's" tan on their faces, necks and arms after a few days exposed to the sun. Grooming varied according to where a person was and how close to a barber shop. Uniform regulations required a haircut to start from zero at the normal hairline to no more than three inches on top. For practical purposes, American Marines did not have sideburns or long hair down the back of the neck. Moustaches were allowed, but not beards, but lack of water sometimes prevented shaving, and "field" beards resulted.

Insignia and Markings

During the war the Marines had 12 enlisted grades and 14 grades of warrant and commissioned officers. The rank insignia was a metal or synthetic pin-on type, with black chevrons for enlisted grades and bright silver or gold for officers. Insignia was worn on both collars, if worn at all in the field. Enlisted rank was at an angle to the front edge of the collar and officer rank was worn centered and parallel to the front collar edge.

Individuals marked personal uniform items with their name at designated places, generally with a stamp or stencil in black block letters. More obvious name placement was used overseas – above the left jacket

Into the valley! Lead elements of the 9th Marines kicked off Operation "Dewey Canyon" with helicopter assaults in the Da Krong Valley to establish fire support bases. Initial landing sites were "prepped" with artillery fire and air strikes. (DOD)

pocket and across the back of the jacket. Mistakes or changes were blotted out with ink, which made for messy uniforms.

Identification tags were aluminum with an individual's name, service number, religion, and blood type. Issued in pairs, they were worn around the neck on a chain or attached to the laces of boots. In case of death, one was taken for reporting and the other was left with the body for identification. Tape or rubber sheaths were used to silence the tags.

The Marines emphasized service rather than unit loyalty. To enhance this, no insignia was worn except the corps emblem. The 1954 branch-of-service "Eagle, Globe and Anchor" emblem was found on the cap and shirt. Most utility jackets were issued unmarked with a service emblem, and the individual used heat transfer or stencils to apply them on the left pocket "over the heart." With unit replacement of clothing in Vietnam, these USMC transfers were not always available.

Headgear

The distinctive sage green utility "cover" was the common headgear. It was an olive-green sateen M58 version of a World War Two design. Rank insignia was fixed at the crown when not visible elsewhere. When not in use, the utility cover was folded and kept in a helmet liner or trouser-leg pocket. During the Vietnam era, tropical ("boonie" or "bush") hats of all types were available in olive-green and camouflage patterns. Versions

Touch down and go! A CH46 Sea Knight of MAG-36 lifts-off after landing a squad of riflemen in a landing zone adjacent to the site of a proposed fire support base to prepare it for follow-on forces, including artillery and supplies. (DOD)

143

were manufactured for the various hot weather uniforms, since the hat provided full cover of the head and neck. Issued or traded on the local economy, they were often worn instead of the utility cover. Sweat rags of olive-green towels or cravat bandages were worn around the neck or head. A sweat band could also be made from the strap and safety pin of cloth ammunition bandoleers.

Utility Uniforms

Marines had some options in field clothing. There were the standard M62 sateen utilities, jungle utilities from 1966 and camouflage utilities from 1968. The first pattern jungle utilities were designed for the special forces, based on World War Two army airborne clothing. The olive-green uniform was durable and fast drying, several modifications evolved, but the basic design remained the same.

The camouflage version of the jungle utilities was in the four-color US Army Engineer Research Development Laboratory leaf pattern. The

jacket and trousers were camouflage, 100% cotton, wind resistant rip-stop cotton poplin (Class 2). The jacket had four pleated bellows pockets and was worn outside the trousers. The trousers had four pockets on the hips and two expanding pockets on the trouser legs. Buttons were plastic and allowed closure at the collar and wrist. Although popular, it suffered the problem of most camouflage uniforms: it was great when you were standing still but drew attention when you moved. Eventually the camouflage uniform was adapted to a distinct III MAF uniform.

Supplementary clothing was held by the unit and used as needed. Some items were commonplace, such as M65 field jackets, raincoats and various other waterproof clothing. Supplemental uniform items allowed for a certain amount of mixing and matching, hence the label "raggedy-ass" Marines, given them by more consistent formations.

Issue olive-green underwear was worn, if any was worn at all, in the field. A standard khaki web belt with an open face brass buckle was also used. Worn with all uniforms, the web belt remained popular, as it was one of the Marine Corps' unique items. The web belt doubled as a cargo strap to secure ammunition boxes or equipment. Extra belts were used, such as "jungle" belts made from suspender straps and a variety of captured NVA belts.

PFC Robert T. Ikner displays blocks of explosives dropped by North Vietnamese Army troops during a sapper attack on a fire support base. He had ducked into his fighting position to reload his rifle when he heard the enemy soldiers on top of the bunker with the charges and shot them in the act. (DOD)

Footwear

The green nylon and black leather tropical combat boots were preferred in Vietnam and were worn as available, again later in Marine units than in army units. Black or olive-green socks were worn – either all-cotton, all-wool or blends with nylon. In the field a spare pair of socks was kept in a plastic radio-battery bag to rotate when one pair was wet. Boot socks were also used to carry ration cans tied to the back or side of the pack and to pad or silence other items of equipment. Trousers were worn bloused around the boot top with "blousing garters" rather than being tucked into the boot top in the army style.

Body Armor

An M1 steel helmet with a separate fiber liner was adopted in 1941 and was in service with the Marines the following year. This helmet, with a single chin strap, was used in Vietnam. It was issued to all hands, and the standard infantry practice was to wear it constantly. In 1962 a defense department standard, leaf pattern, canvas helmet cover with reversible green and brown sides was adopted, and this served through the Vietnam War. It soon faded with use, far beyond that of army units. To hold foliage in place on the helmets, bands made of rubber inner-tube material or army-issue olive-green elastic were used.

The use of body armor varied with the task at hand and was worn by infantry units in Vietnam. Modern body armor was introduced to Marines in Korea with the M51 and M55 protective body armor – the "flak" jacket, with its angular plates, was characteristic, although army

Communist sharpshooters waged a contest with Marines as they moved out of exposed positions. In one-for-two, PFC Ronnie S. Tucker and PFC Robert M. Moxley examine their helmets which were both hit by the same enemy round. Neither was injured in this close call. (DOD)

M69 versions were also used in Vietnam. Metal eyelets on the waist of the jacket allowed equipment to be hooked onto it, so the cartridge belt and harness could be dispensed with. Later models had two pockets added to the lower front. They were designed, like the helmet, to protect from fragmentation and were not bulletproof. Body armor was most suitable for static positions and gun crews, but it became a permanent part of the equipment issue for a number of reasons and was worn over an undershirt or bare skin in hot weather.

Both the helmet and the body armor were described by one 9th Marines company commander as "hard to live with and sometimes impossible to live without." The already overloaded Marine sacrificed mobility for the sake of protection. Although wear was mandatory, the 2nd Battalion, 9th Marines left its helmets and flak jackets behind when it operated in Laos during Dewey Canyon.

Graffiti on helmets and flak jackets included the nine-digit social security number, the older, seven-digit, service number or the four-digit "military occupational specialty" (MOS) number – 0311 for infantryman, 0321 for machine-gunner, 0352 for anti-tank man and so on. These numbers helped identify individual equipment, even though this was not approved. A Marine's surname initial and last four numbers of his social security number would be used to identify his web gear – for example, "M-1488" – a unique method of personalization when the use of a name would be frowned upon. It also became a means of expressing identity or opinion. Names of home states, cities, girlfriends, and nicknames all made this graffiti the ground-pounder's equivalent of aircraft nose art. It was a practice suppressed in the rear areas and was the bane of the junior officer and the non-commissioned officer.

Equipment
The Marine Corps M1941 Pack and Individual Combat Equipment served in World War Two and the Korean War. Equipment with a 1941 date stamp was still being issued in Vietnam, but most had been replaced by army M1956 Load Carrying Equipment (LCE) in olive-green cotton canvas and the later M1967 Modernized Load Carrying Equipment (MLCE or LC1) in olive-green nylon.

Army and Marine Corps gear was intermingled throughout, since equipment was not often issued in matched or complete sets. For the purposes of this book, basic allocations will be considered; model and year designations refer to generations of equipment rather than formal patterns, date of issue or manufacture.

The term "Grunt" meant the same for American Marines as "Marius Mule" had for Roman legionnaires. Despite the desired body-to-load weight ratio of three-to-one, the typical Marine carried in excess of the recommended 50-pound maximum, usually more like 80–100 pounds.

This reflected the belief that if you did not carry something, then you did not have it, as well as limitations of helicopter and vehicle transport once a unit was on foot.

A fighting load in Vietnam consisted of a cartridge belt; a field dressing and first aid kit (the M56 utility pouch held a standard field dressing or cigarettes, compass, whistles etc); two or more M56 universal pouches, each with three M16 rifle magazines; and two or more M62 canteens, with M56 cases worn on the belt or pack. A bayonet or knife and an M16 bipod carrying case/cleaning kit would also be on the belt. This "war belt" was suspended from a pair of M41 belt suspender straps, but the M56 suspenders were superior and preferred by all who used them.

A subsistence load might consist of as little as the M56 combat field pack (or "ass pack") and a case from an M17A1 field protective mask or demolitions and claymore bags for a "day trip." The M41 haversack held the minimum possible that a Marine needed to live for an extended period. (This was a matter of experience, with new men enduring the maximum load and the veteran shedding as much weight as possible.) It generally included a poncho, rations (sometimes stacked in a boot sock and hung off the pack or harness), toiletries and a folding shovel. The poncho deserves mention as a combination groundsheet, tent and blanket for most nights in the field.

Additional items depended upon terrain and weather, and included poncho liners, rain suits, field jackets, sleeping shirts, spare socks and a "rubber bitch" air mattress. Personal touches were seen in bush hats, tiger-stripe shorts, sunglasses, reading material, knick-knacks, extra knives, and pistols. Field modifications included taped or rubber cushioned identification tags, metal canteens covered with boot socks to prevent noise, and yards of black electrician's or green ordnance tape to cushion, fasten or cover equipment. The indigenous ARVN rucksack and the US Army tropical rucksack were popular, and were used when available. Even captured Chinese-made packs were used, and were preferred to the M41 haversack because of their external pockets. A 9th Marines battalion commander, LtCol Elliot R. Laine Jr., observed that he used the M41 pack first, and when it did not carry the load he tried ARVN and even NVA packs. Finally he settled on the tropical rucksack which he got for his battalion through a barter with army units.

Officers and non-commissioned officers carried the same clothing and equipment as enlisted Marines. Differences included the pistol belt, a black leather holster, a pistol magazine pouch holding two magazines, canteens, a first aid kit and "H" harness or belt suspender straps. A "tanker" pistol shoulder holster in black leather was sometimes used; it was designed to be worn with two straps, one around the chest and the other over the shoulder. Compasses, strobe lights, and signal mirrors were carried in

An American sniper team indicates the enemy has shown himself long enough to obtain a shot with an M40 sniper rifle. Cat-and-mouse type engagements characterized the minor tactics of Dewey Canyon's first phase. (DOD)

Battles are won by maneuver as well as fire, with 1st Battalion, 9th Marines moving out from Fire Support Base Erskine just north of the Ashau Valley. The infantry carried everything to fight and survive, while those who remained benefited from a static assignment. (DOD)

either pouches or pockets, often tied to the belt with an "idiot cord" made from a boot lace or parachute suspension line. A watch might be worn with the wrist strap through a button hole of the shirt or breast pocket. Leaders of small units had an assortment of maps, notebooks, radio code sheets and tactical book-keeping materiel necessary for their tasks. As combat became more direct, front-line leaders adapted the uniform and look of the rifleman to avoid standing out. This was hard to do when followed by one or more radio operators and the headquarters element of even the smallest sized unit.

Weapons and Radios

In most situations, units went armed to the teeth, with machine-guns and mortars, because of the need to hold their own without immediate support; they had been trained to "move to shoot and shoot to move" with organic weapons. The general-purpose weapon was the M16A1 rifle, but sometimes pistols and even shotguns were useful. The M16 was an innovative design using aircraft industry manufacturing techniques and material. It was fielded in Vietnam with problems in ammunition, training, and maintenance materials (there was no provision with the rifle to carry cleaning tools), but these had been overcome by 1969.

A battalion weapons coach explained to some replacements the difference between range qualification and fire-fights. He was asked how often they were likely to be surprised when in the field? "Let's just say, too often. You will find yourself pinned down, unable to return fire, or firing and maneuvering for all you're worth." Sight alignment and trigger squeeze were hardly relevant: "He who shoots and kills first is going to win. Shoot low. Push the muzzle down. You can see where the first shot hits. You can get him with a ricochet." These were the instructions given Murphy, Valdez, and Benotz as they sighted their M16s on some 55-gallon drums at the combat base perimeter. Don't

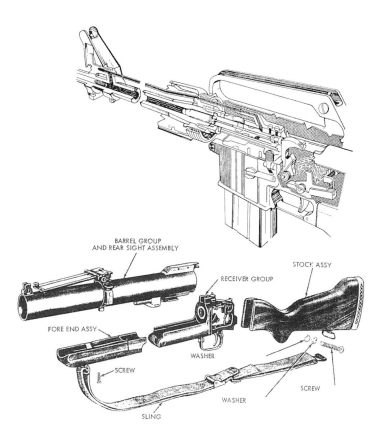

M16 Rifle Schematic – The "Sweet Sixteen" was adapted for use in Vietnam and later became the standard American service rifle. Basic marksmanship training was conducted with the earlier 7.62mm M14 rifle. (USMC)

M79 Grenade Launcher Schematic – The "Blooper" was carried by the squad's grenadier for indirect fire beyond hand grenade range. Handy, if slow to reload, it had a 5 yard fragmentation range. (DOD)

M1911 Pistol Schematic – The "Colt Forty-Five" had been the standard pistol in Marine infantry units since World War One. It was carried by all those not armed with the service rifle. (DOD)

M60 Machine Gun Schematic – The "Pig" was found in the weapons platoon of the rifle company. It was often carried and used at the platoon or squad level to the cry of "guns up!" (DOD)

BARREL GROUP
AND REAR SIGHT ASSEMBLY

STOCK ASSY

RECEIVER GROUP

FORE END ASSY

WASHER

SCREW

WASHER

SCREW

SLING

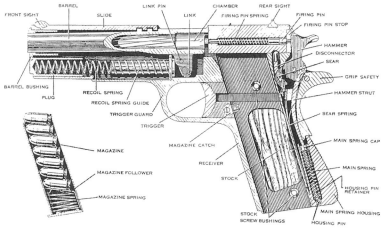

FRONT SIGHT
BARREL
SLIDE
LINK PIN
LINK
CHAMBER
REAR SIGHT
FIRING PIN SPRING
FIRING PIN
FIRING PIN STOP
HAMMER
DISCONNECTOR
SEAR
GRIP SAFETY
HAMMER STRUT
SEAR SPRING
MAIN SPRING CAP
MAIN SPRING
HOUSING PIN RETAINER
MAIN SPRING HOUSING
HOUSING PIN
STOCK SCREW BUSHINGS
STOCK
RECEIVER
MAGAZINE CATCH
TRIGGER
TRIGGER GUARD
RECOIL SPRING GUIDE
RECOIL SPRING
PLUG
BARREL BUSHING
MAGAZINE
MAGAZINE FOLLOWER
MAGAZINE SPRING

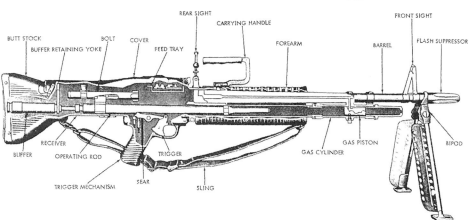

BUTT STOCK
BUFFER RETAINING YOKE
BOLT
COVER
FEED TRAY
REAR SIGHT
CARRYING HANDLE
FOREARM
BARREL
FRONT SIGHT
FLASH SUPPRESSOR
GAS PISTON
BIPOD
GAS CYLINDER
RECEIVER
BUFFER
OPERATING ROD
TRIGGER
SEAR
SLING
TRIGGER MECHANISM

shoot once and look. "Keep firing until the gook goes down, and fire insurance rounds to make him bounce."

Squad-level M79 grenade-launchers were used to knock out direct-fire weapons so riflemen did not have to become exposed in order to throw hand-grenades or to fire rifles at an enemy position. Grenade-launchers are very handy weapons, but are slow to reload. Sgt Black carried his squad's grenade-launcher in order to ensure its use where needed.

Officers, non-commissioned officers, grenadiers, and machine-gunners were armed with the venerable M1911A1 automatic pistol, with its distinctive kick and its large, slow projectile which was designed to knock the enemy down with a body-hit. These pistols were from stocks that had last been procured in 1945. It was considered a back-up weapon, and the feeling was that a rifle was preferable in a real fire-fight.

Hand grenades carried included M26 or M67 fragmentation, M18 smoke, and M15 white phosphorus types. They were used to blast, burn, or smoke the enemy out of his hole or to break up rushes at close range. Grenades could be a problem if left hanging off the webbing, including the M56 magazine pouches designed to carry them this way. The spoons would bend and break after a time allowing the grenade to drop off ("scoring your own goal"). If carried in fibreboard storage tubes or grenade pouches, they were hard to get at in a fire-fight. Other useful weapons were the command detonated M18 Claymore mine, the M49 trip flare, and the M133/135 demolition "satchel" charges.

For "close combat," each rifle came with a bayonet knife and scabbard – the M7 for an M16 – and these served as general purpose knives as well. Marines had a 12-inch all-steel, Bowie-style "Ka-Bar" knife that was issued to everyone who carried a pistol, including machine-gunners, grenadiers, corpsmen, officers and staff non-commissioned officers. Most wore them on the left side of their pistol belt. The fighting knife was used more as a general purpose tool, as everything "from a hammer to a pry bar." The "E tool" folding shovel was a more practical hand-to-hand weapon.

Voice commands and hand and arms signals were common at squad level. Other communications methods included flares, smoke, blinker lamps, flags, air-panels, and runners. The battalion provided radios and operators down to company level, while platoons had to train their own personnel to operate and carry the radio with the platoon leader. Communications equipment included AN/PRC25 very high frequency radios and TA1 telephones for talking with the rear, within a unit, or to aircraft or artillery firing in support. A sophisticated system of communications for their control was present from the highest to the lowest level.

The III MAF commander LtGen Herman Nickerson Jr. wrote that the troop commanders had to "effectively employ weapons that span the spectrum from 60mm mortars and eight-inch naval guns to 2,000-pound bombs. In each confrontation with the enemy, he must determine rapidly what supporting arms are available, which are the best weapons to employ, and then coordinate their use with all agencies involved." Instructions to his subordinates from squad leader to division commander were: "We have the resources. We must use them properly. Those of us who do not use our artillery, air, naval gunfire in seizing objectives are not professional."

SUPPLY AND RESUPPLY

Water, rations, and ammo

One Vietnam veteran recalled that resupply of essentials to frontline units was "frequent and reliable." While regiments and battalions had sections that specialized in furnishing the 10 classes of supplies, at the lower level this was the commanders' responsibility, with help from the gunnery sergeant at the company level and the right guide within a platoon. Both the company gunny and the platoon guide were the second senior non-commissioned officer of their units. Their major concern was provision of rations, water, batteries, and ammunition, and replacement clothing or ordnance items. They accomplished this with working parties drawn from subordinates, and organized carrying parties and landing zones during operations.

The basic allowance of ammunition included 350–420 rounds of 5.56mm rifle ammunition in magazines and cloth bandoleers. There were 21 rounds of .45 caliber ACP ammunition for each pistol and 800 rounds of linked 7.62mm ammunition per machine-gun. Grenade-launcher 40mm rounds were carried in claymore and demolition bags or in special bandoleers and vests. Crew served weapon ammunition was passed out to spread the load. This might include one or two M72 anti-tank rocket rounds, one or two 81mm mortar rounds, between one and three 60mm mortar rounds, illumination flares ("pop ups") and machine-gun ammunition in boxes or belts. The M60 ammunition was carried in the box, bandoleer, or slung across the chest, depending on the situation and unit control. Slung ammunition was easier to carry but was subject to wastage or dirt and damage. Grenades, spare barrel bags, and radio batteries completed the load wherever they could be toted.

Water was as important as ammunition and medical evacuation in the infantry leader's priorities. It was delivered in green metal or black plastic "Jerry" cans to static defensive positions and landing zones, or obtained from local streams and purified with issue halazone or iodine tablets, to be carried in individual canteens. The total number of canteens carried depended on the conditions and early in the war it was

Into the boondocks with Alpha Company as Cpl Smith's men learn what it means to be foot mobile in all terrains and weather. The pickax was "borrowed" from the engineers on leaving the fire support base to supplement individual entrenching tools. (DOD)

found that one canteen was not enough. Water discipline and the use of salt tablets were stressed as rifleman settled for tepid, adulterated and often murky refreshment.

Meals served at base mess halls or from insulated "vat cans" brought to the field were known as A and B Rations. The field ration was the Meal, Combat Individual or "C-Rat." These were issued 12 meals to a case. A Marine would be issued a whole case (22 pounds) to have a four-day supply. He opened the individual boxes, discarded things he did not like or could not trade and packed the rest where he could in his pack or belt. In each case was a supply of can openers, the P38 or "John Wayne" that came with a hole that allowed it to be worn on the dog-tag chain or on the helmet band. A steady diet of three meals a day was about 3,300 calories, but because of the terrain and the weather, fruit, crackers, and one main or heavy meal a day was usually about all most would eat, more like 1,100 calories a day, resulting in weight loss (cold weather improved appetites).

A meal box contained a white plastic spoon (retained in a helmet band or pocket for later use), an accessory pack, a "B" unit (crackers, candy, cheese), and the main meal (or "heavy"). Menus included ham and eggs, spiced beef, ham and lima beans, pork steak, meatballs and beans, franks and beans, chicken and noodles, turkey load and beef slices. Cigarettes were in the rations in packs of four and were useful for trading purposes. Hot coffee was also popular for an early morning or late evening "jump start" drink. Efforts to improve the main meal were seen in the use of hot sauce, worcestershire sauce and peppers or wild onions. In most instances rations were eaten cold, since there was neither the time nor the interest to heat with trioxane fuel bars or a pinch of C4 plastic explosives. Another speculation was that if you mixed cold and hot meals you suffered constipation or diarrhea.

To reduce rations' weight, special dehydrated patrol rations were developed by the army, called the Ration, Long Range Patrol (LRP). These were packed in cloth-wrapped plastic and foil envelopes that required water to prepare. Menus included chili, spaghetti, chicken stew, and beef stew. An accessory pack, candy, a cereal bar, and cocoa were standard additions. A package would be opened, water and seasoning would be added, then it was folded and held down with a rubber band and carried in a pocket, where it marinated until consumed. They were light: three days of LRP rations weighed eight pounds compared to the C rations' 18 pounds. "Lurps," as they were known, were just as dull as C rations to eat and were not fit as long term supplies. In the field, ration issue was by unit. This involved cased meals being

Management of violence was the task of infantry command groups distinguished by maps and radios. Increased enemy resistance required the use of supporting arms, either artillery or air power. Bulky command elements also had to protect themselves from close-in attack. (USNI)

moved from battalion to company to platoon to squad. The company gunnery sergeant, platoon guide or squad leader would up-end a carton so that the contents were hidden and meals would be issued at random. An experienced small unit leader would mix the order of the meals up in the case, since after a while a Marine knew what meal was located in the case by position. Rubbish was repacked in the meal box and returned to the case to be sent back or left.

For Operation Dewey Canyon each rifleman was issued four days of food, an LRP for emergencies, four canteens of water, and twice the normal load of ammunition and batteries. For the seven weeks of the operation resupply and casualty replacement were difficult – units went on short rations or no provisions for a day or two. Ammunition, water, and batteries were a constant resupply problem. It was hard to replenish rifle companies without stopping their movement because finding them from the air was impossible. Once supplies had been delivered, a detail of up to platoon-size had to remain to return cargo nets and empty water containers.

A mortar crew prepares to fire the company commander's "hip-pocket" artillery, the 60mm mortar. This was often the quickest supporting arm to bring into play and could be carried by the rifle companies. (DOD)

Later, supplies were delivered on wooden pallets or in canvas bundles slung from disposable steel cable that could be left behind. The five-gallon plastic water containers were not enough to supply the volume required and they often leaked. Artillery canisters were used, each holding about 13 gallons of water. Beer or sodas were even obtainable at one per man, but were extraordinary enough to be memorable.

MEDEVAC

Shot at and hit

"Combat casualties frequently appear in overwhelming numbers, suffer from multiple fragment wounds and often have waited hours for evacuation and treatment. Add to that austere facilities, equipment and supplies, an echeloned treatment chain, and combat conditions, and it is clear that wartime military medicine presents unique demands," testified a US Navy doctor to the US Senate Committee on Armed Services. This is an accurate description of Vietnam medical conditions.

During the war 14,809 Marines were killed, died or were missing; another 88,635 were wounded. The majority (78%) of those killed were 21 years old or younger in the ranks from private-first-class to corporal (lieutenant to captain for officers). In contrast to World War Two and Korea, small arms fire accounted for 51% of deaths and 16% of wounds to personnel; artillery and mortar fragments were the next most common cause, with 36% of deaths and 65% of wounds; mines, booby-traps and other methods accounted for 13% of the fatalities and 19% of

injuries (mine and booby-traps were not common in Dewey Canyon's remote location). Mortal wounds to the head, torso and groin were most common, while most nonfatal injuries were in the limbs. This provided the medical logic behind digging foxholes and wearing body armor. One company commander during Dewey Canyon observed that many Marines were killed even though they were wearing flak jackets. "They were ambushed at close range with small arms fire which penetrated their body armor."

Because of the nature of the war, Marines had an unspoken conviction that wounded or dead should not be left behind, and they took great risks to ensure this, even suffering more casualties in the process. The Communists recognized this and would often try to trap the wounded near their fighting positions to limit the use of heavy weapons and draw in more Marines to rescue their mates.

In battle, an individual was expected to provide self-aid if injured; his fellow Marines were expected to keep to the task at hand and not care for the wounded. Marines carried one or two battle dressings for their own use, as well as a "jungle" first aid kit with some 10 other items for use if sick or injured. The drill was to always first use the injured man's own dressing, not your own.

US Navy medical corpsmen at platoon and company levels provided follow-up and life saving treatment, often with great skill under trying conditions and at great

Marine Rifleman, Vietnam

Recruit and Drill Instructor,
Marine Corps Recruit Depot, USA

Advanced Training,
Infantry Training Regiment, USA

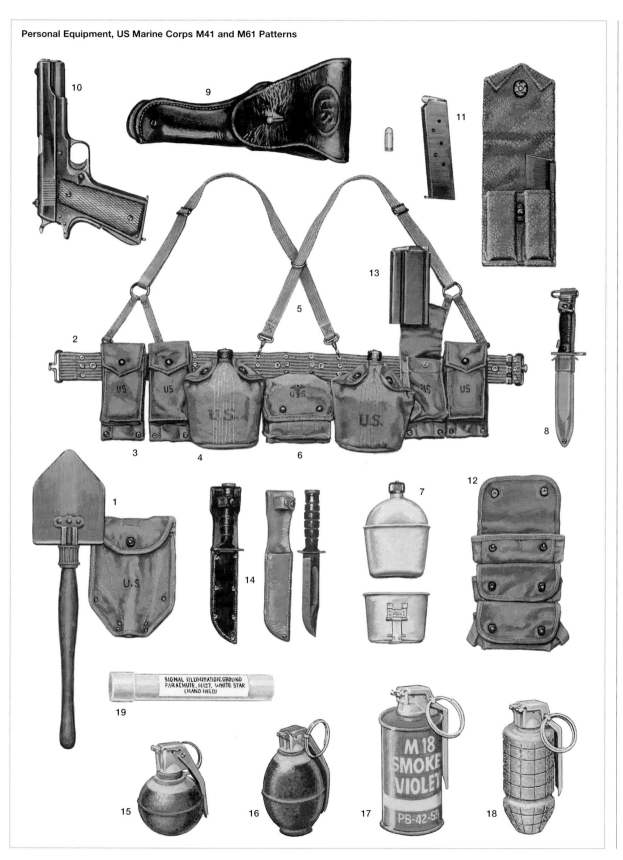

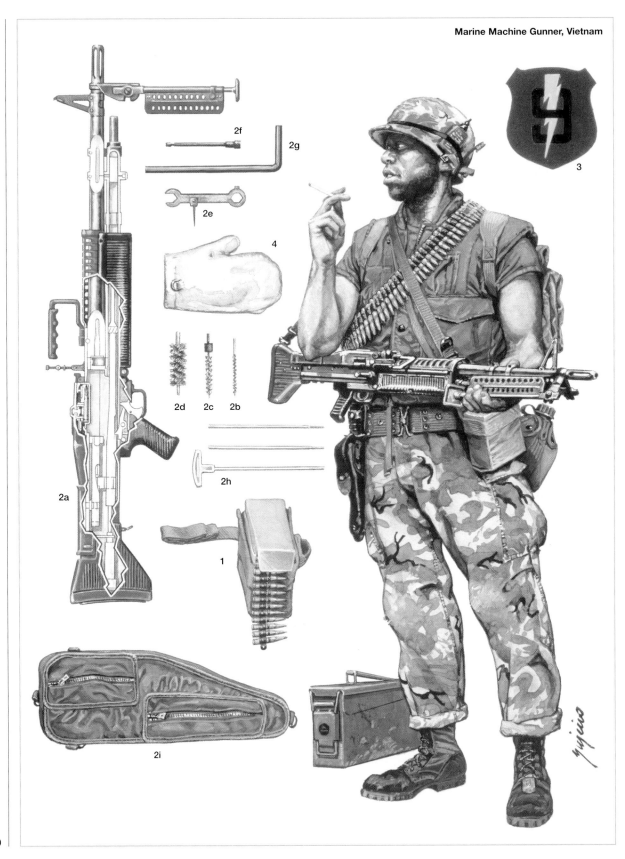

2f

2g

2e

4

2d

2c

2b

2a

2h

1

3

2i

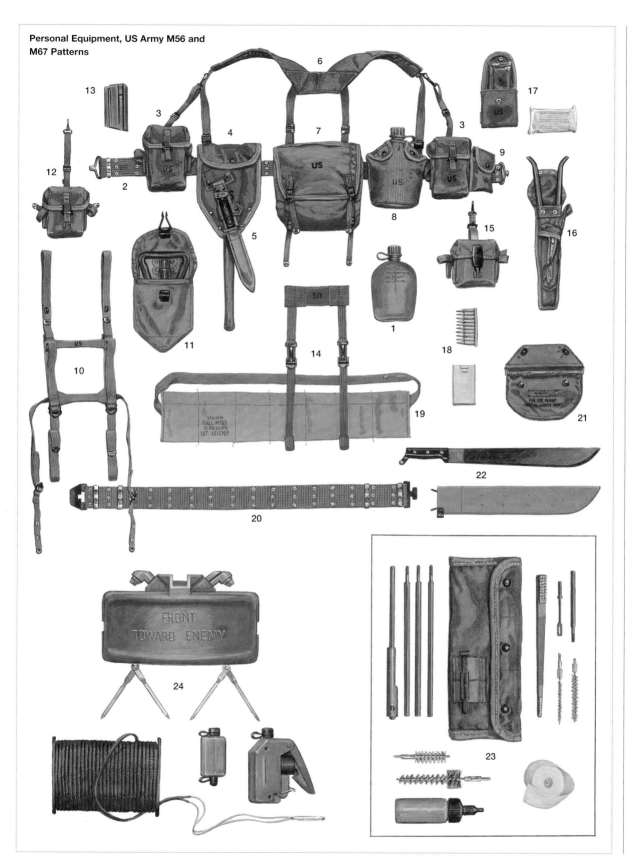

Personal Equipment, US Army M56 and
M67 Patterns

Fire Support Base, Operation Dewey Canyon

162

Fire-fight, Operation Dewey Canyon

The Victor, Operation Dewey Canyon

165

Heads up Charlie! A former North Vietnamese soldier demonstrates with an AK47 assault rifle how to fire at low-flying US aircraft. He was a "Hoi-Chanh" who rallied to the side of the Republic of Vietnam, which explains why the rifle is on "safe."

personal risk. Corpsmen carried a "Unit One" medical instrument and supply set and stocked it with as much extra medical supplies as experience and stamina allowed them to carry. A bit older and more educated than the average Marine, the corpsman's nickname "Doc" was one of respect and hope against needing his attention. Away from combat, corpsmen supervised routine sick calls, medications, and sanitation within the platoon and company area. General concerns were malaria prevention, jungle rot and scratches that led to infections because of lack of soap and water.

The use of helicopters for rapid medical evacuation was an enduring image of the Vietnam War, and saved lives that would otherwise have been lost. The decision to evacuate was made by the unit commander, working with his corpsman and based upon the tactical situation. The movement of casualties paralleled the route supplies and replacements were taking, and was aided by platoon guides and the company gunnery sergeant.

During Dewey Canyon, medical evacuation and replacement of personnel was limited due to the cross-country movement to fire support bases and because of poor flying weather. Casualty evacuation was risky, and the wounded and dead had to remain with the units until evacuation could be arranged, despite the efforts of helicopter crews to get them out – a morale lowering plight for those on the ground. In a number of cases, hoists were used because of the lack of landing sites. Often less serious casualties reduced unit effectiveness in the move southward, until personnel already in the field could be shifted around. One company officer wrote: "If a fire-team sustains only two casualties, or even one in some instances, it simply ceases to exist as a tactical or maneuver unit." This vital cornerstone of the tactical structure had to be reorganized whenever this happened, reducing squads to two fire-teams rather than the normal three.

IN BATTLE

Operation Dewey Canyon

Air and ground reconnaissance tracked the Communist build-up in Base Area 611 and this information was expanded by other agencies available to the 3rd Marine Division. General Davis recalled that 40% of his area was secured by combat forces and the rest was "covered by reconnaissance" with patrols from 3rd Force Reconnaissance Company and 3rd Reconnaissance Battalion. These patrols were used to make contact with the enemy, who were then exploited by a rapid build-up of infantry or air and artillery fire. This was the type of attack called for to disrupt Base Area 611, using a force built around the 9th Marine Regiment led by Colonel Robert H. Barrow.

Elements of two NVA infantry regiments, an artillery regiment, and service-engineer-transportation troops were discovered. With these, the enemy was able to reinforce points under attack, counterattack with small units making considerable use of crew-served weapons, and hit fire support bases. General Nickerson observed that in the North Vietnamese "…we confront a dedicated foot soldier, but a soldier lacking in supporting arms. The test of a North Vietnamese commander then is to counter our overwhelming firepower. And he doesn't mind losing troops to gain his limited objectives." The 9th Marines' commander felt that the NVA was "well organized and formidable" and abundantly supplied and equipped in terrain that helped his defense. "He was strong and he fought hard," Barrow concluded.

To go after the North Vietnamese, the Marines had to operate 20–30 air-miles beyond other allied bases – far from naval gunfire, resupply by road and reinforcement. The battle area was in a remote corner of the mountain highlands, and included the converging valleys of the Da Krong and Ashau watersheds. Two large hill-masses dominated the apex of these valleys, Tam Boi and Co A Nong (Hills 1224 and 1228 respectively from their altitudes on the map), through which Routes 922 and 548 curved. For the infantry, this meant fighting uphill from 600 feet to final objectives of over 3,600 feet, covering an average horizontal distance of just four miles!

During the January to March monsoon season, temperatures were between 71 and 51 degrees – cool compared to the 100-degree temperatures of the lowlands. No significant rainfall occurred, but there were overcast skies and drizzle, with fog and clouds along the mountains and ravines. Barrow recalled that they "experienced

North Vietnamese women soldiers run ammunition and grenades down a trench during the defense of Base Area 611. Communist combat and logistics troops were intermingled in what they considered to be a safe haven from Free-World-Forces ground attacks. (PAVN)

unfavorable weather over fifty percent of the time" and that it "stalled or slowed the momentum of our attack and robbed us of our options."

Headquarters for 9th Marines was at Vandegrift Combat Base. Its battalions assembled there prior to "D-Day" to rest, refit, and rearm. A logistics support area was located at Vandegrift, with all classes of supplies moved by 3rd Shore Party Battalion. The regiment was supported by LtCol Joseph R. Scoppa's 2/12 artillery battalion, an engineer company, and aircraft from the 1st Marine Aircraft Wing and the US Army 101st Airborne Division. Additional units from the 2nd ARVN and 3rd Marine Regiments were later brought into the operation.

Dewey Canyon kicked off on January 18 with the 9th and 12th Marines establishing fire support bases and blocking positions on three previously held hilltops – Henderson, Tun Tavern, and Shiloh. "Built by engineers, defended by the infantry and manned by artillery," the fire support base was an example of

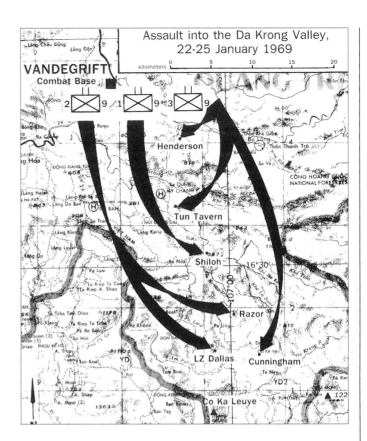

Da Krong Valley, South Vietnam. (MCHC)

Marine flexibility, according to 3rd Engineer Battalion's operations officer, Maj Robert V. Nicoli. Basically, fire support bases were rapidly built artillery positions that allowed infantry to operate within a protective fan of fire that overlapped with other bases in order to fight in forests, jungles, and mountains where ground movement was limited. Infantry moved forward in a classic "fire and maneuver" of forces, rapidly abandoning bases that were no longer needed.

With artillery fire and air strikes for openers, Lt Wesley L. Fox's Alpha Company landed by helicopter at Shiloh on January 21, starting the war for Cpl Smith's fire-team. Not knowing what to expect, the team left the helicopter at the double and took its place in the squad's section of the perimeter, with orders to "spread out, spread out!" The bombs and shells had torn the already constructed parapets and ammunition berms to pieces and everything had a damp moldering feel.

Murphy and Valdez went down the side of the hill "to make a head call," which ended with a cursing Murphy crashing down the slope into barbed wire with his trousers around his ankles. "Honest corporal, I got bamboo in my ass," he said to Smith, who was not impressed by Murphy's inability to defecate off the side of a hill.

Fire Support Base Shiloh proved to have been a "vacation" for Alpha Company as Dewey Canyon unfolded and they were left to guard two 105mm howitzer batteries and a 10-day supply of ammunition, rations, and batteries moved forward from Vandegrift. Working parties improved and built fighting holes, bunkers, and barbed wire obstacles. Mines, grenades, and flares were installed. Observation posts were manned during the day and listening posts outside the lines at night,

The North Vietnamese made effective use of crew-served weapons, whether machine guns, mortars, or recoilless rifles – like this 82mm B10. Note the light scale of personal equipment, including the lack of helmets and body armor favored by the Americans. (PAVN)

with two-man teams using field telephones and flares to warn of attack. The presence of ammunition and fuel meant there could be no open fires. Bunkers were dark and musty, beds were whatever was available to keep off the ground, and there were no windows or electricity. For company there were gnats, mosquitoes, mice, and rats. There was insufficient water for shaving or cooking, and not much more for drinking. Supplies were not plentiful and hot meals a distant memory; most living on canned rations. Mail was infrequent at best, tossed from the resupply helicopters in brightly colored sacks.

Benotz had been sending his $73 overseas and combat pay to his girlfriend to make car payments. Shortly after arriving at Shiloh, a sack

The 2nd Battalion, 9th Marines moved into Laos to secure the right flank of the operation as the regiment entered Base Area 611. This squad moves down Route 922 to disrupt traffic into the battle area. (DOD)

of mail brought him a letter from the finance company repossessing the automobile for non-payment and a "Dear John" letter from his girl saying she was now married and would not be writing anymore. Benotz tore these up and pinned the pieces to the company bulletin board to the cat-calls of "Get some!" from the headquarters clerks. Joe's comments were unprintable.

Enemy threats against these fixed positions were from "stand off" and sapper attacks. The latter were special NVA units designed to conduct raids. The 3rd Marine Division chief-of-staff related that they used unobserved approaches – such as through the rubbish dump – with supporting mortar fire, backed at the last moment by RPGs, Chicom grenades, satchel charges and bangalore torpedoes to cover assaults made with utmost speed, keeping the defenders in their bunkers while the sappers hit ammunition stores, gun positions, fire direction and communication centers. Clearance patrols went out daily, and one platoon routinely left Shiloh for the small river at its foot in order to bathe, with due regard for security in "Indian country." Lieutenant Fox recalled that they would wind up their day by throwing grenades in the deep holes of the river and simply wading out and picking up the fish that floated to the top.

Closing in on the objective from the left flank were infantrymen from 3rd Battalion, 9th Marines moving up a battle-scarred slope in the Ashau Valley complex. Leathernecks advancing against the enemy-held mountain-top near the Laotian border dubbed the peak "Tiger Mountain." (DOD)

Valdez and Murphy attended church-call when a chaplain arrived, mainly to get away from the company gunny and his never ending working parties. The rustic chapel was full, providing a tempting target, and the reading provoked a rejoinder picked up in-country: "Ye though I walk through the valley of the shadow of death I will fear no evil cuz I'm the meanest mutha in the valley."

On January 22 the regiment flew LtCol George C. Fox's 2/9 forward to secure Fire Support Base Razor and Landing Zone Dallas, to move closer to the enemy. Fire and air control agencies were established there and the 9th Marines were now fully committed. Two days later LtCol Elliot R. Laine's 3/9 assaulted the ridge for Fire Support Base Cunningham, a further 6,500 yards beyond Razor. This was home for the forward regimental command post, field hospital and logistics support group.

The fire support bases mounted 155mm howitzers, 105mm howitzers and 4.2 inch mortars. The artillery fan now extended six miles south and southwest to the limits of the operation area. From here, close air support took 30–45 minutes to call in and a helicopter some 45–60 minutes to arrive if the enemy and weather permitted. Because of the enemy antiaircraft defenses in Base Area 611, it was decided to attack cross-country rather than risk an airborne assault onto final objectives – One, Two and Three.

As initial gambits were being completed, 2/9 and 3/9 cleared the areas around the fire support bases and then advanced to Phase Line

Red along the Da Krong River. An outlying company position, Fire Support Base Erskine, was built, and both battalions made light contact with screening forces from units they had believed to be further south. By February 2 an NVA field hospital had been overrun, a heavy company engagement had been fought by 2/9 in rain and fog on Hill 1175, Fire Support Base Cunningham had been shelled by 122mm guns and the bad weather had restricted air support. Company G was the most exposed and encountered a large enemy force as it pulled closer to friendly lines. Rain alternated with drizzle and fog, visibility was reduced to yards, and the ceiling to zero as hard red soil became mud.

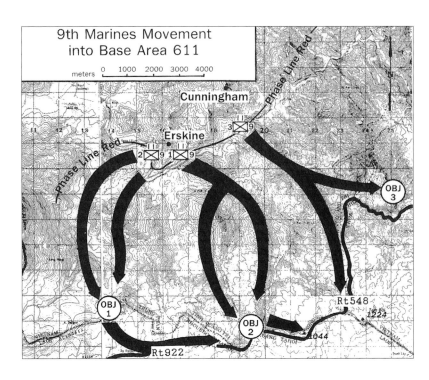

Base Area 611, South Vietnam and Laos. (MCHC)

Barrow decided to hold what ground the regiment had until things improved, and units sat in defensive positions in the rain, with resupply conducted by parachute drops from radar-guided helicopters and C130 transports. Nine days of poor weather cost them the impetus and gave the enemy time to prepare. On February 10 the weather cleared enough for LtCol George W. Smith's 1/9 to be helicoptered forward to Fire Support Base Erskine to take its place on Phase Line Red for the move from the Da Krong Valley up into Base Area 611. The 9th Marines was now on a line from west to east – 2/9, 1/9 and 3/9; each battalion with a zone of action three miles wide and assigned terrain objectives some four to five miles to the southwest.

On February 12 1/9 ran into an NVA force soon after leaving Erskine. Artillery fire and maneuver by three companies killed 25 of the enemy. The other battalions met with machine-gun, mortar, and recoilless rifle fire-fights as they advanced. On February 17 a sapper attack hit Cunningham, which was defended by 2/12 and M Company, leaving 37 bodies behind, 13 within the base itself; however, four Marines had died and another 46 were wounded.

Foot travel brought an all-encompassing cycle of demanding movement or rest, heat and damp, cold and damp, and exposure to the elements 24 hours a day. During the day, two companies advanced up the ridge lines alongside each other, with another company following. The lead units would attack and the rear units would move to the flanks or establish a landing zone for mortar support, resupply, and medical evacuation. Companies rotated through these tasks as the situation permitted. At night, the companies stopped and established defensive perimeters.

Within Black's squad, Cpl Smith proved a competent team leader who saw that his replacements survived the transition into combat with a mixture of force and shrewdness – "attention to detail and mental alertness" was his litany to get their "heads and asses wired together." By example, he demonstrated how to adjust individual equipment, carry rifles and move in a staggered column or extended line. Economy of effort was used during halts, meals and in rigging expedient poncho shelters at night. Benotz, Valdez, and Murphy were able to stay awake on watch without excitement or to fall asleep at the first opportunity. All that was needed was a "baptism of fire" to prove their worth as riflemen.

Alpha Company experienced a number of heavy fire-fights, shortages of water and rations, and exhaustive patrols; it then recalled the "good old days" back on Shiloh. Heavy fighting occurred between February 18 and 22, mostly in 1/9's sector. Company A hit an entrenched platoon on a ridge three miles from Erskine, and the NVA "appeared to want to hold their position at all costs." The position was overrun and 30 Communists were killed. The next morning Company C moved through Alpha and killed as many on an adjacent hill. Lieutenant Archie Biggers' platoon was on "a really well-camouflaged road, about twelve feet wide and better made than anything I had ever seen" when it walked into two 122mm guns and 30 enemy fighting positions (Terry). Charlie attacked and captured the two guns and prime movers, and Alpha then passed through to secure trucks and ammunition stockpiles. The 88 NVA killed were balanced against seven Marines dead and 44 wounded.

As battalions neared the border with Laos, Barrow sought permission to cut Route 922, which was being used to move enemy units in and out of the battle area, despite artillery, fighter bomber, and B52 Stratofortress attacks. It fell to 2/9 to cross the border and ambush traffic on this critical route with infantry, which it did on 21 and 22 February – a story in itself.

By now there was concern about the general level of fatigue on the ground after four weeks of operations. The rugged terrain, tension of combat, and lack of sleep was beginning to tell – in high pulse rates and dehydration. Company and platoon commanders knew that tired riflemen were careless and likely to forget good movement and security techniques as a result.

On February 22, Alpha Company won its commander the Medal of Honor (one of five awarded the 9th Marines during the fighting). As the company neared the border in the center of the regiment's advance, 1st Platoon pushed an enemy squad out of well-positioned bunkers. Since things looked quiet, Lt Fox radioed the battalion to send a detail down to the creek to get much needed water for headquarters and Charlie companies. The 20 men sent for water came under mortar and machine-gun fire, and 1st Platoon went to cover them, kicking off the last heavy engagement of Dewey Canyon.

After Sgt Black showed Cpl Smith where to go on the exposed flank across an open trail, Smith

Alpha Company Marines pinned down in dense growth to await the outcome of the fire fight ahead. Those not engaged took advantage of the delay in movement this offered to take a break and would continue the fight when called forward. (USNI)

Sgt Black directs Cpl Smith to take his team across an open area within a Communist defensive position at Dewey Canyon's climax. Fire and movement in the face of enemy fire was the classic test of infantry in combat. (DOD)

came back and shouted "Benotz with me! Valdez, Murphy, a magazine each, shoot like hell until we're across." He told Valdez and Murphy to follow as soon as they had changed magazines. Smith's final words were: "I will see you on the other side," as he and Benotz broke cover. As Valdez and Murphy raised up to shoot, machine-gun fire and Chi-com grenades blew a storm of fragments and debris into their faces and eyes from the direction the team leader had gone. They both flinched, and Valdez emptied a magazine without raising his head to aim. By the time Murphy lifted up to fire, Smith and Benotz were gone in the smoke and dust. A helmet lay rocking on the dirt trail surface and leaves and debris drifted down. Sgt Black came to see what was going on, bringing the other team for support as the fire-fight continued with grenade and mortar blasts.

After pushing through triple-canopy, undergrowth and banana groves, Lt Malone's men had hit a company-size defensive position, supported from high ground by rocket launchers and mortars. The 3rd

Serious casualties required medical evacuation, a medevac, where speed was essential for treatment of an emergency nature. A CH46 from HMM–262 touches down on an improvised landing zone to receive a litter case carried by his fellow Marines. If halted by weather or enemy action, then the wounded did not get out. (DOD)

In the aftermath of battle, a navy medical corpsman examines surviving NVA prisoners, all of whom were injured and captured in the base area as the Communists withdrew into Laos. Most of the enemy were killed in action. (DOD)

and 2nd Platoons were soon committed in fighting that was so close that artillery and air support could not be used effectively.

The company executive officer took over 2nd Platoon when its commander went down, but was later hit himself. The command group was hit by mortars, killing or wounding everyone, but Lt Fox continued to move through the hazardous area, coordinating aircraft support with the activities of his men. In a final effort, small arms and grenades drove the enemy back. Wounded again in this assault, Fox reorganized his company into a defensive stance. Delta Company came up from behind the NVA position and the two companies linked up to evacuate the casualties – 11 killed and 72 wounded. One of those evacuated was Benotz with a chest wound; Benotz had not seen Smith after he had been hit and a body was not spotted. Some 105 NVA dead were counted, along with 25 crew-served weapons. Murphy found certificates and medals on one corpse that indicated he had killed an NVA war hero. More of these were located as the battlefield was swept clean.

On the regiment's left flank, 3/9 had advanced along Route 548, uncovering maintenance installations and fuel depots. The battalion cleared Hill 1228 (called Tiger Mountain by the Marines) and by February 23 had seized 122mm guns, prime movers, ammunition, a hospital and an underground headquarters complex. Fire Support Base Turnage was established on the Tiger Mountain hill complex to cover this phase of the fighting.

At the border, 1/9 reoriented its march along Route 548 towards Hill 1044, where on February 26 Delta Company found one of the largest supply depots captured during the war – over 100 tons of munitions and 737 weapons. The next few days were spent recovering this materiel and destroying the complex – a massive effort which required two companies.

On the regiment's right flank, 2/9 swung through Laos until March 1, covering 5,500 yards in five days – killing 48 enemy, capturing 20 tons of food, ammunition, and two 122mm guns. This move blocked Route 922 at the time when 1/9 and 3/9 were pushing from the other side. This brought the operation to an end and a phased withdrawal began, and continued until March 18, returning units by helicopter to the Vandegrift Combat Base. Communist forces up to company-size continued to attack in the Tiger Mountain area. The last unit to withdraw was 1st Battalion, 9th Marines and the survivors of Smith's fire-team; they left still under heavy mortar and antiaircraft fire from Base Area 611's tenants.

The Dewey Canyon engagements killed 1,617 North Vietnamese soldiers (more were estimated killed by supporting fire) and took only five prisoners. The captured base area yielded 1,223 small arms, 104 machine-guns, 26 mortars, 73 antiaircraft guns, 16 artillery pieces, 92 trucks, and 14 bulldozers. Completing the haul were more than 800,000 rounds of ammunition – from small arms to artillery, 2,920 land mines, 800 pounds of explosives, 110 tons of rice, and two tons of salt.

Riflemen from Alpha Company stay alert as they move out onto Route 548 in the NVA base complex at the close of Operation Dewey Canyon. The ammunition cans hold extra rifle or machine gun ammunition carried for quick distribution. (DOD)

Marine casualties for the same period were 130 dead, 932 wounded, and one missing. The operation had been supported by 461 close air support missions delivering 2,000 tons of ordnance and some 134,000 rounds of artillery fire. Helicopters had flown some 1,200 sorties to move 9,121 troops and 1,533,597 pounds of cargo, with the loss of one aircraft. For seven weeks enemy resupply and infiltration were blocked and preempted, as were major Communist attacks for the year, so tactical and operational success was achieved. The 9th Marines earned a unit citation for the most successful independent regimental operation of the conflict, retaining their reputation for hard fighting under rugged conditions as "a Marine regiment of extraordinary cohesion, skill in mountain warfare and plain heart." The regimental commander felt the battle was "regarded by many as the most unusual, challenging and successful large-scale operation of the Vietnam War." The credit for this success went to individual Marines, described by one of their battalion commanders as "hard corps – well trained and led, motivated to the highest degree, and undemanding of creature comforts."

Medals of Honor, 9th Marines, Operation Dewey Canyon		
LCpl Thomas P. Noonan	G Co	February 5, 1969
LCpl Thomas E. Creek	I Co	February 13, 1969*
1st Lt Wesley L. Fox	A Co	February 22, 1969
Cpl William D. Morgan	H Co	February 25, 1969*
PFC Alfred M. Wilson	M Co	March 3, 1969*
		* Posthumous

GROUPS AND ORGANIZATIONS

The Regiments Depart

Starting in July with the 9th Marines, the entire 3rd Marine Division had moved to Okinawa by November 1969. The 9th Marines continued to provide the Special Landing Force of the Seventh Fleet until the Vietnam War was finally over, in 1975. In 1979 its battalions returned to the United States on unit rotation, while the regimental headquarters remained overseas. These battalions served in the Persian Gulf and

Somalia in 1990 and 1991. With the reduction in forces in the post Cold War defense structure, the 9th Marines' regimental headquarters was deactivated in July 1994, on the 50th anniversary of its landing on Guam in World War Two. The member battalions soon followed, and the "Striking Ninth" was regulated to the history books until needed again. On September 9, 1995, at the 53 Area of Camp Pendleton, California, the older, wiser, and heavier Joe Benotz and Juan Valdez watched the retirement of the colors for the 1st Battalion, carried by Marines who had not even been born when they had served in Operation Dewey Canyon. Of the others, Leroy Black remained in the Marine Corps until retirement, Pat Murphy died in a bar brawl soon after returning home, and Mike Smith was listed "killed-in-action, body-not-recovered."

Marine Corps Historical Foundation

This organization promotes, through the encouragement of the study of Marine Corps history and traditions, a deeper understanding of the historical role of the United States Marine Corps and the men and women who have served in it. It offers awards, grants, and scholarships, and publishes a directory and newsletter. Membership is open to all interested in the history of the Corps. Contact P.O. Box 420, Quantico, Virginia 22134.

3rd Marine Division Association

This is a fraternal group founded in 1949 to hold annual reunions, raise funds for division causes and to publish a directory and newsletter. It is open to all Marines and corpsmen who served with the division. Contact P.O. Box 297, Dumfries, Virginia 22026.

1/9, 2/9, 3/9 Marines Networks

These are fraternal groups to meet the needs of Vietnam veterans of the 9th Marines through reunions and mailing lists. Contact: 1st Bn 9th Marine Network, c/o 1152 Kensington Avenue, Plainfield, New Jersey 07060; 2nd Bn, 9th Marine Network, c/o P.O. Box 527, Waldo, Florida

Alpha Company Marines uncover the spoils of war from Operation Dewey Canyon in the form of 82mm mortar ammunition in one of many buried caches found throughout Base Area 611 near the Laotian border. (DOD)

32694; 3rd Bn, 9th Marines Network, c/o 33752 31st Avenue SW, Federal Way, Washington 98023.

Vietnam, like Korea, was fought in the shadow of World War Two, by veterans in senior ranks who thought it not much of a war, "but it was all we've got" and they soldiered on. The younger riflemen did not necessarily share this view: they saw it instead as their "big show." This led to a certain amount of dissatisfaction when the war ended, mitigated by personnel assignment policies that put them back into society as individuals without a suitable transition. The war's aftermath was felt strongest by these Marine veterans, who believed "America broke our heart" by denying them either victory or recognition.

Along with the obvious costs of the war, one unforeseen aspect was post-traumatic stress disorder and the impact this had on families and society. This might not be as unique as was first thought. One psychiatrist recently argued that the same sobering impact of war was depicted in Homer's *Iliad*, combat trauma and the undoing of character (Shay). Most veterans readjusted to society in the same way they handled combat, by their own efforts and with their friends and families, but the memory of those days and events remained long after their passing.

Napoleon correctly recognized that it is with bits of colored ribbon that "one leads men." During the Vietnam War, medals and ribbons were awarded for valor, merit, and service. While not a major concern in combat, the impact of the equitable distribution of decorations and awards was of concern in the war's aftermath. Perceptions existed that awards were based on rank, and that an officer had had to be present for a heroic deed to be recognized. The 9th Marines earned five Medals of Honor during Dewey Canyon, out of a total of 57 awarded to Marines during the entire war. Vietnam veterans of lst Battalion recall with pride the more than 43 named operations that saw an estimated 600 battalion members killed and 4,000 wounded to earn the Purple Heart, America's oldest decoration. The Combat Action Ribbon was instituted during Vietnam for participation in battle and was also a personal award earned by Marines.

Unit awards went to specified organizations for significant accomplishment in combat; in Vietnam the 9th Marines earned two Presidential Unit Citations, two Navy Unit Commendations, two

A Marine and corpsman examine a 122mm gun, the largest type captured in South Vietnam. The NVA soldiers had tried to swing the gun from facing down the Ashau Valley to an alternative firing position when overrun by the attacking 9th Marines. The Communists blew the barrel off and left the piece. (DOD)

Meritorious Unit Commendations, and Vietnamese Gallantry Cross and Civil Actions unit citations.

Individual service awards included the National Defense Medal, the Vietnam Service Medal, and the Vietnamese Campaign Medal – the three basic "I was there" ribbons of the conflict. In addition, enlisted Marines earned the Good Conduct Medal for three years of continuous exemplary active service (or "without getting caught," said cynics!).

MUSEUMS AND COLLECTIONS

Marine Corps Historical Center
Located at Building 58, Washington Navy Yard, in Washington D.C., this is the Marine Corps archival and museum facility. It is the starting point for anyone researching Vietnam and any other period of Corps history. It houses a museum which includes exhibits pertaining to the Vietnam era.

Marine Corps Air-Ground Museum
A branch of the historical center located at Brown Field, Marine Corps Base, Quantico, Virginia. The Air-Ground Museum displays large artifacts that include armor, artillery and aircraft, as well as period uniforms and small arms. At present these are in three hangars with exhibits up to the Korean War. Vietnam era exhibits are planned. One of the 122mm guns captured by 1/9 is there, while another is at Fort Sill, Oklahoma. The museum also houses the Marine Corps Research Center, which includes a library and an excellent archive with Vietnam material.

Vietnam Veterans Memorial
The Vietnam Veterans Memorial was dedicated on Veterans' Day Weekend in 1982. Located in Washington D.C. on The Mall near the Lincoln Monument, it is a series of black granite slabs arranged as a wall, with the 58,182 names of the dead and missing from the war. It includes two sculptures depicting three servicemen and women in period

War Trophy DD Form 603-1 – this was used to give an individual permission to keep captured enemy items that had been screened for intelligence value, including some weapons. (MCHC)

uniforms and equipment. The monument was intended to separate the US policy during the war from the issue of those who served as an act of national reconciliation. The cost of the monument was raised through contributions and it is administered by the National Park Service.

Collecting

After a tour in Vietnam, an individual returned to the United States in a service uniform. Few Marines were in a position – or cared – to bring clothing and equipment home afterwards. On Okinawa there were piles of worn jungle utilities and boots left in heaps outside the huts used for processing personnel back home. Customs and military police discouraged efforts to bring anything else home or even to mail articles back.

Marines generally kept the utility cap, belt, and jungle boots which were worn at their next duty station to proclaim status as returning warriors. Since these items were usually unsightly, this lasted until an officer or non-commissioned officer ran the Marine down and told them to send the stuff home. If an individual stayed in the Corps, these items were soon worn out or thrown away. At the time there was not much sentiment attached to clothing and equipment, with the exception of the above items and possibly the Ka-Bar knife. Photographs and captured enemy belongings were valued as souvenirs, and officers kept maps and notebooks as well.

With one third of the Marine Corps in Southeast Asia during this time, the bulk of personal clothing and equipment produced was used elsewhere. At best, a collector will be able to determine an individual item's date of manufacture or contract from markings on the piece. Illustrated are custody and war trophy documents that can authenticate items as Marine Corps issue and captured.

Riflemen were "the combat foundation of the Marine infantry organization." In Vietnam they conducted individual combat tasks using small arms, grenades, mine or demolition techniques, and maintained weapons and equipment in any terrain or weather. (DOD)

GLOSSARY

Actual, Six, Skipper – commanding officer
Arty – artillery
ARVN – Army of the Republic of Vietnam
Charlie, Ngyuen – the enemy
Chow – food
Comm – communications
Conus, The World – Continental United States
CP – command post
Crotch – the Marine Corps
Doc, Bac Se – medical corpsman
FMF – Fleet Marine Force
Grunt – combat infantryman
Head – toilet
High and tight – short haircut
Hump – forced march
HQMC – Headquarters Marine Corps
ICTZ – I Corps Tactical Zone
KIA – killed in action
Lifer – career enlisted
LZ – landing zone
MACV – US Military Advisory Command Vietnam
MAF – Marine Amphibious Force
MIA – missing in action
NVA – North Vietnamese Army
Short timer – first-term enlisted or end of tour
VC, Viet Long – Vietnamese Communist
Ville – village or town
Waste, pop, get some – to kill
WIA – wounded in action

COLOR PLATE COMMENTARY

A: MARINE RIFLEMAN, VIETNAM

Marines at this point in the war benefited from the previous four years of combat in terms of uniforms and equipment to fight with. Older Marine patterns were replaced by army-supplied equipment designed specifically for Southeast Asia. This fire-team leader, Cpl Smith, is going into the field wearing the height of fighting fashion – an M62 utility cover with his rank insignia pinned on the crown, and his M1 helmet is hanging off his "ruck." The camouflage utility uniform has lost its newness and is rolled at the sleeves and legs for ventilation while on the move in the tropics. Fabric and leather jungle boots were essential for the hot-wet conditions, complete with a dog-tag in the laces. His M55 armored vest, a flak jacket, supports the weight of the pack and holds a rifle magazine that was removed from his M16 when not in the field (accidental discharges were frowned upon). He carries a salvaged demolitions bag to hold additional ammunition, grenades or mines; it could also carry rations if packs were not carried. The cartridge belt is an M56 pattern with ammunition pouches and canteens.

When rank was displayed on the utility uniform, it was in the form of metal pin-on insignia. Officers and enlisted rank at the company level were divided into commissioned officers, non-commissioned officers and enlisted men. Insignia were worn in matching pairs on the collars of jackets or shirts. They might also appear singly on the utility cover or on front or pocket of the utility jacket or armored vest. Within a unit, the leaders were known well enough not to need to rely on any outward sign of authority.

The utility cap has a 1954 emblem applied by the manufacturer, while the utility jacket was marked by individuals using a heat transfer decal or ink and stencil, with a larger emblem and the initials USMC to differentiate the Marines from other services which wore the same uniform.

As the jungle and camouflage utilities were theater-issue clothing, markings were at the Marine's choosing. A last name and initials could be shown above the left breast pocket, put there by rubber stamp, stencil, embroidery or hand-written. Helmet covers and flak jackets displayed graffiti depending upon what a unit would tolerate or what an individual could get away with. This was an unofficial means of identifying kit and of expressing opinion, and for identifying hometowns or states, blood type, or the length of time remaining in Vietnam. (After Kevin Lyles) **1** Armored vest. The army M52 type was also available and was constructed from kevlar fabric rather than the plates of the Marine M55. Since it fitted flush against the body, it was hotter to wear. **2** Sleeping shirt. This was kept dry in the pack until needed. Once stopped for the night, wet utilities could be removed and the dry polyester shirt worn until the damp clothing was put back on for the next day's move. It was also worn for warmth under the utility jacket in colder altitudes. **3** Jungle boots. The cure for the curse of heavy, wet leather combat boots was found in the popular "hot weather tropical boot." Even with them, care was required to control the problems of immersion foot. Side vents allowed water to drain out, and a plate in the sole offered some protection against penetration by spike booby-traps. **4** M1 helmet and cover. Another item of personal body armor favored by the Americans because medical research from World War Two and the Korean War indicated it offered protection against injury from fragments. Its utility in mobile situations was debated, but to Marine riflemen it was as essential as boots and a service rifle. The canvas cover was first used in World War Two and was a distinctive item of Marine equipment until the general adoption of helmet covers by the Department of Defense in 1962. **5** Lightweight tropical rucksack and contents. This rucksack replaced the Marine's M41 haversack and knapsack which were not suited to Vietnam service. Fighting gear was carried on the belt, but the pack was the rifleman's home in the field, and the contents of each varied, but revolved around the basics shown here: **a** underclothing, **b** towel, **c** poncho, **d** rations, **e** machete, and **f** air mattress. It did not take long to learn that weight and necessities needed

Riflemen admire their efforts with a captured M49 7.62mm machine gun and antiaircraft mount. Victory on the battlefield was defined by the seizure of territory, material, and eventual withdrawal. Other captured weapons are stacked for disposal with "1/9" marked water cans. (DOD)

Success defined by the infantryman was moving to the rear with the gear and having all major body parts in place. This machine gunner catches up on his reading before going out the next time. The kit and uniform were worn for comfort if not style. (DOD)

to be balanced and mandated loads would often prevent either of these, since unit supplies were also carried. Plates E and G show additional individual equipment and munitions used. **6** Unofficial "beer-can" crest for 1st Battalion, 9th Marines. This design originated during the Vietnam War and was used on patches, hats, shirts, and coffee mugs. **7** M161Al rifle; **8** MX991/U flashlight used since the late war.

B: RECRUIT AND DRILL INSTRUCTOR, MARINE CORPS RECRUIT DEPOT, USA

Like other historical elites, the Marines prided themselves on the severe training that took individuals from diverse backgrounds and circumstances and gave them a sense of common identity. By the mid-1960s, this took on a sharper edge with the return of combat veterans and the reduction in training time to maintain the level of manpower required to support the war. One element that continued to be used to obtain compliance was close order drill. A rather confused Pvt Murphy is being given individual instruction from his DI in the difference between left and right. While physical abuse by instructors was officially prohibited, DIs "laid hands" on recruits to adjust uniforms or to assist in the learning process.

Uniforms were the most visible indicator of status between the two. Murphy wears a silver-painted helmet liner "chrome dome," undershirt, M62 utility trousers, and an M61 cartridge

belt. The recruit is advertised by the ill-fitting newness of the uniform, lack of rank insignia and his trousers hanging over his combat boots. Wearing of a full uniform was graduated to levels of performance. The drill instructor has a campaign hat with its four-dent Montana Peak, an outmoded issue that was limited to instructors and shooting team members. A "duty" belt also indicates his billet. In contrast to the recruit, the sergeant's M62 utility uniform is starched and ironed to a stiff freshness, which necessitates several changes a day to maintain in humid weather. His boots and brass fittings were polished by recruits each night. (After William Mares)

C: ADVANCED TRAINING, INFANTRY TRAINING REGIMENT, USA

Military occupational specialty skills were taught at both Camp Pendleton, California, and Camp Lejeune, North Carolina. In addition, most Vietnam-bound Marines passed through pre-deployment orientation at Camp Pendleton before going overseas, although this was not always the case as the war proceeded.

Orientation consisted of lecture, demonstration, and application as the Marines were introduced to M16 rifles, "jungle-lanes" and "Vietnam villages." These two Marines are practicing the skill needed to search and clear a village with the help of costumed aggressors, including Pvt

For the 9th Marines, Operation "Dewey Canyon" marked the end of the Vietnam War. With its departure on July 14, 1969, the 1st battalion loaded the USS *Paul Revere* for the three-day trip to Okinawa as part of President Nixon's redeployment program. (DOD)

Valdez emerging from the "spider-hole" with a PPSH submachine-gun in his hand. The Marines wear the M62 utility uniform that was standard in the States, with an abbreviated belt order limited to M61 magazine pouches for the M14 rifles carried. Valdez and his companion wear black "pajama" clothing similar to that of rural peasants. Needless to say, the terrain and climate of southern California was very different from that of Southeast Asia, and the training facilities were the same ones that had been used for World War Two and Korea.

D: ARRIVAL AND ASSIGNMENT, VIETNAM

For the majority of riflemen, this was the first time in the replacement pipeline that they were treated as something other than an anonymous group moved in mass from one destination to another. Once in-country, the assignment system narrowed their options until they arrived at a unit. In this case, Sgt Black rounds up replacements assigned to Alpha Company, 9th Marines – including Benotz, Valdez, and Murphy. The whole system was set up for this, to put trained riflemen into the field against the enemy for the next 13 months, unless injury or death brought new replacements. Black wears the early jungle utilities; the replacements wear the later camouflage version, with M56 personal equipment and M16 rifles. Again, the contrast of experience and naivety is apparent. Those leaving at the end of their tour could be heard calling out: "You'll be sorry!"

E: PERSONAL EQUIPMENT, US MARINE CORPS M41 AND M61 PATTERNS

1 Intrenching tool; **2** M61 cartridge belt; **3** M61 cartridge pouches; **4** M44/45 canteen and cover; **5** M41 belt suspender straps; **6** Jungle first aid kit; **7** M44/45 canteen and cup; **8** M6 bayonet knife and scabbard; **9** M1 holster, automatic pistol; **10** M1911A1 pistol, .45 caliber; **11** Pistol magazine and pouch; **12** Grenade carrier for M26 hand-grenade; **13** M14 rifle magazine; **14** Fighting and utility knives made by Ka-Bar and case; **15** M67 hand-grenade; **16** M26 hand-grenade; **17** M18 smoke-grenade; **18** M94 incendiary-grenade; **19** M127 parachute flare.

F: MARINE MACHINE GUNNER, VIETNAM

While riflemen were most common, other infantrymen played a significant tactical role. In the ground combat in Vietnam, the M60 machine-gun team provided the base of fire needed to maneuver rifle squads and formed the backbone of any defense. They operated in a flexible role using a bipod and in the fixed mode, firing from a tripod.

This machine gunner is "loaded for bear" for mobile operations. He carries lubricant and a toothbrush on his M1 helmet. He totes the M60 "black bitch" with a 50-round "teaser" belt loaded into the feed tray and has 200 rounds of ready ammunition slung across the M55 flak jacket, which is worn over an olive-green undershirt. The towel around his neck serves as a sweat rag and cushion. Other individual equipment consists of an M41 pack and poncho, a web belt to hold canteens, and a holster for his M1911A1 pistol with a Ka-Bar fighting knife wedged behind. On his left hip is an M17 gas mask and case to protect him from chemicals that were used by both sides. His trousers are rolled above the boots for air circulation. The jungle boots are laced loose, with an identification tag for easy access.

The 9th Marines was disbanded in 1994. Budget cuts in defense spending accomplished what the enemy could not. At Camp Pendleton, California, the 1st Battalion colors were paraded for the last time on September 9 – until needed again. (1stMarDiv)

The M60 was operated by a two-man team: the gunner and assistant gunner (or "A" gunner). Others were assigned as "ammo humpers," to carry additional belted 7.62mm ammunition. This required the gunner to carry a 24-pound weapon in addition to his personal equipment; his assistant carried another 33 pounds of accessories including a spare barrel; and ammunition weighed 6.5 pounds for each 100 rounds. **1** An "assault pack" of 100 rounds of 7.62mm belted ammunition (one round tracer to four of ball) issued in a cardboard box and cloth bandolier and carried two per metal ammunition container or "ammo can." **2a** M60 machine-gun spare barrel-case and accessories; **2b** Bore brush; **2c** Chamber brush; **2d** Receiver brush; **e** Combination wrench; **f** Ruptured cartridge extractor; **g** Handle; **h** Cleaning rod; rel-case; **k** Asbestos glove; **3** The beer-can version of the 9th Marines regimental crest, designed in World War Two by regimental commander Col Lemuel C. Shepherd Jr. The design was used as the basis for informal equipment and clothing.

G: PERSONAL EQUIPMENT, US ARMY M56 AND M67 PATTERNS

1 M62 canteen; **2** M56 individual equipment belt; **3** M56 universal small arms ammunition case (M14); **4** M56 entrenching tool carrier; **5** M7 bayonet knife and scabbard; **6** M56 suspenders; **7** M56 combat field pack; **8** M62 canteen and M56 cover; **9** M56 case and compass; **10** M56 sleeping bag carrier; **11** M67 entrenching tool and carrier; **12** M56 universal small arms ammunition case (MI6); **13** M16 rifle magazine; **14** M56 adapter assembly; **15** M67 universal small arms ammunition case (MI6); **16** M16 automatic rifle bipod and accessory case; **17** M56 case and individual first aid field dressing; **18** 5.56mm ammunition and stripper clips; **19** 5.56mm ammunition bandolier; **20** M67 individual equipment belt with quick release buckle; **21** Rifle grenade sight case (M14); **22** M42 machete and M67 sheath; **23** M67 small arms cleaning kit; **24** M18 Claymore anti-personnel mine.

Proud warriors of the 9th Marines, including those who fought during Dewey Canyon a quarter of a century before. For many this completed a cycle begun as recruits, performed as riflemen in combat, and finished as veterans. (1stMarDiv)

H: FIRE SUPPORT BASE, OPERATION DEWEY CANYON

The airmobile operations by the 9th Marines established fixed fortified positions to provide helicopter and artillery support to infantry units moving by foot without supply lines in rugged mountain terrain. The fire support bases also provided command and control, communications and medical backing. They were subject to enemy attacks by fire and raids the longer they remained in one place. While not as primitive as in the maneuver companies, these outposts were still subject to harsh conditions and exposure to weather.

I: FIRE-FIGHT, OPERATION DEWEY CANYON

The classic engagement for infantry in Vietnam was the close-range, violent and unpredictable fire-fight that saw opponents pitted against each other with small arms until one side or the other could bring to bear a decisive weight of supporting arms or maneuver. Weather, terrain, and surprise were all critical influences for both sides, and the infantry's job was to fight, win or lose. In these conditions skill-at-arms, tenacity, and effective small unit leadership were needed – to hit the deck, return fire, and dominate the situation. A grenadier fires an M79 in support of his squad in the initial stages of a contact, while the riflemen seek to return effective fire under the control of the team leader on the right.

J: THE COST, OPERATION DEWEY CANYON

Pte Benotz is treated for a sucking chest wound by "Doc," a company corpsman who had a number of others to take care of while the company organized evacuation. Casualties were dead and wounded from enemy fire, friendly fire, and accidents in the maelstrom of combat. The appalling damage caused by projectiles, fragments, blast, and concussion were magnified by the effects of weather, filth,

and evacuation. Navy corpsmen had to triage the injured and conduct the field surgery necessary to stabilize the wounded until they could be evacuated to the rear for treatment – by helicopter if possible and by stretcher parties if necessary. The normal course of evacuation was along the same lines as ammunition, water, and food being brought forward.

K: THE VICTOR, OPERATION DEWEY CANYON

A Marine rifleman at the end of the day, in possession of the field in enemy territory, in this case on a blasted artillery prime mover in Base Area 611. Pte Murphy and his fire-team have accomplished the task of the infantry, to close with and destroy the enemy. Murphy gave a noncommittal look at a very dead Communist driver and pronounced: "Whose hill now, Charlie?" The score for his four-man unit was one missing, one wounded and two left to hold the ground until the 9th Marines withdrew from the area. These events in the first half of the year would be the highlight of their military "careers."

L: NAVY MEDICAL CORPSMAN, VIETNAM

In each rifle platoon and company were individual field medics or hospital "corpsmen" who were members of the US Navy. At this level the "Doc" assumed fabled proportions with that of the squad leader and platoon commander. A recent veterans reunion was dedicated solely to "grunt corpsmen" because of the impact they had at the small unit level. Navy medical doctors and staff ran aid stations at the battalion and regimental levels.

This platoon corpsman is dressed for the field the same as a Marine rifleman, and in fact often carried an M16 instead of the issue pistol. While his helmet, flak jacket, utility uniform, and boots are prosaic, this corpsman is distinguished by a "Unit One" bag and ammunition bandolier stuffed with extra field dressings. 1 Identification tags. One symbol of service was the issue of "dog-tags," which stayed with a Marine throughout his service in case he was killed or wounded. The stamped aluminum plates were issued in pairs and worn on a metal chain around the neck. In the field a tag might be laced onto a boot. 2 Medical instrument and supply set, the Unit One, carried by platoon-level corpsmen with supplies to treat wounds and illness. The standard issue was modified to fit the unit's mission and circumstances – such as extra field dressings, morphine, and plasma. It was worn, ready for use, across the chest with a general-purpose carrying strap. 3 Medical instrument kit, used in field surgery for life-saving procedures in addition to the Unit One. 4 Jungle first aid kit. It had plastic strip band aids, elastic gauze bandages, individual field dressings, water purification tablets, salt tablets, anti-chap stick, sodium chloride-sodium bicarbonate for burns, and an eye wash solution. Often these supplies would be unavailable and the case would be used to carry cigarettes and snacks instead. 5 First aid individual field dressing, carried to be used for one's own wounds. First aid was intended to clear airways, stop bleeding, treat for shock, and protect the wound until medical treatment and evacuation could be arranged, often after the fighting was over. 6 A beer-can emblem for the 3rd Marine Division that was designed and worn in World War Two as a shoulder insignia. The three points of the tetrahedron symbolized the division's three infantry regiments and number.

FURTHER READING

Albright, John, Cash, John A., & Sandstrum, Allan W., *Seven Firefights in Vietnam*, Vietnam Studies series, Department of the Army, Washington, D.C. (1970)

Appy, Christian G., *Working-Class War*, Chapel Hill (1993)

Baker, Mark, *Nam: The Vietnam War in the Words of the Men and Women Who Fought There*, W. Morrow, New York (1981)

Barrow, MajGen Robert H., "Operation Dewey Canyon," *Gazette*, pp84–89 (November 1981)

Burkett, B. G., & Whitly, Glenna, Stolen, *Valor: How the Vietnam Generation was Robbed of its Heroes and its History*, Verity Press, Dallas, TX (1998)

Clark, Gregory R., *Words of the Vietnam War: The Slang, Jargon, Abbreviations, Acronyms, Nomenclature, Nicknames, Pseudonyms, Slogans, Specs, Euphemisms, Double-Talk, Chants, and Names and Places of the Era of United States Involvement in Vietnam*, McFarland, Jefferson, NC (1990)

Commandant of the Marine Corps, *Dewey Canyon*, video, Washington D.C.

Davis, 1stLt Gordon M., "Dewey Canyon: All Weather Classic," *Gazette*, pp32–40 (September 1969)

Dawson, Capt David A., *The Impact of Project 100,000 on the Marine Corps*, Washington D.C. (1995)

Ebert, James R., *A Life in a Year: The American Infantryman in Vietnam 1965–1972*, Ballantine Books, New York (1993)

Fleming, Dr. V. Keith, "Welcome to the Marines," *The Marines*, pp8–15, Harrisburg, PA (1989)

FMF Pacific, *A Marine's Guide to the Republic of Vietnam*, MCBul 3480 (1968)

FMFM 6–5, *US Marine Rifle Squad*, various editions, Washington, D.C.

Halberstadt, Hans, *War Stories of the Green Berets: The Vietnam Experience*, Motorbooks International (1994)

Herr, Michael, *Dispatches*, New York (1977)

HQMC, *The 3rd Marine Division and its Regiments*, Washington, D.C. (1983)

HQMC, *US Marine Corps Uniform Regulations*, various editions, Washington, D.C.

Kelly, Francis J., *U.S. Army Special Forces 1961–1971: Vietnam Studies Series*, US Government Printing Office (1973)

Kelly, Michael P., *Where We Were in Vietnam: A Comprehensive Guide to the Firebases, Military Installations and Naval Vessels of the Vietnam War 1945–75*, Hellgate Press, Central Point, OR (2002)

Lanning, Michael Lee, *Vietnam at the Movies*, Fawcett Columbine, New York (1994)

Lyles, Kevin, *Vietnam: US Uniforms in Colour Photographs*, Europa Militaria Special No. 3, Windrow & Greene, London (1992)

Maga, Timothy P., *The Complete Idiot's Guide to the Vietnam War*, Alpha Books, Indianapolis, IN (2000)

Mares, William, *The Marine Machine*, New York (1971)

Marshall, S.L.A., *Battles in the Monsoon: Campaigning in the Central Highlands, Vietnam, Summer 1966*, W. Morrow, New York (1967)

Miraldi, Paul W., *Uniforms and Equipment of U.S. Army Infantry, LRRPs, and Rangers in Vietnam 1965–1971*, Schiffer Books, Atglen, PA (1999)

Moore, Harold G. & Galloway, Joseph L., *We Were Soldiers Once ... And Young*, Random House, New York (1992)

Nickerson, LtGen Herman, *Leadership Lessons and Remembrances from Vietnam*, Washington, D.C. (1988)

Shay, Dr. Jonathan, *Achilles in Vietnam*, New York (1994)

Sigler, David B., *Vietnam Battle Chronology: U.S. Army and Marine Corps Combat Operations, 1965–1973*, MacFarland, New York (1992)

Simmons, BrigGen Edwin H., *Marines*, New York (1987)

Simpson, Charles M. III, *Inside the Green Berets: The First Thirty Years*, Presidio Press (1983)

Smith, Charles R., *US Marines in Vietnam, 1969*, Washington, D.C. (1988)

Stanton, Shelby L., *Anatomy of a Division: The 1st Cav in Vietnam*, Presidio Press, Novato, CA (1987)

——, *Green Berets at War: U.S. Army Special Forces in Southeast Asia 1956–1975*, Presidio Press (1985)

——, *The Rise and Fall of an American Army: U.S. Ground Forces in Vietnam, 1965–1973*, Presidio Press, Novato, CA (1985)

——, *Special Forces at War: An Illustrated History, Southeast Asia 1957–1975*, Howell Press (1990)

——, *U.S. Army Uniforms of the Cold War 1948–1973*, Stackpole Books, Mechanicsburg, PA (1994)

——, *U.S. Army Uniforms of the Vietnam War*, Stackpole Books, Harrisburg, PA (1989)

——, *Vietnam Order of Battle: A Complete Illustrated Reference to U.S. Army Combat and Support Forces in Vietnam 1961–1973*, Stackpole Books, Mechanicsburg, PA (2003)

Summers, Harry G. Jr., *The War Vietnam Almanac*, Presidio Press, Novato, CA (2003)

Sutherland, Ian D. W., *Special Forces of the United States Army 1952/82*, R. James Bender Publishing (1990)

Terry, Wallace, *Bloods*, New York (1984)

TM10–276, *Hot Weather Clothing and Equipment*, Washington, D.C. (1970)

5th SFGA, *The Green Beret Magazine* (5th SFGA monthly publication 1966–70) Vol. I–V. Complete reprint set available from RADIX Associates, 2314 Cheshire Ln., Houston, TX 77018-4023, USA.

INDEX